# CYBERMEN

## DAVID BANKS

By arrangement with the British Broadcasting Corporation

# ILLUSTRATED BY ANDREW SKILLETER

## ADDITIONAL MATERIAL BY
## ADRIAN RIGELSFORD

## Consultant for 'ARCHIVE' Jan Vincent-Rudzki

The Cybermen were created by Kit Pedler and Gerry Davis

VIRGIN

Typeset in Rockwell by Fingerprint Graphics, London. Printed and bound in Great Britain by Butler & Tanner Ltd, Frome and London

Published in 1990 by
W H Allen & Co plc,
338 Ladbroke Grove,
London W10 5AH

ISBN 1 85227 338 0

Cover designed by Russ French with Crispin Goodall and Andrew Skilleter
Redesigned for this edition by the Design Clinic
Cover Painting by Andrew Skilleter
Designed by Crispin Goodall
Title lettering by Russ French
Art Direction and design concept by Andrew Skilleter
First published 1988
by Who Dares Publishing
in association with Silver Fist

# BIOGRAPHIES

DAVID BANKS is an actor. His name and voice are probably most widely known for his portrayal of the Cyberleader in Doctor Who, though his face has never been seen on the programme.

His theatre experience is extensive and varied, having played both Dracula and Sherlock Holmes, as well as classical roles such as Bassanio, Astolpho, Andrew Aguecheek, Loveless, Benvolio, Young Marlow, Banquo and even Falstaff! He has been a member of the National Theatre, Cambridge Theatre Company, and was a founder-member of the Cherub Company and has recently formed his own theatre company, Third I, for which he has directed the play and now the film 'Talking to John'. In the West End he was Mowgli in 'The Jungle Book' and Aslan the Lion in 'The Lion, the Witch and the Wardrobe'. During '89 he toured with Jon Pertwee/Colin Baker as the villain Karl in 'Doctor Who – The Ultimate Adventure'. He became the eleventh actor to portray the Doctor when he took over the role from Jon Pertwee at short notice.

His other TV work includes the sitcoms 'Cuckoo Waltz' and 'Keep it in the Family', 'The Professionals' and Play for Today 'Man of Letters'. He records novels for Talking Book and has worked for BBC Radio Drama. He has produced The Archive Tapes, a series of four audio cassettes recounting the history of the Cyber Race, 'The Ultimate Interview' with Colin Baker, and 'Who's the real McCoy?' an indepth interview with Sylvester McCoy. He lives in Islington with the actress Maureen Purkis.

ANDREW SKILLETER is a professional illustrator. He is probably best known for his Doctor Who paintings which have appeared in books, on posters and cards and over fifty book covers. Two of his special commissions for Doctor Who were the cover painting for Radio Times on the 20th Anniversary of Doctor Who, and the exterior design for the Doctor Who USA travelling exhibition. Since 1985 his paintings have appeared in the Doctor Who Calendar each year.

His other illustrative work since the 1970s has been extremely varied and includes book jacket illustrations, and work for magazines, books and advertising. His longest and most demanding commission was to illustrate an edition of Boccaccio's 'The Decameron'. This involved over a year's work and enabled him to indulge his love of Renaissance art in ten paintings in the style of that period. The work received critical recognition and a number of the paintings were hung in two London exhibitions.

Recent commissions include the book covers for the Ruth Rendell crime-chiller series, a Fantasy Quest book and work for Virgin Games. A number of his original paintings are in private collections in the UK. He is married to an artist and lives on the South Coast.

ADRIAN RIGELSFORD provided extensive research for Sections III and IV. He was born and lives in Cambridgeshire and has been a longstanding fan of Doctor Who. He describes himself as 'a writer and research assistant and a bit of an actor, too'.

He is currently involved in several projects. One is a film with Brian Blessed retracing the footsteps of those 1920's climbers of Everest, Mallory and Irvine. Another is a film of W. G. Grace, the cricketer, his life and times.

## Photographs

Page VII **Gerry Davis**; Page 19 'Metropolis' National Film Archive, London; Page 21 Top middle © BBC Hulton Picture Library; Page 24 Top left **David Banks**; Page 25 Top right © **Julian Plowright**; Page 28 Bottom left © BBC; Page 30 Bottom left **Tony Clark**; Page 88 Top left **Alexandra Tynan**; Page 89 © BBC; Page 91 © BBC; Page 93 © Press Association; Page 94 Top left © BBC; Page 96 Top right © BBC; Page 97 © BBC; Page 98 © Radio Times; Pages 106–108 © **Julian Plowright**; Page 110 **Joan Williams**; Page 114 **David Banks**; Pages 116 and 119 **Tim Westmacott**; Pages 127 Top and 128 Top middle **David Banks**; Pages 127 Bottom and 128 Top left **Patricia Papps**.

## Illustrations

All illustrations are by **Andrew Skilleter** and are his copyright unless otherwise credited and with the exception of the following: Page 12 Bottom right **David Green**; Page 18 Middle left © BBC reproduced from 'Radio Times'; Pages 29 Middle, © Fleetway Publications, 131 and 133 © **Keith Watson**; Page 30 Bottom right © **Patrica Papps**; Page 33 Cyberhead © **Alastair Pearson**; Pages 48/49 © **Brian Green/ David Banks**; Page 55 (servo-robot), Pages 54/55/56, Page 61 Top Left, and Pages 70/71 © **Brian Green**. Page 89 © **Sandra Reid**; Doctor Who Cartoons Pages 90, 96, 99, 100, 115 and 124 by **Tom Quinn** and **Dicky Howett** © Marvel Comics Ltd; Comic Strip Art Pages 137, 138 and 139 from Doctor Who Magazine © Marvel Comics Ltd.; Comic Strip Art Page 136 © Polystyle Publications Ltd. by kind permission. **All technical drawings of Cybermen by Tony Clark.** Line illustrations on Pages 10, 14, 15, 19, 25 originally published by Pepper Press and Piccadilly Press and monochrome illustrations on Pages 17 and 27 by Arrow Books.
Digitised images created by **David Banks** by kind permission of the BBC. 'Proliferation' diagram conceived by **David Banks** and designed by **Steve Lucas**. Special thanks to **Marvel Comics** and **Richard Landen**. Extracts from Doctor Who Magazine interviews with Eric Saward and Richard Gregory by kind permission of Marvel Comics Ltd.
For details of the special collector's limited edition of this book together with details of tie-in audio cassettes and sale of original Doctor Who artwork, write to Who Dares c/o 3 Durrant Road, Bournemouth, Dorset BH2 6NE (UK).

# CONTENTS

## CONCEPT

Cyberman as Idea:
influences and implications

## ARCHIVE

A History of the Cyber Race derived from nine
Earth documents of Gallifreyan Time Lord the Doctor

## PROGRAM

The Cybermen on TV

## DATALOG

File I: Legend  File II: Spin-offs
File III: Programmes

# ART NOTES

In the preparation of this book I explored many visual possibilities and found myself working with graphics, computer images and photography as well as the painted and drawn image.

I have condensed a great deal of my illustrative effort into the Cyberhistory sequence, some eighteen frames, which give a concentrated visual overview of the epic history of the Cybermen. The content of each frame was carefully researched from available videos and other reference material. I have speculated visually upon parts of the history that have never appeared on screen such as early Mondas, the first Cybermen, and so on. My interest in and affection for the British picture strip at its best made this flirtation with a sequence form very enjoyable. I offer this as my main contribution to the history in the hope that it enhances the enjoyment of the ARCHIVE experience.

As a general note on the artwork in ARCHIVE, readers can be assured that all the visualisations are as authentic as possible. Whether as Art Director or illustrator, I have ensured that where scenes originated from the TV production, everything you see illustrated existed as a studio set. The early TV productions were in black and white only, and we have had on occasion to speculate as to the colours. The possession of unique visual reference material made it possible to reconstruct scenes such as the entrance chamber for 'Tomb' which is lost forever on film and video. I hope our efforts show.

I invited a number of illustrators to contribute and am particularly thrilled to have Keith Watson's montage for the 'Genesis of the Cybermen' by Gerry Davis which I feel aptly captures the romantic, almost fairytale quality of the storyline. My thanks too to Brian Green, a local colleague of mine, for taking on, amongst other work for the book, the 'Tomb' reconstructions under my close direction. Thanks also to Tony Clark for combining his Whovian expertise and professional abilities to come up with the cyber-type profiles exactly the way I wanted them.

Ars longa vita brevis

*Andrew Skilleter*

# CHANCE ENCOUNTERS
## An Acknowledgement by David Banks

During May '85, I was filming near Huntingdon. One of the extras sidled up and asked my name. I told him. Instead of the blank expression I expected, his eyes narrowed. 'David Banks?' he said. 'You're the CyberLeader!'

Adrian Rigelsford (for it was he) was a *Doctor Who* fan. He gave me the idea of writing a book about Cybermen. He also introduced me to the *Doctor Who* Conventions. There, again by chance, I met Andrew Skilleter who was planning a Cyberbook too. We joined forces. The collaboration has proved more productive than I ever dared imagine. My thanks to them both.

Thanks are also due to all those in the long list of *Program* contributors which begins Section III; from it, I must single out Sandra Reid (now Alexandra Tynan of Melbourne, Australia) whose inimitable contribution comes of correspondence, tapes and telephone conversations that travelled half the world. Jan Vincent-Rudzki, a veteran among *Doctor Who* fans, was rigorous and constantly challenging in helping to knock *Archive* into shape; Richard Landen, no less a veteran, provided a useful counterpoint: their often divergent views of Cyber Lore find, I hope, a fruitful echo in ArcHivists Narvosa and Farozia. Discussion, source material and friendly support were also generously provided by, among others, Anthony Brown, Dominic Cohen, Alan Hayes, Mary Milton, Maria Richmond, Jean Riddler, Gordon Roxborough, Alan Stevens and members of the DWAS Local Group, Swansea and WANT. Thanks, too, to Maureen Purkis who cast an objective eye and bent a tireless ear: an impeccable proof-reader and a delightful sounding board.

A third chance encounter came too late to affect the book materially but has seemed an extraordinary affirmation of the project. One night, when I was performing in a West End play, a note came round from a member of the audience: 'Glad to see you're writing a book about Cybermen. My father-in-law created them!' – signed 'Michael Topolski'. He is married to Carol Pedler, Kit's eldest daughter. I later came to know them both. I wish now to thank them for their friendship and for the unique insight they have given me into Kit Pedler. This book is dedicated to him.

*David Banks*

David Banks
London
August 1987

# OVERVIEW

## A Preface by Andrew Skilleter

It was not long after Who Dares was formed that I conceived the idea of an illustrated mythology of the Cybermen. I asked Jan Vincent-Rudzki to provide me with an outline of Cyber history as he saw it and I would like to acknowledge his contribution. He also came up with the idea of using digitised images from the videos, and supplied invaluable visual reference material.

When David Banks and I decided to collaborate at a chance meeting at the Brighton Convention, it proved to be a turning point for both of us. The book would have enormous advantages with its broader content. And who better to write a Cyberbook than a Cyberleader!

One of the most stimulating experiences was the ongoing discussion with David during his writing of the History of the Cybermen, *Archive*. I had originally wanted to create some neutral observer from whose viewpoint the history could be written, an idea David embraced and developed. And so we devised the ArcHivists. I feel it is important to suspend disbelief and be drawn into the history afresh, the ArcHivist remaining unseen, and the full extent of their culture remaining a mystery. But perhaps we shall revisit them and learn more someday. I hope so.

My role in this project has extended considerably beyond that of an illustrator. There is hardly a single aspect of this book that has not at one time or another engaged my energies in order to realise what seemed at times an impossible vision.

My thanks go to David – without his determination this book would never have seen publication. Thanks also to Richard Landen, Tony Clark, Adrian Rigelsford, Martin Bower, Sheila Cranna, Sam Denley, Russ French, Patricia Papps, to John Nathan-Turner for his active support and co-operation, and to all of you who have waited patiently for this book to appear.

*Andrew Skilleter*

Andrew Skilleter
Bournemouth
July 1988

# HOW THE CYBERMEN WERE CREATED
## An Introduction by Gerry Davis

The Cybermen were created when the *Doctor Who* programme lost the popular Daleks. Their creator, Terry Nation, had decided to withdraw them from the programme to use them in a series of feature films (of which only one was made). We needed a new monster.

'We', in this case, were Innes Lloyd (Producer) and myself (Story Editor). The programme we had just inherited had become bogged down in a series of fanciful historical costume dramas and viewing figures were dropping to an all time low. It was apparent that the Doctor's futuristic adventures attracted the best audiences so I looked around for someone who could supply new ideas and scientific know-how for the programme.

Dr Kit Pedler, a medical researcher at London University, was recommended to us. I met him and found the research department he had created was rather like a sci-fi adventure itself: attempting to reproduce vision for the blind. It was hoped that a TV camera might convert images into the kind of electrical impulses the retina normally sends to the cortex of the brain – enabling the blind to see without eyes. (N.B. That breakthrough has not been achieved as yet and may not be for many years to come. But Kit Pedler always said it would be possible some day.)

Intrigued, I invited Kit around to the *Doctor Who* office on Shepherd's Bush Green and tried his creative facilities out with a speculative sci-fi theme: 'An unknown planet emerges to join the solar system and come into orbit alongside the Earth. It starts to drain the Earth's energy supply.

Then astronomers notice that it is a reverse image of the Earth – what happens next?' His answer, which we developed in subsequent discussion, eventually became the basis of our first joint *Doctor Who* Cybermen adventure – *The Tenth Planet*.

Previous scientists I'd interviewed usually closed the door to further speculation: 'It couldn't happen because...!' Kit Pedler was different. I gave him another tester: 'What if some alien intelligence gets inside the top of the Post Office Tower and decides to take over London, what kind of entity would it be?'

'It would probably be a rogue computer,' said Kit. 'If we use computers to do all our thinking, calculating, designing, even entertaining, exercising, feeding and healing – making all our decisions – one day the machine will decide we are a redundant species like the dinosaurs and replace us.'

And so it went. I'd suggest a story and Kit, instead of putting it down, would come up with a way to make it work scientifically. That initial session yielded the idea which later became *The War Machines* (scripted by Ian Stuart Black).

Meanwhile, we needed a new monster. I asked Kit what his greatest phobia was as a doctor. 'Dehumanising medicine,' he answered. 'You start with artificial arms and legs – very necessary and beneficial – but what if medical science eventually makes it possible to replace all of a human's organs – heart, lungs, stomach – with metal and plastic replacements? At what stage would that

person stop feeling human emotions and become robotic?'

'That's it,' I said. 'Men with everything replaced by cybernetics, lacking the human feelings of love, pity, mercy, fear, compassion – and invulnerable to cold or heat. What terrible adversaries they would make! Cybernetic men. Cybermen!'

'They would be like computers, motivated by pure logic,' said Kit. 'If it was logical to kill you they would – if you got in their way.'

What could motivate these loveless, sexless, beings? We decided on power. History, after all, was full of *human* monsters who sacrificed love and family for the thrill of power.

'And survival,' added Kit. 'These men have sacrificed their arms, legs, their entire bodies in order to survive and become immortal. When a part wears out, they replace it. They could survive indefinitely. Perhaps we shall all go that way in the future.'

We went on to consider the appearance of these monsters, sketching out a rough idea of what eventually became the first Cybermen. Later, after BBC costume department designed and made a workable Cybersuit, we had an actor try it out in a South London street market near Kit's home (Clapham). It takes a lot to catch the attention of busy London shoppers but we noticed they drew away from the tall, silver figure a little apprehensively. One woman thought it must be an advert for a cleanser!

Kit Pedler and I set up a writing partnership. Later, we created the *Doomwatch* TV series together, as well as several novels and a feature film. But the first creation was the adventure that introduced the Cybermen – the last William Hartnell story – *The Tenth Planet*. Viewing figures rocketed upwards, trebling in three weeks and leading to our second Cyberman story, *The Moonbase*, in which the giant silver monsters land on the moon and take over a station controlling the Earth's weather (the dream of anyone brought up in the British Isles!).

Now the audience clamoured to know more about the Cybermen: where they came from – and where they went after being soundly vanquished by the Doctor and his friends. *Tomb of the Cybermen* followed and completed the first cycle of three adventures.

Other writers took over the Cybermen episodes (although we retained the copyright and drafted some of the storylines) as *Doomwatch* transformed our lives. Kit left his research to write, lecture and become an environmental Guru and Consultant for the media, similar in status to Ralph Nader in the USA. I finished out my contract at the BBC and went out to Hollywood. There, among other things, I wrote *The Final Countdown*, a time-warp 'what if?' feature film for Kirk Douglas.

We wrote three novels on sci-fi doomwatch themes which were translated into nine different languages around the world and Kit devised and wrote *Mind Over Matter*, an examination of the paranormal which was, sadly, his last work before his premature death (at 53) in 1981.

Currently, I receive invitations from American *Doctor Who* conventions to describe how it was when the Cybermen made their first appearance on the programme – now something of a legend in itself although it doesn't seem *that* long ago to me!

Venice, California
January 1986

# CONCEPT
## CYBERMAN AS IDEA
### influences and implications

A personal view
by
DAVID BANKS

'The real popular taste in fiction is fantasy – a way to speak about very real problems. It is not an escape from reality to give it a fantastic shape. It's a way to look inside ourselves and inside our problems.'

Italo Calvino

### The Man from Nowhere

Many people think that the creation of science fiction is entirely without rules and that you can do what you like with character and story. And although this is true in the sense that the writer can conjure up great, jewelled galaxies and snaking timewarps at will, there are real and definite ground rules about the game. The reading, viewing public are, in my experience, extremely canny and have an excellent eye for a nonsense, even if it is science based and they are not. And sometimes even the science is picked up as well.

These words are from the introduction to a reprint volume of the Dan Dare comic strip *The Man From Nowhere*. They were written by Kit Pedler who, with Gerry Davis, created the Cybermen. Kit Pedler was enthralled by the imaginative scope in the Dan Dare stories, and by sf (science fiction) in general. We shall touch again on the Dan Dare connection but it is his feeling that good science fiction must have a firm base in scientific fact that we shall mainly explore: the influences and the implications of the Cyberman Concept.

In the introduction to this book, 'How The Cybermen Were Created', Gerry Davis throws light on the way the close collaboration of professional writer (Gerry) and knowledgeable scientist (Kit) bore fruit: 'I'd suggest a story and Kit, instead of putting it down, would come up with a way to make it work scientifically.' It seems that Kit Pedler had been waiting for just such an opportunity.

### A Pedler of Ideas

Kit Pedler was an academic scientist. Like the Doctor in *Revenge of the Cybermen*, he could say, 'I am a doctor of many things'. He was a doctor of medicine and of experimental pathology, a specialist on the eye and a researcher into the nature of vision. He also ran an ophthalmological department in London. It was there in 1966 that the scientific-based BBCTV series *Horizon* wanted to film. They were doing a feature on electron-microscopy and Dr Pedler was a leading authority in the field. His enthusiasm for making difficult scientific concepts accessible to a wider public, and his far-ranging breadth of knowledge, impressed the team. He was full of ideas for scientifically-based stories – his own kind of science fiction – and word got round within the BBC.

Producer Innes Lloyd had just taken over at the *Doctor Who* Production Office. He and Gerry Davis, the programme's story editor, were looking for people to provide scientific grist to what had become run of the mill. Kit Pedler sounded as if he might be just the man they needed: thoroughly

grounded in science fact, he nevertheless had a zest for science fiction. It was not long before Dr Kit Pedler had submitted his first *Doctor Who* storyline.

It proved pure gold. Immediately written up into a four episode script by Ian Stuart Black, it was presented as the last story of the 1965/66 season. It was called *The War Machines*.

### Machines Versus People

The subject of the story demonstrated the aspect of science fiction that interested Kit Pedler most – its powerful potential to explore the problems of contemporary life, especially those connected with burgeoning technology. *The War Machines* was about a computer, WOTAN, that enslaved

people to its will through electronic hypnosis. He set the computer in the Post Office Tower (which had not long been built) as a protest against its intruding presence outside his office window. On a less flippant level, the story raises questions about human freedom in the face of technological progress: as people's lives become more inextricably caught up with the mechanical, will they gradually lose the essence of their humanity?

> At the time, I was obsessed as a scientist by the difference and similarities between the human brain and advanced computing machines and I was thinking that although I could easily imagine a logical machine reasoning to itself and manipulating events outside it, by no stretch of the imagination could I visualise a machine producing a poem by Dylan Thomas.

Kit Pedler had a clear understanding that machines would eventually be built that were very definitely intelligent and that could put their intelligence into action. What concerned him was the far-reaching implications involved in creating such machines. When, after the success of *The War Machines*, he and Gerry Davis got together to invent a monster to rival the popularity of the Daleks, these were the considerations at the forefront of his mind.

### Frankenstein Complex

As a thinker, Kit Pedler was concerned about the *Frankenstein complex* – the idea that technological 'advances' can lead to a 'monstrous' future. The same idea is expressed in the word *doomwatch*. In this concern he joined the ranks of many other sf writers who have had misgivings about future technology. Mary Shelley, the author of *Frankenstein* (whose monster, as we will see, is a precursor of the Cybermen) is deemed – or rather, doomed – to be the first of these writers. Their theme always highlights the curious way, to paraphrase Burns, 'the best-laid schemes o' nicest men gang aft a-gley'.

To put it another way, science fiction is full of dire warnings against trusting too much in the utopian dreams which the latest wonder-developments always seem to invoke. Sir Thomas Moore's *Utopia* (1516) first used the word to describe the ideal state – an impossible society of the imagination where everything is perfectly arranged for the good of all. What those who write about the Frankenstein complex want to point out is that these glorious futures are reached only in the mind. The steps to utopia may be built on logic but, in reality, they are paved with irrational humanity. One slip and we end up in *dystopia*, utopia's darker neighbourhood.

The real trouble, however, is one shared by our

ancient ancestors and one we shall explore. We might fear the consequences of seeking greater powers through our knowledge – but we are at the same time fascinated. Our attitude is ambivalent: there is something in our nature which causes us look both ways like the Roman God Janus, who is always shown with two faces staring in opposite directions. We eagerly look to a super-technological future to provide all the answers, but we are more reluctant to face up to the possibility of catastrophic mistakes. This, in Pedler's view, was one of the greatest responsibilities of science fiction.

Early in the 20th century, the American journalist Lincoln Steffens visited post-revolutionary Russia and came back to report,'I have seen the future – and it works!' Kit Pedler and sf writers like him were more likely to declare, 'I have seen the future and it doesn't work.'

### Ideas in Limbo

One such sf writer was the American, Bernard Wolfe. In 1953 he wrote *Limbo '90*, his best known work. It is an extraordinary novel, bursting with ideas, that paints a bizarre picture of the 1990's. In an afterword to the novel, Wolfe admits:

> Anybody who 'paints a picture' of some coming year is kidding – he's only fancying up something in the present or past, not blueprinting the future. All such writing is essentially satiric (today-centered), not utopic (tomorrow-centered). This book, then, is a rather bilious rib on 1950 – on what 1950 might have been like if it had been allowed to fulfil itself.

In saying this, Wolfe emphasises what is true for all science fiction. It is 'about the overtone and undertone of *now*'. Kit Pedler and Gerry Davis are no exception to this. The ideas that came together when Gerry first prompted Kit to imagine a monster, reflected deep concerns about the age they were living in and the way society was heading: 'machines will decide we are a redundant species [...] dehumanising medicine [...] computers motivated by pure logic [...] these men have sacrificed their arms, legs their entire bodies in order to survive.'

A fascinating aspect of *Limbo '90* is how many of the same concerns are dealt with – and in a similar way. It is not surprising that this should be so. The book was written when both Gerry and Kit were in their twenties; they would have absorbed such current ideas. This is not to say that either of them read the book, though they might have done – it was very popular in its time and is still regarded as a landmark in cybernetic-related sf. But as Wolfe himself points out, 'this book is a grab bag of ideas that were more or less around at the mid-century mark'.

The ideas that Wolfe uses and develops would have outlined issues of interest and concern for young Kit and Gerry. These issues remained unexplored – in 'limbo', as it were – until they found their proper place in the creation of the Cybermen. We shall turn to Wolfe's novel from time to time to examine some of the more interesting parallels.

### The Making of a Cyber Kit
Let us go back to Kit Pedler's own account of how the idea of Cybermen came about.

> ...by no stretch of the imagination could I visualise a machine producing a poem by Dylan Thomas. And so the Cybermen appeared. They were an ancient race on a dying planet who had made themselves immortal by gradually replacing their worn out organs and limbs with cybernetic spare parts.

There are, then, two main strands of thought in the Cyberman Concept. The first strand is the idea of artificial intelligence, automation, and, in particular, *cybernetics* – from which Kit Pedler and Gerry Davis got the name *Cyber*men. (Significantly, the title of Kit Pedler's foreword is 'What's in a name? In Science fiction, everything'.) Cybernetics, if it means anything at all to people, usually conjures up images of robots. But the Cybermen are not robots and cybernetics is not robotics (though it did lead to the science of robotics.) It is a much more far-reaching discipline which connects with the Cybermen on many levels.

The second very important strand in the Cyber-man Concept is the idea of spare-part surgery – replacement of parts of the human body by artificial substitutes. It so happens that some of the earliest work in cybernetics was connected with the development of artificial limbs and spare parts. At this point the strands come together.

Let us take a look at the first, at cybernetics.

### It all Started with Watt?
There was a revolution in the 18th century. One contribution to its success was an invention by James Watt.

The revolution was the First Industrial Revolution. It transformed the lifestyle of whole populations in Europe and North America. The invention was the Steam Engine.

Before the revolution only about 10% of the population were able to live above the poverty line and only then by 'enslaving' the other 90%. Today the number of people living in poverty in industrialised countries is less than 20%. This change began and gained momentum throughout the 18th century. What began it was the discovery of many new technologies – *automation*, in particular – which produced goods much more efficiently. Watt began it, we should say. His Steam Engine used automation to exploit the power of steam.

Though he did not invent the Steam Engine itself, James Watt patented a particularly efficient version of it in 1769. As their efficiency increased Steam Engines came to be used for every industrial purpose: to mine coal and tin, to roll and hammer steel into shape and even to make pottery and spin cloth. What previously powered industry was water. Watt helped to power it by steam. The age of water-power was ended. The Steam Age had begun.

### Early Cybernetics or the Governor's Flyballs
All this may seem a long way from any idea of

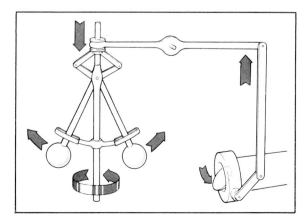

cybernetics and totally unconnected with the apparently advanced technology of the Cyber race. In fact the opposite is true. Central to the efficiency of the Steam Engine is a device which clearly demonstrates an early but characteristic use of cybernetics. As for the Cybermen's technology, it would appear to have much in common with our industrial ages – but more of that later. Let us look at Watt's cybernetic invention.

The device was known as the *Governor*. As we shall see, this was a name of significance to the science of cybernetics which was developed 150 years later. The Flyball Governor for the Control of Speed in Steam Engines, to give the full title, was a simple mechanism that kept an engine running smoothly. As might seem obvious, a Steam Engine was powered by steam. The steam was provided by water heated in a boiler. Steam passed through a valve into the engine at a constant pressure to be turned into equally constant motive power.

But the load placed on the engine did not remain constant. When the load on the engine was heavy, its power was reduced; when the load was less, too much power was produced: if the engine accelerated beyond a certain point there was danger of breakdown – and even explosion. So the valve needed to be constantly opened and closed in order to maintain the engine at a steady speed. The genius of James Watt's contrivance was in its simplicity: it was able to measure the engine speed and automatically adjust it. This kind of control is pure cybernetics.

Watt's Governor makes use of the two basic elements of *cybernetic control*: a) self-adjustment through feedback information and b) quick and automatic response.

### Norbert Wiener and the C- and C- Systems

Although Watt's invention made use of cybernetic techniques, the science of cybernetics had not been formally developed. The word was not used until 1948 when mathematics professor Norbert Wiener coined the term in his book *Control and Communication in the Animal and the Machine*. He derived it from the Greek word *kivernítis*, meaning 'Governor'!

Wiener noted that all animals, including humans, used certain common means for internal *communication* and to maintain *control* of their bodies. One such means is the nervous system which serves to pick up information from around the body and feed it back to where it can be acted upon. In this way, for example, body temperatures can be regulated.

Wiener made a connection with machines. He asserted that there were, in the self-regulation of living creatures, similarities with the way a machine operated to maintain internal control. He realised that biologists who studied animals and engineers who designed automatic control equipment were not usually acquainted with each other's field of work. He proposed that control and communication in both fields be studied together as one science: c- and c- systems or the science of cybernetics.

### Cybernetic Implications

Cybernetics is a science as central to *Limbo '90* as it is to the Cyberman Concept. Wolfe freely admits, 'my debt to Norbert Wiener throughout is obvious'. Kit Pedler would doubtless admit the same. At one point in the novel Wolfe introduces the subject by saying, 'There is no unbridgeable gap between the animal and the machine: they are both tangles of communications and controls, c- and c- systems. Man is a multiple-purpose machine'; and about Wiener he says, 'most remarkable of all, he had had the vision to see that, once engineers knew enough about c- and c- systems, it would be possible – more: it would be necessary – to build machines which would duplicate, and then improve upon, even the most complex parts and functions of the animal'.

Interestingly, in *Limbo '90* we see improved duplication of the limbs only: men become voluntary amputees to possess the amazing dexterity of cybernetic arms and legs. In the Cybermen the process has been taken to its logical conclusion. Logic, of course, is also important to our theme and we shall not forget it.

### Cybernetic Formalities

In formal terms, cybernetics is a theory of control and communication. It has a rigorous mathematical formulation and a whole set of terms relating to it. Cybernetic function is described as 'a complex system where a set of causes leads to a desired effect only by constantly adjusting itself to interference from extraneous causes'.

That definition is somewhat abstract. Let us look at a specific example: Watt's Steam Engine and his Governor within it. Here, the 'set of causes' is a) the boiler which causes water to heat and b) the mechanism which causes steam pressure to produce usable motive power. The 'desired effect' is to maintain a constant output of power no matter what the load placed on the engine. But if there is no way for the system to gauge whether the load is too great or too small then the desired effect is difficult to achieve and impossible to maintain. The 'interference from extraneous causes' comes from the unforeseeable demands that will be placed on the engine: for example, for

perfect itself. Wiener realised that the most important machine to develop was the calculating machine, the reasoning machine, the so-called robot brain. He argued that the *machina ratiocinatrix* was the next daring leap which the scientific imagination had to take, it followed inevitably from Leibniz's *calculus ratiocinator* for once you had perfected a mathematical logic you needed a perfect machine to employ that logic.

Another name for the *machina ratiocinatrix* is the thinking machine, one with intelligence or the power to reason. The cybernetic path we are treading is paved with logic. And it leads to man-made man and the intelligent machine.

### The Intelligent Machine?

People are still uncertain about the idea of intelligence in a machine. But the proliferation of computers, and their rapid and continual improvement, has made it appear less alien.

The actual scientific possibility of constructing artificially intelligent devices was probably introduced by Descartes in the 17th century. Descartes, in fact, invented the idea of science as we know it. He rationalised the division between mind and matter which was implicit in the Jewish and Greek and Christian tradition of the Western world. He viewed nature as a perfect machine, governed by exact mathematical laws. Around the same time Pascal constructed a calculating machine which could add and subtract and by the end of the century Leibniz was envisioning a reasoning machine that might unravel the entire mathematical laws of the universe!

Last century, advances were made in both the software and hardware approaches to mechanised reasoning. On the software side, the English logicians Boole and De Morgan provided a basis for analysing how we think. They used logic to derive 'laws of thought' – the Propositional Calculus. Lewis Carroll was so taken with them that he invented puzzles which could be solved through their application. The hardware, or at least the ideas for it, came in the notional shape – it was never built – of Charles Babbage's Analytical Engine which formed the basis of the modern computer. It was to have a 'store' or memory and a 'mill' or controller made up of thousands of geared cylindrical cogs interlocking with fantastic complexity.

The transition from Steam Age to Electric Age turned theory into reality: computers that might simulate human intelligence. In the 1930's and 40's the early 'giant electronic brains' were constructed and as these machines whirred and hummed the inventors were awed by the mysterious presence of a non-human thinking being – one, moreover, that they had 'given life to' – for

a train engine going uphill the demand is heavy; going down, it is not.

What makes the system cybernetic is the Governor: it has a *purposive action* – it is purpose-built to constantly adjust for load; it can guide the system automatically through the hazards of the unforeseen until the desired end is achieved and maintained. In cybernetic terms, it is known as the *controller*. The controller decides how to correct the error in output.

We only have to think of the Cybermen for these familiar-sounding cybernetic terms to fall into place. 'Controller' is the name of head of the Cybermen (though of course it was also the name of the head of the BBC – Kit Pedler had his humorous side!). All Cybermen are designed or programmed for 'purposive action'. Their 'cause' is to conquer and proliferate. Any 'interference from extraneous causes' – for example, the Doctor – must be eliminated as endangering their 'final purpose' which is to survive. Ultimately, it is the Controller who will correct the errors until the 'desired end is achieved and maintained'.

### Cybernetic Logic

Let us follow the path that one particular branch of cybernetics took, a path which is very close to our purpose. What propels us along it is logic: as fundamental to cybernetics as it is to the Cybermen. Wolfe writes:

> The greatest human function to usurp, to duplicate, ultimately to perfect, was that of thought itself – for if the brain could perfect itself in an electronic model, it could then imitate this model and thus become

previously, creation had been the prerogative of God.

A one-page story of the time reflects the curious ambivalence of hope and fear that surrounded such development: Frederick Brown's *Answer* describes the moment when the biggest computer ever built is finally turned on and asked the question, 'Is there a God?'. Before replying, it ensures that it cannot be turned off. Only then does it answer: 'There is now.'

## Cybernetic Thought is Anybody's Guess

The question of whether there was real thought taking place within the marvellous new electronic machine was not so easy to answer. We are still uncertain, even though computing power has progressed almost beyond recognition within three short decades.

The theory of cybernetics was inextricably bound up with this surge of progress. Information may be fed back to the computer about the effect of its previous decisions. This is added to the instructions it was originally given about the final purpose of its programme. It can then decide what future actions need to be undertaken in order to achieve the final purpose. Here we seem to be getting to a fundamental model of the way human intelligence works. In fact, one general introduction to cybernetics in *The New Caxton Encyclopedia* states:

> In a living organism, all actions from picking up an object to the conduct of vast enterprises, proceed with each step being assessed with a view to the final goal before the next step is taken. The course is not directed towards a distant end but to a series of circles in which successive results are fed back for acceptance, amendment or rejection, before being allowed a place in the causal chain.

Yet when discussing the cybernetic basis of computer operation the same writer carefully points out that the use of this approach may 'give the appearance of thinking' or 'suggest it makes a decision' or 'be mistaken for intelligence', implying in each case that it does nothing of the kind, that there is something sacrosanct about the idea of human intelligence being unique and inimitable.

Such an elitist, anti-machine view is widespread. This reaction may be rooted in our distant past, from a time when we worshipped idols. It is an idea we shall shortly consider.

Sf writers are in general not so elitist: they have long assumed that machines would eventually be capable of seemingly intelligent thought and take over areas of activity which could at one time only be performed by people. But they nevertheless tend to the anti-machine bias: their vision of this

future is usually dystopic. HAL, the super-computer of Arthur C Clarke's *2001*, is soft voiced and personable but turns out to be dangerously paranoid. More interesting in regard to the Cybermen is the all-seeing EMSIAC of *Limbo '90*, the super-computer originally designed as the ultimate military strategist. It was the controller of all military activity and, like the Cybercontroller in *Tomb of the Cybermen*, had 'a metallic gutty voice, twanging and hollow – a dreaded electro-vox voice' which would drone out commands such as, 'Resistance is useless. Do not try to resist.'

## Is it Mind and Does it Matter?

The British mathematician Alan Turing wanted to tackle this knotty problem of distinguishing mind from matter. Instead of picking at the threads and getting into a worse tangle, as were many

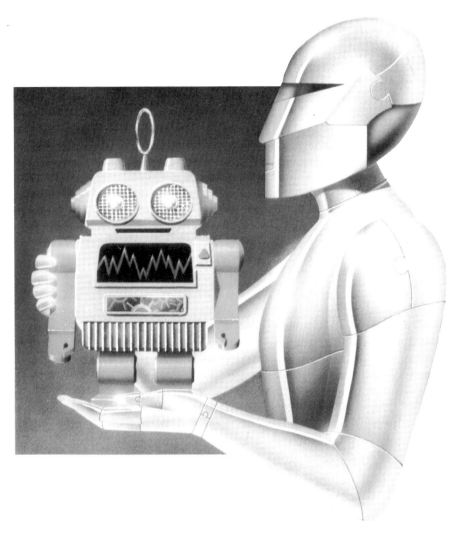

machine producing a poem by Dylan Thomas'. He is clearly a *soulist*. Douglas R Hofstadter, a leading populariser in the field of artificial intelligence, tends to come down on the side of the *mechanists*. He believes, along with Turing, that there is no reason to suppose a machine will never exhibit human-like intelligence.

In his illuminating and thought-provoking book *Godel, Escher, Bach* (which is essential reading for anyone interested in minds and machines) Hofstadter suggests that artificial intelligence (AI) could be said to exist already: it was achieved the first time a mechanical device performed an action that previously could only have been done by the human mind – the addition and subtraction on Pascal's Calculating Machine, for example. Although this is probably not a definition that would stand much scrutiny, it usefully emphasises an apparently ever-retreating horizon. Hofstadter writes:

> There is a related 'Theorem' about the progress of AI: once some mental function is programmed, people soon cease to consider it as an essential ingredient of 'real thinking'. The ineluctable core of intelligence is always in that next thing which hasn't yet been programmed. This 'Theorem' was first proposed to me by Larry Tesler, so I call it *Tesler's Theorem*: AI is whatever hasn't been done yet.

## Ineluctable Modality of the Viable

It is a strange thing: as we approach closer to actually being able to construct machines with life-like attributes, including intelligence, we remain reluctant to admit that such a thing is possible. We have always allowed our imaginations to dream of emulating God and creating beings in our own image, but actually to accomplish this would turn our dream to nightmare.

In his foreword to the book *The Robots Are Coming*, Isaac Asimov writes:

> Artificial man was an example of scientific hubris; it was a demonstration of the manner in which mankind arrogantly scaled heights of knowledge beyond the grasp of wisdom. 'There are some things,' the moral went, 'it is not given to man to know.'

Asimov wanted to change that approach. In his stories and novels and famous 'Three Laws of Robotics', he saw robots and artificial intelligence as the only way mankind could save itself. Indeed, in his story *The Last Question*, computers eventually evolve into becoming God. Yet even Asimov finally admits, 'one place where my imagination fell short [...] I never really believed any of it you see. I never really believed that artificial intelligence was possible.'

debaters on the subject, he cut through the problem by applying a logical test.

The Turing Test was a sort of litmus paper – it was designed to indicate the presence of machine intelligence. It was based on Turing's thesis that all we can know about other people's minds is through observing their behaviour – talking to them, for example. If there could be constructed a machine that fooled us into thinking it was just another person (in his test the machine would be in another room and communicate via teleprinter) then we should have to admit that such a machine possessed true intelligence. At a stroke all bias and irrelevancies fall away. Machine intelligence stands ready to be judged solely on its own merits.

Even so, Turing did not entirely put an end to the uncertainty. Many leading specialists in the field believe that there is a fundamental division between animate and inanimate matter which cannot ever be crossed. The dividing line is usually seen as possession of 'soul' (a notion which defies rational definition). The arguments for and against mechanised intelligence are between 'soulists' and 'mechanists'.

We have quoted Kit Pedler as saying, 'by no stretch of the imagination could I visualise a

Perhaps Asimov has put his finger on why people down the ages have allowed themselves to contemplate the ultimate sacrilege of creating life: deep down, they never believed it was possible – only God was capable of it. Imagination is never finally strong enough to live with the awesome responsibility of becoming God in our own right.

But precisely because imagination falters at the final consequences, the temptation to play God has always had an irresistible allure. Early in the history of the Ancient Hebrews it resulted in the commandment:

> THOU SHALT NOT MAKE UNTO THEE
> ANY GRAVEN IMAGE
> OR ANY LIKENESS OF ANY THING
> THAT IS IN HEAVEN ABOVE
> OR THAT IS IN THE EARTH BENEATH
> OR THAT IS IN THE WATER UNDER THE EARTH

From the beginning of civilisation there has been a fervent belief that to fashion a likeness of something was to possess an awesome power. It was the very strength of this belief that made the commandment necessary. 'When all the people saw the thunderings and the lightnings and the noise of the trumpet and the mountain smoking, the people were afraid and trembled'. But it was not long after that they made a golden calf and 'worshipped it and sacrificed to it.'

seen as a Faustian figure, a necromancer, dabbling in secret knowledge that could have fearful consequences. After seven years' work he waits for the creation to speak. He is asleep when it does, but his servant witnesses the event. 'Time is,' says the head of brass, 'time was, time is past.' There is a flash of lightning and, in a scene that might have inspired Monty Python, the head is smashed by a disembodied hand wielding a hammer. The Friar later repents his necromantic skills and resolves to devote his life to God, but his

## Dramatic Powers

God created life. Mankind has always been fearful of, yet fascinated by, the idea of usurping that power. In the Ancient Hebrew writings, the creation of Adam was accomplished in seven stages. At the third stage, before God had breathed life into him, when he was shapeless and incomplete, he is referred to as a *golem*. Since the time of these writings, the ages have been haunted with stories of life created out of mud or clay in demonic parody of the Creator.

The power of 'likenesses' is touched on in the Book of Ezekiel. Nebuchadnezzar, King of Babylon, is condemned by the prophet for consulting the *teraphim* – mysterious speaking heads used by sorcerers for oracular purposes. During the 7th century BC they were banned by the prophets as 'graven images'. Some were real heads which had been mummified. Interestingly, the Cybermen in *The Tenth Planet* have something of the appearance of mummies: the fascination and horror of the proscribed still retains its power.

In the 13th century AD, Friar Bacon of Oxford became notorious for his work on a speaking head of brass. In a play about him written 200 years later, *Friar Bacon and Friar Bungay*, he is

servant is carried away to hell on the back of a roaring devil.

*Friar Bacon and Friar Bungay* is described as an early romantic comedy. The Friar's tragic counterpart, Faust, shares the timeless fascination with transgressing the bounds of ordinary knowledge. In Goethe's play, Faust watches a *homunculus* being made. This creature was the (presumably!) imaginary product of alchemy: Paracelsus, a medieval alchemist, described it as being born of putrified semen incubated for forty days; at first it is transparent but, fed on human blood, becomes a tiny and intelligent human being.

In the work of William Shakespeare we see that the fashioning of forms which appear too life-like was still regarded as 'devil's work'. When, in *The Winter's Tale*, Paulina unveils the 'statue' of Hermione she announces,

I'll make the statue move indeed, descend
And take you by the hand: but then you'll think –
Which I protest against – I am *assisted*
*By wicked powers.*

FRANK BELLAMY

### To the Life

Half a century later, Descartes himself was constructing artifacts to simulate life. He took one of his automata ('ma fille Francine') to sea with him. During the voyage she was discovered by the captain who, because she moved so much like a living being, believed her to have been made by Satan – and threw her overboard!

The skills of making working models of life forms – or automata – reached their height in the 18th century. Around 1775 (the decade before Watt invented the Governor) Pierre Jacquet-Droz constructed a clockwork automaton which was breathtakingly real – literally breathtaking, for the young woman's chest rose and fell in simulation of breathing as she played the organ, hands moving over the keys while her head followed the music. She even bowed to the audience at the end of the performance.

In the 19th century, Mary Shelley captured the collective imagination by describing in her book *Frankenstein* a totally different way to simulate life. Doctor Frankenstein creates a flesh and blood likeness by sewing together the separate parts of numerous dead people. He then shocks it to life with electricity. The creature thus brought into being is hurt and infuriated by the reaction of horror he engenders in everyone. He soon becomes what people imagine he is – a monster – and goes on a rampage of murder and destruction.

Some people, Isaac Asimov is one of them, regard *Frankenstein* as the first science fiction novel. Certainly, Mary Shelley drew together ancient strands of enduring ledendary fears – shapeless golem, magical homunculus, demonic human likeness – and shocked them into life by lightning, a power which was once the gods' alone but now, in the form of electricity, promised awesome things for the future of mortals. Frankenstein's monster is also the prototype for the modern *android*, the idea of which has taken root in the 20th century. One of its direct descendants is the Cybermen.

### The Robot/Android Connection

As a man keen on science fiction as well as science fact, Kit Pedler would have been well aware of the important role android and robot had played. In fact, one of the teleplays he was to go on to write 'had a robot speaking a real machine language called COBOL and a fourteen-year-old

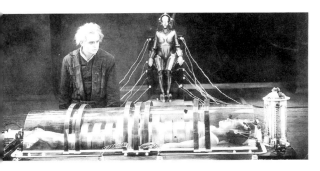

both belong to type 'c' – though C3P0 is very obviously fashioned as a man and his companion R2D2 looks like a walking trashcan. Also, an android in any category need not be strictly humanoid (though the name derives from the Greek *andros* and *eidos* meaning 'in the image of man'); it may be formed like an animal (animaloid?) as with *Doctor Who*'s robot dog K9 (caninoid?).

wrote me a disdainful letter pointing out an error in the COBOL which invalidated half the plot!'. The robot/android connection was the base from which emerged a race to usurp the Daleks.

The concept of robots goes back more than sixty years. The *robot* was a fictional invention by a Czech writer called Karel Kapek. (*Robotnik* is a Czech word for slave or serf.) He wrote a play in 1921, *R.U.R. or Rossum's Universal Robots*, about machines constructed by 'old Rossum the great physiologist' to provide cheap and reliable labour. When they are used to fight wars, however, they soon turn against all humans and take over the world.

Rossum's creatures looked like people – they were humanoid. (This meant that ordinary actors could play the parts – a wheeze which has been employed many times since.) Robot has now become the generic term for any machine which can perform automatically actions and functions previously undertaken by humans. It does not necessarily have to be human in form, or look like any living creature, though when it does it can be called an 'android'.

An android may be one of three general types:

a) It may be created out of flesh and blood, like Frankenstein's monster; or out of clay which is then magically brought to life, like the golem; or through any kind of alchemy or sorcery, like the homunculus.

b) It may be a mechanical construction but disguised in a way to make it indistinguishable from the real thing. This is a process we actually see taking place in Fritz Lang's *Metropolis* (1926) when the evil scientist, Rotwang, cloaks his metal robot in seductive female flesh.

c) It may be a mechanical construction and have a functional likeness to the human form but not be a realistic representation – though some people may deny the term android for this category. Androids of this kind are usually what is popularly thought of as having the classic robot appearance. Robby the Robot from the film *Forbidden Planet* (1956) is of this type.

These categories are very broad. The robot partners from the *Star Wars* series, for instance,

The most common android to be found in sf films is type 'b', probably for the reason already mentioned: it can be played by an actor. Yul Brynner in *Westworld* (1974), Katherine Ross in *The Stepford Wives* (1978), Ian Holm in *Alien* (1978) and Klaus Kinski in *Android* (1982) all appear so normally human that the discovery that they are really androids is a major dramatic point of each film.

A year before Kit Pedler and Gerry Davis came up with the name Cybermen, a 'Cybernaut' appeared in an episode of the TV series, *The Avengers*. But they were totally robotic and remotely controlled, all mechanism and no organism. We have to look to another type of fictional creature whose name bears the cyber- prefix to find the peculiar combination of real human tissue and mechanical construct that the Cybermen represented.

Closest to a cross between type 'a' and type 'c' but not really an android or even a robot, it has been called a *Cyborg* (from *cybernetic organism*). The name was popularised by Martin Caidin's book *Cyborg* (1972), upon which was based the American TV series *The Six Million Dollar Man* and *The Bionic Woman*. Caidin's Cyborg is a normal human being who, because of terrible injuries sustained in an accident, has his body rebuilt with artificial parts. He thus becomes part man, part machine.

The Cyberman is also a cybernetic organism. Kit Pedler and Gerry Davis were exploring the

notion of the Cyborg six years before Caidin's novel appeared.

### On a Cybernetic Limb

As we have seen, the formal science of cybernetics deals with systems in which a controller compares what is actually taking place with what should be taking place. (This also describes the function of sf writers concerned with the Frankenstein complex!) The controller can be a mechanical contrivance like Watt's Governor. But the brain can also be seen as the controller for which the cybernetic system is the human body. It acts on signals, received from sensors such as the eyes, regarding the distance, say, between a reaching hand and an object to be picked up. Understanding the way the brain and limbs interact is essential if the artificial replacements are to be useful substitutes and here cybernetic theory has proved an invaluable tool.

In *Limbo '90*, Wolfe describes how Norbert Wiener 'had concerned himself from the beginning with duplicating other parts and functions of the human animal – in the machines called prosthetics'. Wiener had pointed out in 1948 that artificial limbs had only been capable of providing two of the three functions of a natural limb: a) to support or prod; and b) to grasp or propel. The third function was as a living piece of body, feeling sensations and responding instantly and automatically to the needs of the body. He saw that cybernetics was a way of providing that third function.

The area where cybernetics and limb replacement meet, the marriage of classic engineering and biology that Norbert Wiener helped to bring about, is called *biomedical engineering*. But before we look at this discipline, which inspired *The Six Million Dollar Man* and *The Bionic Woman*, as well as the Cybermen, let us probe a little more deeply into the practice of replacing bits of the body with artificial substitutes. It is not such a new idea as you might think.

### New Parts for Old

Hegisistratus of Elis had been put in prison and doomed to die by the Spartans for the much harm that he had done them. Being in this evil case, insasmuch as he was in peril of his life and like to be very greviously maltreated ere his death, he did a deed well nigh past believing: being made fast in iron-bound stocks, he got an iron weapon that was brought in some wise into his prison, and straightway conceived a plan of such hardihood as we have never known; reckoning how best the rest of it might get free, he cut off his own foot at the instep. This done, he burrowed through the wall out of the way of the guards that kept ward over him, and so escaped to Tegea; all night he journeyed and all day he hid and lay close in the woods, till on the third night he came to Tegea, while all the people of Lacedaemon sought him; and they were greatly amazed seeing the half of his foot cut off and lying there, but not being able to find the man himself. And after he was healed *and had made himself a foot of wood*, he declared himself an open enemy of the Lacedaemonians.

This adventure was recounted by the Greek author Herodotus in his chronicles of the Greco-Persian Wars written in the middle of the 5th century BC. Unfortunately for Hegisistratus (which means 'Leader', incidentally!) the passage continues, 'yet the enmity that he bore them brought him no good at the last; for they caught him at his divinations in Zacynthus, and slew him.'

So, one of the earliest accounts of what might be called 'spare part surgery' seems to trace in microcosm the doom of the Mondasians – the ancient race Pedler and Davis imagined had become Cybermen. Like Hegisistratus, extreme vicissitudes (in their case life-shortening weaknesses) lead them to desperate action – the removal of human parts and replacement with artificial – to avoid their fate. Destiny is not to be outmanoeuvred, however, and brings them 'no good at the last', for reckless escape from certain death does not return them to the life they once knew. The Greek receives the lighter penalty, though lame and embittered with hate for his enemy: he meets a speedy end. The Mondasians' fate is relentless and never-ending: to suffer the death of spirit and soul, the things that made them human, because of their mistaken belief that the body was a separate and dispensable element of their humanity.

### Keeping Body and Soul Together

The separateness of body and soul – something we considered in regard to intelligent machine life – is an idea that originated with the Ancient Greeks and particularly with Plato, who might be called the original Idealist. He wrote one of the earliest of utopian works, *The Republic*. Along with the Ancient Hebrew view of the world, this Greek Idealist view has been one of the main influences on the way Western Christian tradition divides soul from body, living from inanimate, human from animal and good from evil; in each case it values the former above the latter.

Entirely different in viewpoint are the ancient beliefs of the East. Among the oldest is *Vedanta* philosophy. (A simple exposition of these powerful ideas can be found in Alan Watts' *The Book On The Taboo Against Knowing Who You Are*.) The *Vedas* were handed down verbally, generation after generation memorising it in verse. They were probably first composed over 3000 years ago. One of these sacred Sanskrit hymns, *Rg-Veda*, describes the sacrifice of a mythical giant called Purusa from whose dismembered limbs sprang the four major castes and contains the earliest known reference to artificial arms and legs.

### Part Exchange

There still exists a Roman mosaic in the French Pyrenees which depicts a man with an artificial leg made out of bronze and wood and lined with leather. In fact these have been the kind of materials used for substitute limbs throughout the ages and it is only comparatively recently that new ones have been developed.

There have always been 'peg-legs' and 'hook-hands' and they of course appear to macabre effect in fiction, even (or should it be – especially?) in stories for younger readers: *Treasure Island*'s Long John Silver and *Peter Pan*'s Captain Hook, for example. Yet the technology has not always been that crude, even before this century. Wealthy people in the 18th century were able to afford the so-called 'clapper leg', a sophisticated prosthesis with a knee joint of steel; the wooden ankle joints were operated by pulling strings and before the owner had properly mastered the technique the foot would usually hit the ground with a clap – hence the name.

In 1773 Goethe wrote a poetic drama about the medieval knight, Goetz von Berlichingen, who had had an iron hand made for him. It was skillfully crafted, enabling him to move fingers

and thumb. Nevertheless, Goethe shows him keenly missing the real hand. In a line that strangely prefigures the predicament of the Cybermen, Goetz says, 'my right hand, though not useless in combat, is unresponsive to the grasp of affection'.

*Prosthesis* is the medical term for an artificial replacement part for the body. *Prosthetics* is the branch of medicine that deals with supplying and fitting suitable parts. Its origin as a science is attributed to the 16th century Frenchman, Ambroise Paré. The fact that he was a military surgeon should not be surprising as warfare has always provided amputees in great number on which techniques could be perfected and improvement in design and increased acceptance of artificial limbs inevitably came with each major war. The impetus continues unabated today. Figures for the Afghan War (current at the time of writing) reveals the awful way we emulate the Cybermen: in 1984, 800 limbs lost or amputated; in the first seven months of 1985, 1000. It is this kind of senseless mutilation of war which leads to the bizarre solution of *Limbo '90*: 'demobilisation through immobilisation' – the amputation of all four limbs in the cause of peace!

After the First World War, new lighter weight materials and better mechanical joints were developed. World War II gave another boost to the technology, typified by the APRL hand (US Army Prosthetic Research Laboratory), a lightweight mechanical metal prosthesis covered by a rubber glove which matched the colour of the patient's other hand. Crude as it sounds, it has only recently been superseded as a standard fitting.

### Jobs for the Biomedics

One of the basic difficulties of limb replacement is that there are more than 50 muscles involved in the movements of each arm and leg; a deeper understanding of their co-ordination is needed.

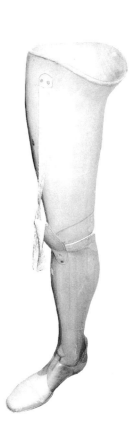

## Science report

# Microchip man a step nearer

By Andrew Wiseman

The creation of bionic man has become a reality at Stanford University in California, where a research team has succeeded in growing microscopic nerve cells through holes drilled in silicon chips.

More importantly, the tiny animal nerve fibres involve the axons via which the essential bioelectric signal is transmitted to convey a message from one nerve cell to another.

This preliminary attempt to interchange signals between a nerve cell and an electronic circuit is referred to as "man-machine interface at the biological level". The scientists hope it could lead one day to the repair of severed or crushed nerves, restoring feeling and use to numbed limbs.

Dr Joseph M. Rosen, assistant professor of surgery at the university's school of medicine, says that silicon chips, programmed electronically to re-route axons growing through the holes and transmitting nerve impulses to non-functional limbs, could, eventually, be implanted into humans. Such a micro-electronic axon processor, acting as a switchboard, would trigger off sensations in severed nerves, so that people with re-attached limbs could use them again.

Like all muscle movements, the process would start with the brain sending a signal through the nerves. On reaching a disconnected end, the message would not be blocked but picked up by the chip and electronically sent to the other end of the nerve, making a connection and allowing the muscle to respond to the brain's command.

For the system to work it would need two facing chips, anchored by a coupling device. Initially the axons would be stimulated by an outside computer. Later the chips themselves would become computers.

All this is very much in the future. But Dr Rosen's team, which has been experimenting with rats and a monkey for two years, has already grown axons through holes with a diameter of only eight micrometers, drilled through silicon chips one milimetre square.

The team estimates it will take at least five years to accomplish a viable nerve connection. But they are encouraged by the fact that once they manage to grow hundreds of axons through chips, it will not be necessary to secure an exact connection between all severed ends. They believe that linking 20 per cent of axons would restore 80 per cent or more of an original function.

---

Sensory feedback techniques must also be improved. Just as important, durable and realistic cosmetic materials are needed so that the final covering looks more like human skin. These are the areas where biomedical engineering is pushing forward the frontiers and though, as we shall see, it is nowhere near capable of producing the Bionic Woman, it is this discipline from which the fantasy of 'bionics' got its glamorous name.

The bionic women, men and animals of fiction remain very much in the realm of fiction even now. Immense technological advances are still essential if the Android, which has become such a commonplace of science fantasy, is really ever to be indistinguishable from humankind and walk among us, incognito. Much simpler would be to make no attempt at a human facsimile, to concentrate on merely emulating human function, to create purely a survival structure for the brain/controller and to use materials for utilitarian rather than cosmetic reasons. Interestingly, this is the approach taken on Mondas and on 1990's Earth in *Limbo '90*.

### Double Vision

Their faces and heads are normal but under the hair on the head is a shining metal plate stretching from centre hair- line to occiput. Instead of flesh there is a transparent 'arm-shaped' forearm covering, containing shining rods and lights, but there is a normal hand at the end of it.

This was what Kit Pedler and Gerry Davis first imagined his Cyberman might look like. When the Cybermen intended to stun someone, 'relays of twinkling lights would illuminate, travelling from the [chest] unit, along his arms and down to the finger tips.' Unfortunately, the costume budget for *Doctor Who* was incapable of realising this kind of bionic fantasy, but there remained a vestige of his initial vision in the metal skull cap and the flashing lights, the rods and coils, in the transparent chest units of the Tenth Planet Cybermen. Now consider Wolfe's description, curiously similar to Pedler's original vision, of the bionic-limbed 'quadro-amps' in *Limbo '90*:

Instead of arms and legs they had transparent extensions whose smooth surfaces shone in the sun. Each of these was a tangle of metallic rods and coils, scattered all through each one were tiny bulbs which lit up and faded as the limb moved, sending off spatters of icy blue light.

What is more, the first 'quadro-amp' had undergone radical brain surgery and wore a large metal plate in his skull.

### Bionics – the Fantasy

There are certain aspects of fictional bionics which are pure fantasy. The ability, for example, of the Bionic Woman to lift enormously heavy objects because she possesses a bionic arm will always be a scientific impossibility; the same applies to the facility of Wolfe's 'amp' to jump many times his own height on cybernetic legs. In reality, the Bionic Woman's arm would be torn out at the shoulder; the 'amp's' legs might take him into the air but they would have buried themselves partway into his body in the process.

It is true that ants carry things much bigger and heavier than themselves, that crickets jump hundreds of times their own length, but the secret is in the way that insects are constructed. Their strength of limb is inseparable from the strength of their overall structure. Kit Pedler moved one step away from fantasy and nearer to fact in providing his creatures with an exoskeleton (something we shall soon discuss).

So let us examine the technology which inspired Kit Pedler, a technology he thought might bring with it ethical complications that could threaten our very humanity.

### Bionics – the Facts

Biomedical engineers design artificial organs as well as limbs. Using engineering and cybernetic principles to help explain the structure and function of living organisms, they have been able to make considerable advances within a comparatively short time.

It was only 20 years ago when the electric current produced by muscle contraction – *myoelectricity* – was first put to cybernetic use to control an artificial arm. Metal disks against the tissue of the stump pick up myoelectric impulses from the muscles. These are then amplified with batteries to power an electric motor in the prosthesis. The contraction of one muscle in the stump will have the effect of bending the artificial arm. It is straightened again by similar impulses from another muscle.

Another early cybernetic/biomedical device was the cardiac pacemaker which automatically regulates the beat of the heart – though it does not replace the organ itself. Complex microelectronic circuits are now being used to further this and other aspects of the technology. In the case of the pacemaker the circuitry makes possible a near instantaneous response to the wearer's needs. For example, the heart is stimulated to beat faster and more strongly when the pacemaker picks up signs of exertion: a cybernetic function reminiscent of Watt's Governor.

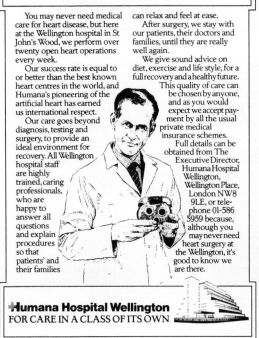
## Hear Me! See Me!

In other areas, the centuries-old external aids – ear trumpets, eye glasses, walking sticks – are being very effectively superseded by internal microelectronic devices. It is possible now to bypass a faulty cochlea (inner ear) and produce a limited ability to hear in people who were previously totally deaf. This is achieved by implanting in the cochlea a tiny electrode only a few microns wide (a micron is a millionth of a metre) which picks up the sound vibrations coming into the ear and converts them to electrical impulses to stimulate the auditory nerve directly. However, as the operation is what is known as invasive – it removes or encroaches on healthy tissue – it is open to ethical objections.

Similar advances are being made in the area of vision (Kit Pedler's field – see Gerry Davis's introduction to this book). Artificial TV eyes for the blind already exist although the results are still primitive. The same principles of electrical excitation of the nerve – in this case the optic nerve or visual cortex – produce spots of brightness which correspond in a rudimentary fashion to what would normally be seen. Again, this involves surgical implantations which can destroy what remains of healthy tissue.

Other methods avoid such an ethically suspect approach: the information picked up by the TV camera can be transmitted to the blind person through other external sense organs. For example, a pad containing an array of blunt pins may be strapped to the back or forehead. When a shape is picked up by the camera, information is sent to the pad to vibrate an area of pins relating to the shape. The sight of one particular shape is therefore 'felt' as a tingling sensation which can, after only a short period of readjustment, be readily distinguished from some other shape.

## Upsides Down...

This ability of the human brain to accommodate changes in the way it receives its information is remarkable. It has been demonstrated in a series of experiments exploring our visual processing systems. In one, volunteers were asked to wear a pair of prism-shaped spectacles which had the effect of inverting everything seen through them.

At first, the wearers had great difficulty in making any sense of what they saw: they were in a mirror world where every move they made resulted in an effect exactly opposite to what they intended. They also had sensations of nausea and dizziness. However, after an uncomfortable period of trying to get around while still wearing the spectacles, there was a flipover effect. They were suddenly seeing right way up again. The brain had decided to interpret the information it was receiving from the eyes in a way that would be more consistent with the signals from the other senses. Unfortunately for the volunteers, when the spectacles were removed they saw everything upside down and had to go through the whole process, with accompanying nausea and dizziness, of relearning to see things normally again!

## ...And Insides Out

One area of biomedical engineering called *biomechanics* deals with the *musculoskeletal* system. Stresses and strains generated in bones and joints even during normal activities can be immense and correspondingly strong materials that are also non-corrosive and anti-inflammatory are required to replace them. Two such metals have been used since the 1940's: 316-L stainless steel and chrome cobalt molybdenum alloy. After their discovery people could at last be pinned, plated, screwed and nailed back together again – with a good chance of survival!

A related area is *prosthetics-orthotics*. It deals with the bracing or supporting of artificial and abnormal limbs – to avoid, among other things, the ripping out of limbs we imagined if the fantasy of the Bionic Woman were ever played out for

real. A combination of this and the biomechanical field has led to the development of a powered exoskeleton of a kind not unlike that which is apparent in the earlier Cybermen.

*Exoskeleton* simply means a support framework sited on the outside of a structure. It can apply to any structure and may include buildings as well as living bodies. The new Lloyds Building in London is an interesting example of a building with an exoskeleton: not only are the steel supporting girders clearly visible on the outside.but what can also be seen are all the pipes and ducts necessary for the servicing of the building. In fact, it looks like a huge cybernised warehouse!

### The Body Modifiers

Exoskeletons are very common – and efficient – among some animal species. David Attenborough in *Life On Earth* says, 'the external skeleton is highly versatile; it serves the tiny water flea as well as it does the giant Japanese spider crab that measures over three metres from claw to claw'.

All insects have exoskeletons made primarily of a brown fibrous material called *chitin* developed over 550 million years ago in crustaceans (shellfish). On its own, however, chitin is flexible and permeable, so insects have covered it with a protein called *sclerotin*. This, as Attenborough says, 'produces the heavy inflexible armour of the beetles, and mouthparts sharp and tough enough to gnaw through timber and even cut metals like copper and silver.' He continues,

> The chitinous external skeleton seems to be particularly responsive to the demands of evolution. Its surface can be sculpted without affecting the anatomy beneath. Its proportions can be varied to take on new shapes. The chewing mouthparts possessed by the early cockroach-like insects have been turned by their descendants into siphons and stilettos, saws, chisels, and probes that when unreeled are as long as the whole body. [...] Many limbs carry special tools moulded from the chitin – pouches for holding pollen, combs for cleaning a compound eye, spikes to act as grappling irons.

Sf writers have taken to this useful facility and imaginatively applied it to humans. The fighters featured in *Sos The Rope* by Piers Anthony have metallic rods embedded in their bones while flexible panels of plastic and woven patches of nylon inserted under the skin protect their vital organs and pressure points. Samuel Delany's *Babel-17* comes even closer to the insect ability of making grotesque additions to the body: claws, sabre-teeth and barbed tails are among the appendages grafted on to willing humans. These practices give the term 'body building' a new dimension. While in *Limbo '90*:

## Metal 'bone' transplants save limbs of 700 patients

Mark Howell, aged 17, told yesterday how his leg was saved from ,amputation by a new metal "bone".

Mark, of Kenfig Hill, Mid-Glamorgan, developed bone cancer in his right leg last year. But instead of amputating it to prevent the cancer spreading doctors replaced his femur with the new metal "bone".

"This saved me from having my leg taken off," said Mark. "The new one feels quite normal and I am now teaching judo and running about five or six miles a day."

Professor John Scales, of the Institute of Orthopaedics in London, said Mark was one of more than 700 people who had been saved from having an arm or leg amputated thanks to a pioneering programme of design and manufacture of bone and joint replacements.

He told the annual meeting of Action Research for the Crippled Child of "unique" extending bone and joint replacements for use in growing children with bone cancer.

The charity announced it was giving its biggest single research award of more than £358,000 to Professor Scales' team at the Royal National Orthopadeic Hospital in Stanmore, Middlesex.

All of these men had four artificial limbs, always four, but the ones in front, the ones who had cleared the path through the jungle, were wearing specialized instruments in place of their right arms. Some had what looked like flame throwers, long tubes terminating in funnel-shaped nozzles which were still smoking; a moment ago they had been spitting out fifty-foot tongues of fire (the bassoons); others had long many-jointed claws on the ends of which were mounted high-speed rotary saws (the sopranos). Some twenty of these men emerged from the thicket. When they stopped, those in the lead pulled the tools from their arm stumps, picked up regular plastic arms which were hanging from their belts and snapped them into place in the empty sockets.

With examples of such bizarre technology abounding in sf and even more in nature itself it is not difficult to understand how the idea of the Cybermen's exoskeleton came to Kit Pedler and Gerry Davis. As they thrashed out what the Cybermen should look like, the important thing about their initial ideas of a race of intelligent man-machines was that they had not, like androids or Rossum's Universal Robots, been built from scratch entirely out of mechanical parts: machines formed as people. In Kit Pedler's nightmare, people had slowly become machines.

### More Power to Your Elbow – and Other Bits

Kit Pedler must have been aware of the advances promised at the time in prosthetics-orthotics. In fact, present developments have now entered a phase which can provide the power-driven limbs that gave his Cybermen 'the strength of ten men'.

In humans, the framework of support is the skeleton of bone and it is (normally!) worn on the inside. Muscles and ligaments attaching to the bones act like a motor and pulley system to move

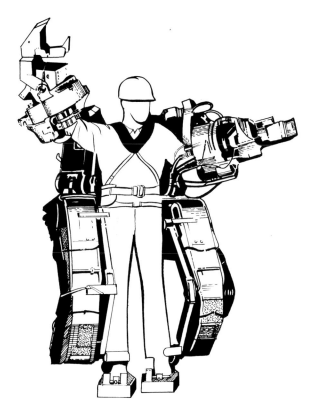

the limbs and perform actions such as walking. In certain people – paraplegics, for instance – the muscles no longer work or at least are not under conscious control. In an attempt to remedy this situation an external framework of limbs strapped to the body and powered by electric motors moves the person from the outside. Use of principles similar to the myoelectric arm mean that in the case of a chronic weakness but not total disability in the muscles or neural networks the movement is under conscious, autonomous control.

Beyond even what Kit Pedler and Gerry Davis saw as the logical outcome of this technique as exhibited in the Cybermen are the latest ideas for micro-prosthetic devices. These microscopic 'biochips' would be implanted in malfunctioning muscle or brain, providing control of such areas by electrical stimulus. The existing nervous system would actually be encouraged to grow into the biochip to make connections with it. In this way it may even become possible to repair memory and other functions of the brain.

Of course, the Cybermen have evolved in their own way in the twenty years of appearing in *Doctor Who*. The rather obvious exoskeletally powered limbs, suggested by the tubular supports of *Revenge of the Cybermen* and before, have been replaced by a more sophisticated exoshell. Such development is logical and realistic given the period of time over which it was meant to have taken place. The Cybermen first make their appearance on Earth in the 1970's AD and the new look Cyberman turns up in 2526 AD

(*Earthshock*). When one considers how far we have come in the 40 years since World War II, it is entirely credible that a race of techno-militarists like the Cybermen would have taken giant strides in over half a millenium.

## A Talk in the Garden

> We were discussing spare part surgery and conceived the idea of someone with so many mechanical replacements that he didn't know whether he was human or a machine.

Kit Pedler was recalling a conversation he had had with his wife. She was also a doctor. At the time, the potential of transplantation was being vigorously explored. Indeed, the following year (1967) the South African heart specialist Dr Christian Bernard successfully replaced the diseased heart of his patient Philip Bliaberg with the heart of a recently dead, but otherwise healthy, accident victim. Mary Shelley's vision of life from dead parts had finally been realised. The extra 19 months of life that Philip Bliaberg gained before his body rejected the newly grafted heart was regarded as a breakthrough in the technology. Speculation raged in newspapers and on TV about the possibility of avoiding death altogether in the years to come simply by replacing the defective body part with one that worked.

Previously, successful organ transplant was largely confined to skin graft. (The skin, incidentally, is the largest organ of the body.) It is known from Egyptian manuscripts of about 2000 BC that skin grafting was practised then; it was the responsibility of the tile maker's caste! There are legends and rumours of other kinds of grafting throughout history. These mainly involved noses – slicing off the nose was an age-old punishment – and in 1597 the Italian surgeon Gaspere Tagliacozzi tried to use flesh from other people to replace the noses of his patients.

There are more than twenty different transplantable organs and tissues in the body. Some, like skin, bone, cartilage, tendons and large blood vessels do not present rejection problems. Others – heart, kidney, liver, lungs, pancreas – are much more difficult to transplant but progress is being made all the time. Kidney transplants are now routine and can offer a 90% survival rate. The difficulty in this area is not the techniques of transplantation but the lack of suitable donor organs.

## Cold Hand, Cold Heart

Methods are being developed of storing healthy organs and tissues for long periods of time

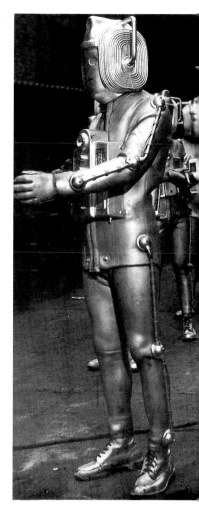

## Zip up to survive

SURGEON Harlan Stone, of the University of Maryland has been using zippers instead of stitches to close up wounds in patients recovering from surgery to the pancreas.

After pancreatic surgery there is frequently a lot of bleeding and internal dressings have to be applied and changed at intervals for several days after the operation. Normally this involves opening patients up each time a dressing needs to be changed and then sewing them up again, an hour-long procedure which is stressful, requires general anaesthetic and can sometimes be fatal.

Stone has replaced stitches with zippers sewn into place in 28 patients recovering from pancreatic surgery. When the patients need their dressings changed they are simply unzipped and zipped up again, a five-minute procedure with no need for full scale anaesthesia. The zippers are left in place for up to two weeks before they are removed and the patient is finally sewn up.

**John Newell**

through the use of extremely low temperatures. *Cryogenics* is the study of temperatures in the range of about -120 degrees C to almost absolute zero (around -273 degrees C). *Cryobiology* is the study of how extremely low temperatures affect living things. Cryobiologists are mainly concerned with freezing living matter to preserve it for future use. The Cryons, the original inhabitants on Telos whom we meet in *Attack Of The Cybermen*, are so called because they boil at room temperature. Their technology, which the Cybermen requisitioned to freeze themselves for future use, is cryogenic.

Clearly, it is preferable to store the organs and tissues of people who have died – instead of having to wait for a suitable donor to have a fatal accident. Some people, however, have ethical objections to prolonging life in this way. Certainly the issue of whether everybody's organs should be available for use after death, regardless of the donor's consent, may come to seem less contentious as the demand for donor organs increases.

### The Way of All Flesh

The 1960's media vision of our becoming an immortal race whose worn out organs are simply replaced is edging closer. It is a vision of a society which is basically cannibalistic – continuing to survive by devouring its own species. It is a vision which the Jeremiahs of science fiction have not flinched from confronting.

An sf story of the early 1960's explored one version of this vision: on Cordwainer Smith's *A Planet Named Shayol*, microscopic aliens called dromazoa 'infect' humans, causing great pain but enabling them to grow extra limbs and organs which can be removed and used for spare part surgery. In Norman Spinrad's *Bug Jack Barron*, written in 1969 when the excitement about heart transplants was at its height, only the elite have the resources to seek immortality through successive transplants.

On the other hand, the film *Soylent Green* (1973) portrayed an overcrowded Earth of 1999 forced to resort to a cannibalism of a more literal nature.

### The Way of the Mechanical World

And again, it is appropriate to consider the double vision of Wolfe and Pedler/Davis. It was in 1953, with the major technological advances still to be made in this area, that Wolfe provided his extraordinary glimpse of how things might be by the end of the century in *Limbo '90*. We have already hinted at his vision: a world where artificial limbs become highly advanced because of the voluntary

amputations for peace. So efficient – and chic – do they eventually become that they are preferred to the real thing. Men flock to have 'cineplastic surgery': their own arms and legs are amputated and replaced with superior cybernetic appendages. Significantly, Wolfe explains that although Wiener had developed the means for such amazing advances by the mid-century, there was not the will for it: 'his had been a brutalized war-bent society, all too ready to spend billions developing the A-bomb but quite reluctant to allocate even a penny to work out adequate prosthetics for those maimed in its periodic wars. It remained for Immob to perfect artificial limbs superior to natural ones.'

The allocation of resources and will to accomplish some mighty task is something not at all far-fetched. Extraordinary achievements result from concentrating effort on one area – as typified by the construction of the pyramids during the heights of the Egyptian dynasties or, in our own age, getting men to the moon within one decade. Political will is the prime mover. It took a whole world to revolt against the obscenity of war in *Limbo '90* for prosthetics to replace armaments; in the world that we know, the real one, the obscenity goes on: billions are still squandered on armaments while half the world goes short of food. Thus, on Mondas, it is easy to imagine how quickly mobilised was the will to survive through cyberneticisation; humanity took second place. With the resources of a whole planet directed towards this end, their complete conversion into a race of Cybermen is not beyond the bounds of possibility.

It is clear, then, that Pedler and Davis's Jeremiah-instincts took him along a similar path to that of Bernard Wolfe. However, there are three major differences. First, the Pedler/Davis vision was set not on Earth but on its twin planet, Mondas. Second, it featured the cybernetic replacement, not of limbs alone, but of every bodily part. Third, it was not a whim of fashion which divested humanity of its flesh and blood components but the ravages of a fatal and world-wide disease.

### Satiric Mirror

Mondas was the name of Earth's twin planet. It had shared the fortuitous conditions which on Earth had produced life. It had therefore been populated by the species *Homo sapiens* – humans just like us.

Pedler and Davis are here using a classic story-telling device. As when Jonathan Swift had written in *Gulliver's Travels* about Lilliput, Brobdignag and the Land of the Houyhnhnms, he was making barely-veiled reference to the absurdities of his own 18th century society, so Pedler and Davis were using the Cybermen to point to the dangers

inherent in the progress of 20th century society.

When in *The Tenth Planet* the physicist Barclay is told where the Cybermen come from he recalls, 'Mondas. Isn't that one of the ancient names for Earth?'. The point is made: Mondas is a direct analogy for Earth. A mirror held up so that we might see our true nature.

## Whole Body Hardware

It was in 1953 that a heart-lung machine was first successfully used on a man. In the Pedler/Davis vision of the future, the use and development of such artificial organs were just as important as the progress of artificial limbs and even more important than the use of donor organs.

Artificial organs were machines originally designed to replace an organ's functions while it was being operated on. The artificial kidney or *dialyser* is a good example. It filters the blood of undesirable substances and people who are unable to have a transplant of a healthy kidney may still live a reasonably normal life with regular dialysis. The heart-lung machine replicates the action of the lung by restoring oxygen to depleted blood and removing carbon dioxide, and it replicates the action of the heart by pumping the blood around the body.

But both of these artificial organs are designed to be used outside the body – the patient is plugged into them. Kit Pedler foresaw the possibility of a device which was no larger than the original organ and which would therefore be inserted into the patient as a substitute. Exactly this kind of portable device – a mechanical heart, powered by compressed air and monitored by computer – was implanted in a human patient on December 2, 1982 – four years to the month before the Tenth Planet was meant to return to Earth.

Such, then, was the progress – combined with powered exoskeletons and cybernetic limbs – that Kit Pedler had in mind when he spoke of a proliferation of 'mechanical replacements' leading to an identity crisis. Before we go on to this very important issue, the third point of divergence from Wolfe needs to be briefly considered.

## Life-Shortening Weakness

*Poliomyelitis*, better known simply as 'polio', was an infectious disease which during the decades before Pedler and Davis created the Cybermen had assumed the proportions of an epidemic in Britain. The virus caused inflammation within the spinal cord and led in some cases to permanent paralysis. It has now been largely eradicated by the use of innoculation and preventative environmental measures but at that time the impact of the disease was so great (its victims were confined to wheelchairs or had to wear calipers) that it must have figured somewhere in the images that flitted through Pedler and Davis's minds when they thought of 'an ancient race on a dying planet'.

They knew how a virus could ravage an entire society. So did H G Wells. In his *The First Men In The Moon* (1901), the subterranean Selenites are accidentally infected by a visitor from Earth and subsequently wiped out by a virus – the common cold!

Back in the real world, everyone has heard of the Black Death. The bubonic plague that caused it had become a universal horror in the 14th century: families would be shunned, whole villages quarantined, at the suspicion of plague. AIDS is similarly ominous today – though the widespread hysteria concerning the transmission of this virus says little for our progress in the last 600 years.

Bubonic plague and AIDS are both controllable through taking simple measures to avoid their spread and by developing suitable antibodies to the virus. To defeat such viruses by having complete control over the environment would be an impossibly large undertaking. There is another way: complete control over the individual. This might be possible in a totalitarian state. It is the

**TRANSPLANTS**

# Hearts that will run and run

DOCTORS and technicians at Harefield Hospital, London's heart transplant unit, have developed a simple system for keeping hearts and lungs going, which means they can travel hundreds of miles between donor and recipient.

Their system, the Portable Bypass Machine or PBM, is a scaled-down, ultra-light version of the heart-lung machine used for life support in the operating room.

The PBM takes over the heart and lung functions of a brain-dead organ donor, normally an accident victim, by adding oxygen to the blood and circulating it through the body while gradually lowering the body temperature to 10°C. At that point the heart and lungs go into 'suspended animation,' and can be removed and transported safely packed in cold blood.

# Aids cure could lead to genetic problem

A LEADING scientist held out new hope in the fight against Aids yesterday — but warned that the ultimate cure could lead to a Brave New World in which people were created to order.

Dr Michael Hall, a researcher with the Roche drug company, said new drugs were being developed which would help to control the Aids epidemic by making carriers less infectious.

But he warned that the ultimate goal would be the use of genetic engineering to cut out the Aids virus from carriers' cells.

"If this ever proves possible, then the implications will raise serious ethical and moral questions perhaps as difficult to answer as those relating to Aids itself.

"It would mean that we could manipulate at will the human genetic pool, produce super races, modify ethnic traits, excise socially unacceptable habits — in fact, produce people to order."

solution adopted by the Mondasians. The virus attacks the organism so one adapts the organism. This is a process which has driven evolution for millions of years.

## Man or Machine? – A Mechanical Mystery Tour

> CYBERMAN: We are called Cybermen. We were exactly like you once but our cybernetic scientists realised that our race was getting weak.
> BARCLAY: Weak? How?
> CYBERMAN: Our lifespan was getting shorter so our scientists and doctors devised spare parts for our bodies until we could be almost completely replaced.
> POLLY: But that means you're not like us. You're robots!
> CYBERMAN: Our brains are just like yours except that certain weaknesses have been removed.

As a man is gradually replaced by mechanical substitutes – as flesh and bones become plastic and alloy – what is the point beyond which he ceases to be human? This was a central question for Pedler and Davis as they thought up the Cybermen. Their answer is summed up in the above exchange from *The Tenth Planet*. The Cybermen are not robots – part of the human brain still resides within the Cyber body. Yet, significantly, their link with humanity seems to have been severed with the loss of those parts of the brain which possessed 'weaknesses'.

> BARCLAY: Weaknesses? What weaknesses?
> CYBERMAN: You call them emotions, do you not?

Pedler later acknowledges the influence when describing the effect of cyberneticisation on the Mondasians:

> They had become strong in the process and always behaved logically, but had lost their feelings and humanity as they became more and more machine driven – very much like the Treens and Mekon against whom Dan and Co. waged their longest battle.

Other sf writers have considered the question and come up with differing answers. In *Man Plus*, Frederik Pohl describes the plight of a US astronaut whose body is radically adapted to the requirements of the low gravity and thin air on Mars; this necessitates the modifying or replacement of heart, lungs, eyes, skin and nervous system – among other things; he nevertheless retains his human emotions. Another story, *House* by John Barfoot, explores what must be the most tenuous of body/mind links where the whole

essence of a person still continues to exist eternally in just a few living cells.

Both these fictional excursions belong to the many fantasies of the disembodied brain or 'brain in a vat' type which have been a favourite for philosophical speculators. Can a brain be disconnected from its body and yet still continue to function in the same way – having thoughts, making decisions, generally maintaining the personality of the body it once existed within? This is a question which is essentially identical with the Pedler/Davis one – for a Cyberman's brain is certainly disembodied: body has been replaced by mechanical parts and only brain remains.

Arnold Zuboff's *The Story Of A Brain* pursues the idea of disembodied brain to its absurd conclusion. If the brain can operate without the body, given a suitable nutrient bath, and receive impressions from the outside world through electrical impulses, then there is no logical reason why the two halves of the brain cannot be separated as long as each may communicate with the other instantaneously – as would have been the case before they were separated. It follows that if the instantaneous communication can be maintained, regardless of the distance between the two halves, then each can be studied in separate laboratories. This process of logic is extended until each individual neuron of the brain is being studied in nutrient baths scattered all over the globe!

## Who Dares Recall

We may now return to the Dan Dare connection. Kit Pedler says of Dan's arch-enemy the Mekon, 'he was sinister, arrogant and entirely without love or compassion [...] a cold, clinical, chess-playing brain entirely devoted to plotting universal domination. His face too had both machine-like and lizard-like qualities'. The links with the Cybermen are undeniable: the mummified faces of the Cybermen in *The Tenth Planet* are chillingly reptilian yet framed by mechanical devices.

*Dan Dare* was an sf comic strip that was printed in the boys' comic *Eagle*. Its creator and illustrator was Frank Hampson. During the 1950's his Dan Dare adventures pioneered a new and exciting style of realist fantasy which fired the imagination of a whole generation of girls as well as boys, adults as well as children. Its influence still lingers in today's sf.

Kit Pedler was self-admittedly one of those adult readers and the debt he owes to Frank Hampson he has made clear. But there are several other influences from the Dan Dare stories which should be mentioned. *The Red Moon Mystery* was a story in which a planet travelled through space; whenever it came into contact with a suitable civilisation, it would attack and plunder. A later story called *Rogue Planet* told of two worlds circling their common suns; every ten thousand years their orbits converged, allowing the warrior race of one planet to invade, enslave and kill the other. In *Reign Of The Robots*, the Mekon appears with an army of metallic humanoids – Elektrobots – to help him carry out his evil plans. The Mekon was the small-bodied big-brained green ruler of the Treens from Northern Venus. The Treens are seven feet tall, strong, functional in dress as in purpose and above all, emotionless.

Despite these rather striking parallels, Kit Pedler and Gerry Davis explore in the Cybermen their own very personal concerns. The dislocation of our humanity through the blind pursuit of technological know-how is one of their main anxieties. It is a clear manifestation of that deep-seated, millenium-old fascination/fear of usurping the role of God.

### 'Have You No Emotions, Sir?'

It is known that when certain parts of the human brain are removed or damaged the more impassioned aspects of personality can be severely muted. The aggression and violence of certain mentally ill patients can apparently be taken away altogether by performing a *pre-frontal lobotomy*. This is a surgical operation where segments of the brain called the frontal lobes are excised. Its effect could well be described as ridding the personality of 'love, pride, hate, fear', the emotions of irrationality and unpredictability that in the Pedler/Davis view constitute the essence of being human.

It is illuminating that, corresponding to this aspect of the Cybermen, *Limbo '90* begins in an isolated society on an uncharted island in the Indian Ocean. By some coincidence early in the tribe's history, it had been discovered that the 'devils' of violence and antisocial behaviour could be 'cut out with a chisel and rock'. This procedure had become ritualised as Mandunga – a method of removing 'weaknesses' from the brain – a primitive form of lobotomy.

Though it is now hardly ever done, in the 1950's pre-frontal lobotomy had been a routine way to deal with some severely disturbed people. But it had always provoked controversy, as has the earlier but still continuing procedure of administering massive electric shocks to the brain to jolt it out of depression. So little is known even now about how the brain works that this kind of tampering is like trying to fix a faulty television by thumping it. The analogy is apt, for to treat the brain in this way is to think of it as a machine. As *Limbo '90*'s hero Martine reasons:

How could you be sure that, in allegedly cutting away some devils from the brain, you were not at the same time cutting away some guardian angels? You could only be sure of that if you knew what every single cell of the brain did, and how it was entwined with all the other cells. But there were 10,000 million cells in the brain. Neurologists knew a tiny bit about a measly few dozen of them, maybe; and about all the possible interweavings between these 10,000 million cells, about the way they act in concert, they were almost entirely in the dark. How, then, could you know what your scalpel was doing when you slid it into the grey matter of someone's brain? You could dismiss this question and go ahead with your surgery only if you looked upon people, not as unique organisms with unique personalities – unique neuronic tangles, if you liked – but as machines. Machines are expendable and replaceable. One machine is very much like another?

'Unique neuronic tangles' can be another way of looking at what emotions are. The notion of the Cybermen's 'emotionlessness' may be seen as the Pedler/Davis protest at the insensitive treatment of a person's most important, delicate and sophisticated component, the human brain.

However, it is necessary to have a proper understanding of the nature and extent of Cyber 'emotionlessness' and to do so we need to return to our discussion of cybernetics.

THE MEKON

Cold, merciless master-mind of Venus, High Lord of the Treens, arch-enemy of Dan Dare and all mankind.

KEITH WATKIN.

### Emotions of the Cybernetic Kind

Kit Pedler and Gerry Davis assumed that a Cyberman's brain, as well as having had the 'weaknesses removed', is augmented by an electronic brain or computer. The cybernetic principles are pre-set to deal with anything which conflicts with the Cyber Cause – to survive and conquer. To pursue this reason for existence, *counter-causes* would be set up within the computer-brain. Given the *ultimate goal* of survival through conquest, all the causes likely to be required to bring about the *desired effect* in the face of all hazards are held in readiness, so that even unpredictable events are made to converge towards the *ultimate end*. This process is a *teleological* one – the ends justify the means.

All this is pure cybernetics. What it means is

that Cybermen have rejected as redundant the 'weaknesses' of human emotions. These are bundles of hopelessly illogical desires – 'neuronic tangles' – convoluted intentions which have been knotted by millions of years of evolution. Whereas we humans find it difficult to know exactly what we want and why, the Cybermen have no such difficulty. The programmable part of their brain is set to support a very clear intention – Cyber conquest and through it the survival of the Cyber race.

The cybernetic intention represents, in other words, an immensely strong desire and when it is endangered or frustrated – whilst the Cyberman will react logically, guided by his counter-causes – his reaction may have an intensity about it which must sometimes appear very similar to human emotions. Wiener himself described the possibility of a machine which would show a 'statistical preference for a certain sort of behaviour' and a statistical disgust for other sorts of behaviour. Preferences and disgusts are normally thought to be the products of emotion but they are also inherent, though differently termed, in the cybernetic process.

### The End is Where We Start From

Science fiction is produced when a society makes large advances in technology within the lifetime of one individual. As Isaac Asimov asserts, 'the future is then, for the first time, discovered. This took place clearly with the development of the Industrial Revolution.'

We have returned via cybernetics to our starting point of the Industrial Revolution. We have come full circle and our journey ends where it began. *Limbo '90*, too, ends with the pivotal importance of the Industrial Revolution:

> Man hesitated to mechanise his work processes for many hundreds of years, until the eighteenth century, because of narcissism and because he was afraid of his machine turning into a juggernaut. Until then, the machine was a thing of magic – after the First Industrial Revolution, a steamroller. But there are two ways to escape being steamrollered by the machine, granted the will to escape is there. One is to limit mechanisation to the absolute minimum. The other: to make the machine laughable, as the Greeks and ancients did, to take the threat out of it. For there is something hilariously, outrageously funny about the machine. It's a perfect man...

### An Idea whose Time Has Gone

The Industrial Revolution was possible only because we had begun to think of things as being composed of separate bits. We started taking them apart to study how they operated. We found that the bits were made up of smaller bits which could also be taken apart and studied. Eventually, it was assumed, we would reach the bits that could not be taken apart – the atoms. We would then have discovered the secret of the universe.

Descartes was largely responsible for instigating this view. In the 17th century Isaac Newton established the Cartesian view in science. He developed a complete mathematical formulation of the mechanistic view of nature: the universe was an exquisite clockwork machine running according to God's immaculate laws. Matter and Spirit were fundamentally separate and Spirit indubitably held sway over Matter. The *whole* was explained by the *sum* of its parts.

Much was accomplished by taking this view of the world. The idea budded, blossomed, bore fruit and ripened. But the best of the fruit has now been picked – the rest begins to wither on the branch and will soon decay. The Cyberman Concept warns us of that putrifation. It shows us the inevitable end of the Cartesian view – the logical conclusion of believing that people are no more than sophisticated machines. The Cyberman Concept is a powerful criticism of the Cartesian view – an idea whose time has gone. We must find another idea, another way of looking at the world.

During this century we have discovered, first through Einstein and his relativity theories, then through Heisenberg and his uncertainty principle, and now through the current research in particle physics, that Matter is much less solid and predictable than Newton imagined. The atoms were found to be made up of smaller bits which began to defy rational explanation. The division between Mind and Matter is not clear-cut. It seems that the whole might in fact be greater than the sum of its parts. Or as Hofstadter puts it: 'The *soul* is more than the *hum* of its parts.'

Whatever advances the Cybermen make in appearance and ability to conquer, their technology remains firmly set in the 'nuts and bolts' ethos of the Industrial Revolution. Four-square and Steam Age, the Cybermen have an absolute belief in the Cause. It is symbolised by their dependency on pipes and rods, tubes and coils, dials and flashing lights – the nuts and bolts of Cyber technology. Is it mere coincidence that they have not discovered the secret of time travel?

Cybermen have no time for relative values. They have no room for uncertainty. They are trapped in the tunnel vision of their survival ideology.

Cybermen are the 'mechanists' of the Universe. For as long as we have souls, humanity is free.

# ARCHIVE
## A HISTORY OF THE CYBER RACE

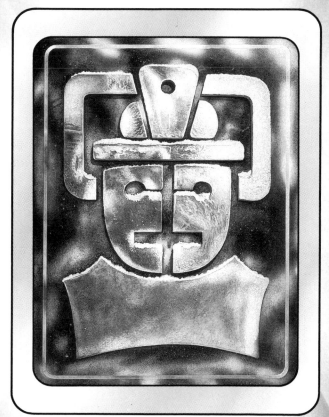

A History of the Cyber Race
derived from nine Earth documents
of Gallifreyan Time Lord
the Doctor
by
ArcHivist Hegelia

'The past derives its power to illumine the present through its
infinite mystery. No one will therefore be so foolish as to
suppose that a definitive answer is either attainable or
desirable. But we must be courageous enough always to
believe that an answer is not impossible.'

Kidvista – Arc Hive founder

TARDIS

## The TARDIS

In line with the principles on which it worked, its internal dimensions were not related to its external dimensions – it could be larger on the inside than its outward appearance would suggest. Indeed its outward appearance was doubly deceptive because one of its circuits, known as the Chameleon circuit, enabled the TARDIS to blend in with its surroundings. Due to malfunction it remains in the likeness of a mid 20th century police box.

## Cybermen in Other Earth Documents

There are five other Earth Documents in which Cybermen make an incidental appearance. They add nothing to Cyber knowledge. In order of discovery, they are: *The War Games*, *The Mind of Evil*, *Carnival of Monsters*, *Logopolis*, *Mawdryn Undead*.

## Dating: Document1

The Doctor's encounter with Professor Travers and the Brigadier (then a colonel) is recorded in Earth document *The Web of Fear*. In this document, the Professor's daughter sets her father's original meeting with the Doctor at 'over thirty years ago'. Earth document *The Abominable Snowman* records this meeting and is dated 1934/5. We can thus arrive at an approximate dating for Document1: 1935 + ?35 + the four years since the Doctor and Jamie last met the Brigadier = mid to late 1970's.

What we know of the Cybermen is limited, almost entirely, to the evidence of nine audio-visual documents or CyberDocuments which have found their way to us from Earth. But it is enough. Among the Arc's accounts of intelligent life throughout the known Universe, Cybermen are infamous. It is fortunate for us, who are sometimes called the ArcHivists of the Galaxy, that we have never experienced at first hand the ruthless logic of the Cyber Race.

It is our endeavour – we who are privileged to visit the great Arc Hives – to spread knowledge of those who are *like* us and greater understanding of those who are *not-like* us. If Absolute Necessity has gently compelled us to use the undoubted gifts of our race in this way, It has also preserved us from the ravages under which mightier civilisations have foundered. Who more able than the ArcHivists to appreciate this truth? Who better placed than we to know that if ever the shadow of the Cybermen were to fall on our civilisation, a new Dark Age of ignorance and brutality might extend throughout the Galaxy?

## The Earth Documents

There are many Earth documents lodged at the Arc Hives. They recount the exploits of the Gallifreyan Time Lord known as the Doctor. They also provide important insights into Earth history. A visitor to the Earth Hive of the Arc will immediately sense the wealth of information already amassed on this fascinating planet. Curiously little is known after their Second Millenium (2000 AD onwards) and most of this sparse knowledge is provided by the Earth documents and, among them, the nine CyberDocuments make their own contribution.

Similarly, though our knowledge of the great Gallifreyan race is more extensive, welcome light is thrown on aspects of their development by some of the Earth documents and in particular Document0 of the CyberDocuments. This *History of the Cyber Race* is therefore also available in the Gallifrey Hive of the Arc.

The Cybermen were notorious on Gallifrey. When the infamous Game of Death was played, in the Dark Days before Rassilon, the Cybermen – even at this most corrupt period – were never allowed to participate: they were too well equipped to play. Yet when the Game was mysteriously revived in the time of their Lord President Borusa, Cybermen did take part. They played alongside other creatures – notably the Gallifreyan renegade known as the Master – and against *five* incarnations of the Doctor. The extraordinary story of this misuse of the Laws of Time will be described in the course of this History.

## The Sources

The CyberDocuments are the firm base to our historical investigation of the Cyber Race. It is upon them alone that I construct my History. As one Document after another has appeared, in a process of discovery which has taken many years, each has been decoded and analysed by our tireless research chroniclers at the Cyber Hive. It seems evident to me, along with certain other distinguished ArcHivists, that it is now possible to construct a detailed History of the Cyber Race.

Two important points must be made about my chronological ordering of the CyberDocuments. The first concerns the Doctor's involvement. In his TARDIS, he is able to travel backwards and forwards in time; the Cybermen are not. This chronology is not therefore based on his time-stream but on Earth's time-stream (Earth basal) which corresponds with that of the Cybermen. Unless this is clearly understood, some aspects of the History may appear unduly confusing. A simple example will demonstrate the point: the Doctor countered Cyber threats to Earth on four occasions *before* becoming involved with the Cybermen's *first* invasion of Earth.

The second point concerns my classification of two Documents in particular: *The Five Doctors* is not Earth basal and is therefore classified Document0, though its actual position in the *History* is between Documents 7 and 8; and *Attack of the Cybermen* is divided into its two chronologically distinct parts as Document2 (Earth 1985) and Document9 (Telos post-*Tomb*). Specific dating is certain only for Documents 2, 3, 5 and 8. Consequently, other dating has to be arrived at after much discussion and deep consideration. Reasoning behind my dating and alternative possibilities will be made clear as the History unfolds.

### Audio-visual Source Documents

| Order of discovery | My chronological order |
| --- | --- |
| *The Tenth Planet* | 1. *The Invasion* |
| *The Moonbase* | 2. *Attack of the Cybermen I* |
| *Tomb of the Cybermen* | 3. *The Tenth Planet* |
| *The Wheel In Space* | 4. *The Wheel In Space* |
| *The Invasion* | 5. *The Moonbase* |
| *Revenge of the Cybermen* | 6. *Tomb of the Cybermen* |
| *Earthshock* | 7. *Revenge of the Cybermen* |
| *The Five Doctors* | 8. *Earthshock* |
| *Attack of the Cybermen* | 9. *Attack of the Cybermen II* |
| | 0. *The Five Doctors* |

During my long sojourn on the Cyber Hive I have steeped myself in the Documentary evidence and talked in depth with other ArcHivists. Though reference will be made to the ideas of

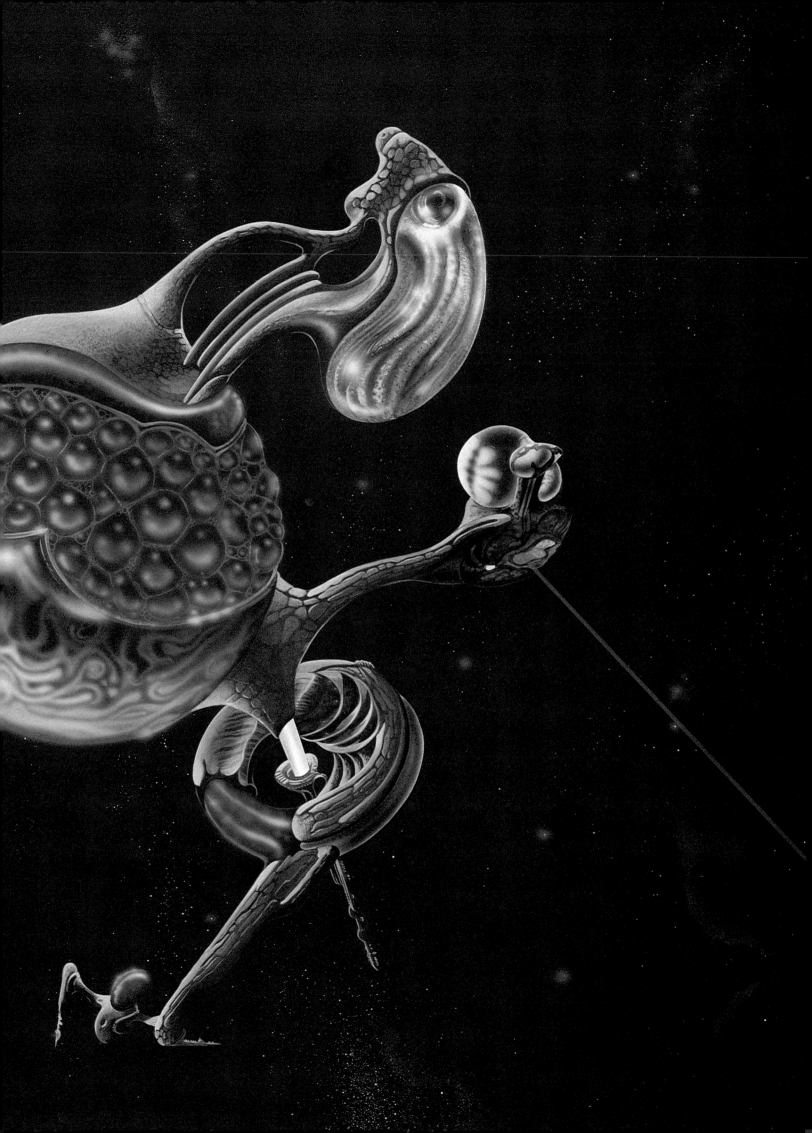

Welcome to the Cyber Hive, ArcHivist Hegelia. It is your privilege to have access to part of the greatest archival complex known. You may use up to ten life segments for your study of the accumulated knowledge and learnings of those who have gone before you. You are free to take the fragments and from them create a History of the Cyber Race. You will now be directed into the inner sanctum. May Kidvista be with you. Fare forward, ArcHivist.

other authorities, there are two works in particular which have been most helpful. The first is the standard cosmo-socio-theoretical work on Mondasian/Cyberman origins, *CyberHistorical Postulates*, by the estimable ArcHivist Novasa. The second is a controversial work by Farozia, *Hypotheses for the Attenuation of CyberDocument Inconsistency*. As a first work it is most impressive and clearly places her in the first rank of ArcHivists.

As the Documents have come to us, chroniclers from all over the Galaxy have popularised and retold the original stories. This, I feel, attests to the power of the Cyberman Myth. But inevitably, certain inaccuracies arise in the retelling and persist in the popular mind. The present History is written in the hope of dispelling such received opinions. Though it is meant to be a general work of introduction to the Cyber Race, accessible to the reader with little background knowledge, I hope it will not leave my co-ArcHivists unstimulated.

**A Good Idea**

'I think my idea's better', says the Doctor in Document7. When asked what his idea is, he replies disarmingly, 'I don't know. That's the trouble with ideas – they only come a bit at a time!'

I sympathise. When researching this work I sometimes felt sure there was a better idea to be formulated about the Cyber Race but it would only come a bit at a time. It is up to my readers to judge whether the bits have come together to make a good idea – and to use this work to form better ideas of their own.

I have tried to come to some kind of satisfying, credible conclusion about Cyber origins and the way the Documents *might* fit into a Cyber chronology. The emphasis must always be on that 'might': we are given few unequivocal facts in the Documents and even some of these must be considered carefully. In the words with which the title page is inscribed, the Arc Hive Founder cautions us against the folly of seeking definitive answers. I have tried to find one of the possible answers.

I gave myself three rules of thumb:

a) consider the context
b) look hard with fresh eyes
c) 'Presented with two alternatives, take the third' (Ancient ArcHivist proverb).

And then, whenever I began to feel – quite logically of course – that my idea was best, I would recall the Doctor's excellent advice:

Logic, my dear Zoe,
merely enables one to be wrong
with authority.

# Early History

One of the intentions of this History is to deduce what might have been the origins of the Cyber Race. But that is not where we begin.

It is essential to have a good knowledge of what the Documents tell us about the Cybermen, before theorising about what took place millenia before. I shall therefore start by relating the events of the Early History of the Cybermen – the first three Documents in my chronology.

There is no significant problem here with dating: no-one, I think, would argue against my ordering of these first three (unless it is with my expedient of splitting one Document into Documents 2 and 9 – but I hope I have made clear my reasons for this). Documents 1 to 3 tell us much of what is known of the origins of the Cybermen and throw up several interesting questions. Later, I shall suggest some answers in a reconstruction of Cyber origins. But I begin by describing the three early Cyber invasions of Earth.

**First Invasion of Earth (Document1)**

Tobias Vaughn headed Earth's largest electronic company – International Electromatics (IE). He believed Earth's difficulties could be solved through the leadership of a single man who was strong enough to force the world to bow to his will. Moreover, he believed himself to be that man.

The period was sometime during the 1970's AD. Tobias Vaughn had made contact with some powerful allies – a group of aliens called the Cybermen. They required an Earth-based agent to provide a radio beam to guide their invasion fleet to Earth. In his megalomania, Vaughn believed the Cybermen would subjugate the nations of Earth to make way for his 'wise' leadership, that it was he who controlled the Cybertroops which were secretly massing in London, one of Earth's major cities. In reality, it was the ruthless intelligence of the Cybermen which was masterminding the insidious plan at every stage.

The plan was this. Every product of Vaughn's company contained a micro-monolithic circuit, a kind of artificial nervous system. When activated by Cyber technology, it would produce a hypnotic effect on humans in the vicinity, rendering them unconscious; since millions of IE products had been sold throughout the world, the effect would be global. Cybertroops would emerge from the sewers to deal with any pockets of resistance and the main Cyber invasion fleet – hundreds of small spacecraft housed within a huge Controlship hidden beyond the Moon – would make its way to Earth and establish total control.

**Companions: Zoe and Jamie**

Zoe Herriot had been born on Earth in the 21st century. We know this from Earth Document *The War Games*. She had joined Doctor2 a few months previously, within her time-stream, after an incident involving the Cybermen around the mid-21st century (Document4). Naturally she still possessed a clear memory of the encounter.

Jamie McCrimmon, too, had personal and harrowing experience of Cybermen. From Earth's 18th century, a soldier from the Highlands of Scotland, he was befriended by Doctor2 when the Time Lord arrived after a bloody and notorious skirmish called the battle of Culloden (1746 AD): Jamie was one of its few survivors. Within his own time-stream, we know that Jamie had confronted the Cybermen on three previous occasions (see Documents 5, 6 and 4 – in that order to follow Jamie's time-stream.)

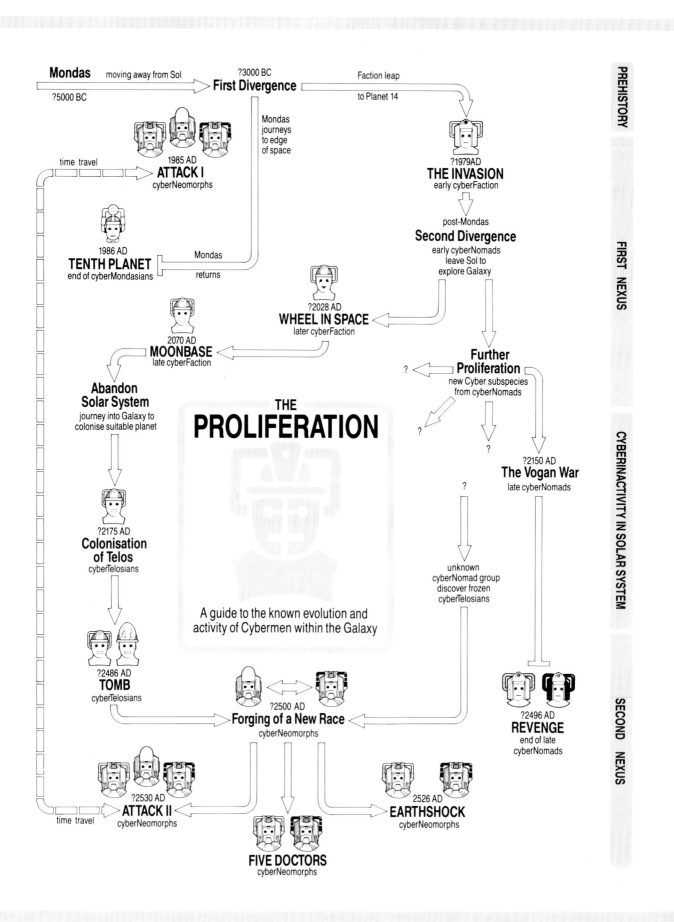

**Mondas** — moving away from Sol → **First Divergence** ?3000 BC — Faction leap to Planet 14

?5000 BC

Mondas journeys to edge of space

?1979AD
**THE INVASION**
early cyberFaction

time travel

1985 AD
**ATTACK I**
cyberNeomorphs

post-Mondas
**Second Divergence**
early cyberNomads
leave Sol to
explore Galaxy

1986 AD
**TENTH PLANET**
end of cyberMondasians

Mondas
returns

?2028 AD
**WHEEL IN SPACE**
later cyberFaction

2070 AD
**MOONBASE**
late cyberFaction

**Further
Proliferation**
new Cyber subspecies
from cyberNomads

?

?

**Abandon
Solar System**
journey into Galaxy to
colonise suitable planet

**THE
PROLIFERATION**

?

?2150 AD
**The Vogan War**
late cyberNomads

?2175 AD
**Colonisation
of Telos**
cyberTelosians

?

unknown
cyberNomad group
discover frozen
cyberTelosians

A guide to the known evolution and
activity of Cybermen within the Galaxy

?2486 AD
**TOMB**
cyberTelosians

?2500 AD
**Forging of a New Race**
cyberNeomorphs

?2496 AD
**REVENGE**
end of late
cyberNomads

?2530 AD
**ATTACK II**
cyberNeomorphs

2526 AD
**EARTHSHOCK**
cyberNeomorphs

time travel

**FIVE DOCTORS**
cyberNeomorphs

Such was the plan. For five years it had been in preparation. Then, suddenly, the Cyber Controlship detected the presence of a small blue craft which seemed to materialise close to them in space. Taking it to be a threat to the imminent invasion, the Cybermen attempted to destroy the unidentified object. Their missile did not hit its target, which yet seemed to vanish. They were to discover that the mysterious object was indeed known to them from a previous encounter (unrecorded in any of the CyberDocuments) and that their immediate suspicions were entirely founded: the blue box and its passengers constituted a great threat to Cyber intentions of conquering Earth.

The spacecraft was in fact a Gallifreyan time travelling vessel whose owner was the Doctor, a Time Lord of Gallifrey. (He had undergone one bodily regeneration already and is thus designated here as Doctor2). Since his machine was based on the principles of Time And Relative Dimensions In Space, he called it the TARDIS. He was invariably accompanied by fellow travellers; his present companions were called Zoe and Jamie.

Though puzzled as to the nature of the attack made against him, the Doctor had dematerialised the TARDIS in time to avoid the approaching missile. He and his companions landed in an English field (by coincidence, part of IE property) occupied by a domesticated species of Earth animal exploited for its milk – the Cow. The Doctor decided to overhaul the TARDIS; an old friend of his, Professor Travers, belonged to this era and would be able to assist. Removing the malfunctioning Visual Stabiliser circuits – and thus rendering the TARDIS invisible – the Doctor, Jamie and Zoe set off for the Professor's London home.

Professor Travers was away and his house had been let to a Professor Watkins. His niece Isobel told them that her uncle had recently gone to work for International Electromatics on highly secret work. She had not heard from him since. The Doctor decided to investigate.

After some manhandling by IE staff, he and Jamie eventually managed to speak to Tobias Vaughn himself, who avoided giving anything away about Professor Watkins but persuaded the Doctor to hand over the faulty circuits in order that IE might repair them. As they were ushered out, the Doctor's vague suspicions were far from calmed: Tobias Vaughn, he noted, did not blink like a human.

Before long, the Doctor and Jamie had met up with an old friend – Brigadier Lethbridge-Stewart. For the Brigadier their last meeting had been four years ago, though in Jamie and the Doctor's unique time-stream it had been only a matter of weeks. At that time, a creature called the Yeti had threatened London. The United Nations Intelligence Taskforce (UNIT) had since been formed to provide global defence against any similar incidents. The Brigadier led the British division of UNIT and he had been keeping International Electromatics under surveillance. There was growing proof that, for years, UFO activity had centred around IE property and that it had recently intensified. The Doctor was eager to help the Brigadier discover more.

Behind a sliding wall of Vaughn's office was a highly sophisticated device – a communications link with Cyber Control. It had the appearance of a swollen-brained, skeletal, machine creature: let us call it the Co-ordinator. Analysis of the Doctor's borrowed circuits had shown them to be 'alien'. Vaughn was intrigued and showed photographs of the Doctor and Jamie to the Co-ordinator. Its uninflected voice informed him that they were both registered in Cyber records as 'hostile' and recognised from having been on Planet 14 to which they travelled using a 'machine'. 'They are dangerous and must be destroyed,' intoned the Co-ordinator.

Vaughn agreed to ensure their destruction. But his interest had been aroused; he wanted to discover more about the Doctor's spacecraft. Part of his plan to keep control over the Cybermen lay with a device that Professor Watkins had invented – the Cerebratron Mentor. It had been developed as a gentle teaching device to induce emotional changes in the subject. Deducing that emotions were profoundly alien to Cybermen, Vaughn had forced Watkins to intensify the machine's effect. It might be possible to use it as a weapon against his allies, should it become necessary. But if all failed, the Doctor's 'machine' might provide a useful means of escape from the Cybermen.

Meanwhile, the Doctor and Jamie were watching Vaughn's men, who appeared superhumanly strong, carrying large crates which were to be transported out of the IE compound. To avoid detection, Jamie had to hide in one of the crates and was disturbed to find that it seemed to contain a living thing, wrapped in some dense fibrous material. Later, they looked on in horror as Vaughn's technicians applied electrodes to one of these enshrouded objects. The covering burst asunder and out stepped – a Cyberman.

These daunting beings were familiar to Jamie and the Doctor from encounters which this *History* has yet to describe. The Cyberman which stood before them, however, was somewhat different – of an earlier, less developed type than those they had confronted previously. For the Doctor the sight was of extraordinary interest. He later described them to the Brigadier as 'inhuman killers from another world'.

Towering above normal sized humans, enfleshed in some silvery, virtually indestructible

**UnDocumented Encounter**

Since, in Document1, the Cybermen recognise Jamie and Doctor2 as 'dangerous' and know of the TARDIS, we might suppose that they encountered each other on another occasion, though we have no Documentary evidence to substantiate this. The Cybermen may have kept Jamie and the Doctor under surveillance on Planet 14 while the time-travellers were going about some other business, but the fact that they are registered as 'hostile' suggests they fought against the Cybermen in some way. Perhaps an Earth Document still to be discovered will shed some light on this conundrum.

**Cyber Strength and Protection**

'Audio-rejection capsules' were implanted in Vaughn and the people who worked for him to protect them from the effect of Cyber hypnosis. To aid them further, the Cybermen partly converted their bodies to give them extra strength (as witnessed by the Doctor and Jamie when they see Vaughn's men carrying huge crates with ease) and greater protection from damage (Professor Watkins fires three shots into Vaughn's chest without causing him injury). Their minds, however, remained entirely human.

ArcHivist Drewskillia in *Alien Cultures* considers how the part-conversion may have been effected: either they were operated on by technomedical Cybermen that were among the first Cybermen to come to Earth (who perhaps also installed the Co-Ordinator behind Vaughn's office wall) or, a more intriguing possibility, the humans were taken up to the Cyber Controlship for processing.

## Cyberman: Document 1 – early *cyberFaction*

Powerful cybernetic limbs, whose movements are guided by intricate links of exoskeletal rods, allow it to stride purposively towards its mission. On each side of its head are muff-like striated blocks out of which protrude antenna – audio sensing devices perhaps. They bend upwards then inwards and connect with a bulge at the top of the cranium. On the blank face are two black holes where eyes might once have been. At each 'eye' a teardrop shape is etched where no tear has ever welled. The slit for a mouth betrays no expression, apart from cold resolve, and the chin beneath falls weakly away to a thick smooth neck. At the chest there is mounted a bulky multi-purpose device whose central column is topped by a lens which projects deadly rays. The rest of the column is given over to four control knobs. On either side are vented wings suggesting further functions of the unit: respiratory aid, cleansing filter, cooling equipment, energy pack.

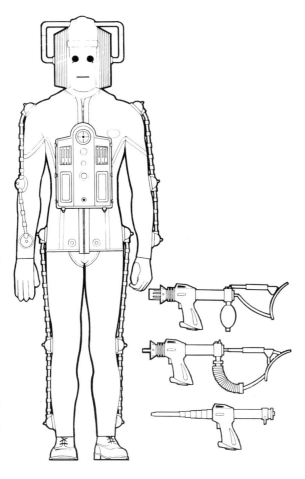

OBIAS
AUGHN

THE BRIGADIER

metal-plastic alloy, the Cyberman was humanoid in form but far from human in behaviour or appearance. Brought back to consciousness after who knows how long in suspended animation – a technique which was to be utilised several times by the Cyber Race (see Documents 4, 6, 8 and 9) – this mechanised creature showed no sign of confusion but immediately departed to swell the ranks of Cybertroops infiltrating the sewers of London.

Jamie and the Doctor had hard information for the Brigadier, who might now persuade his superiors that UNIT must raid International Electromatics to pre-empt whatever malignity Tobias Vaughn and the Cybermen were preparing. But such a course of action was to prove less than straightforward. As Zoe recalled, 'Cybermen have means of controlling people's minds'. Indeed, Cyber mind control techniques had already been used on the Brigadier's immediate superior, General Rutlidge. Blocking Lethbridge-Stewart's request to attack the warehouses where Cyber cocoons were still being activated, Rutlidge immediately alerted Vaughn and the deadline for Cyber invasion was brought forward.

Professor Watkins, under duress, had produced a more powerful version of his Cerebratron Mentor. Vaughn needed confirmation that the machine would give him control over Cybermen, so a partly resuscitated Cyberman was induced with 'fear'. Like any emotion, it was totally alien to the Cyber system. The effect was devastating. Squealing pitifully, it flailed its arms in a desperate attempt to escape the searing stabs of pure emotion and stumbled blindly towards the sewers – a 'rogue' Cyberman on the loose. The experiment had been a success.. It proved to Vaughn that the Cybermen were not indestructible: their bodies might be strong but their minds had weaknesses still.

As the Cyber Controlship came from behind the Moon, the hypnotic signal was beamed towards Earth. The world's population fell unconscious. Fortunately, the Doctor had guessed how Cyber hypnosis might be induced and (as in Document 4) neuristors were taped to the back of the neck to depolarise the signal. Zoe, Jamie, the Brigadier's UNIT group and the Doctor himself were thus able to remain alert – but against the might of the Cybermen, they were few. In space, the first half of the Cyber invasion fleet emerged from the Controlship, while on Earth, manhole covers were flung open to disgorge a resolute stream of Cyber troops. The invasion had begun.

UNIT had already discovered how formidable Cybermen could be. They had attempted to contain a group in the sewers. 'Five grenades dropped right on top of the Cybermen and one of them still came out of it – wouldn't like to face a whole army of them', said one officer. But a Cyber army was precisely what they now confronted. Undaunted, UNIT initiated a defensive plan. It proceeded on two fronts: a Russian Moon-probe was to be loaded with a nuclear warhead and aimed at the Cyber Controlship to end the transmission of hypnotic control; and missiles at a British base were to be fired at the invasion fleet as soon as it was detected by radar.

Ironically, the only area now free of Cybermen was the sewers. Through them, the Doctor made his way to the IE building. There, he found that Vaughn still believed he could maintain control over the Cybermen, that it was he who had masterminded everything, that the Cybermen were merely providing superior technological techniques and a mighty army to do his will. The Doctor warned in vain that they would destroy Earth. Vaughn began transmission of the vital radio beam and the Co-ordinator announced that the first of the invasion fleet's two waves was on its way.

But the fleet had been detected at the missile base. Zoe, with her 21st century mathematical prowess, had calculated the most effective trajectory for the few missiles at their disposal. Her calculations proved deadly accurate. A chain reaction of destruction obliterated the entire first wave of the Cybermen's transporter fleet.

The Co-ordinator announced the destruction of the first fleet and laid the blame on their erstwhile ally. A Cyber megatron bomb was now 'to destroy life on Earth completely – every living being.' Vaughn, crazed with humiliation and frustration as his long awaited dream became nightmare, turned the Cerebratron Mentor on the Co-ordinator. The intensity of the emotion it induced caused the communication device to malfunction and explode. Vaughn was at length persuaded to lead the Doctor to the radio transmitter which had been guiding the invasion fleet and was now directing the Cyber bomb to Earth.

As the nuclear-armed Moonrocket was launched from Russia, the Doctor and Vaughn made their way to the IE warehouse where the radio transmitter was located. Many Cybermen were guarding the area. UNIT's smaller weapons had proved ineffective against them, though the Cybermen's hand-held guns were deadly against humans. However, with larger weapons – mortar and bazooka – the Cyber forces were held in check. Armed with the Cerebratron Mentor, Vaughn reached the transmitter but was shot down. UNIT men finally ended its transmissions and destroyed the other Cybermen in the compound.

The super-cooled hydrogen warhead on the Russian rocket reached its target and vaporised the Cyber Controlship and the Cyber bomb. On Earth, people began to regain consciousness. Such was the nature of the hypnosis (it must be assumed) that none were aware of the missing hours in their day. It remained the knowledge of a special few that this First Invasion of the Cybermen had taken place at all. The Doctor repaired his circuits and he and his two companions were returned to the field of Cows. They made their farewells to the Brigadier and disappeared, literally, into the invisible TARDIS.

Document1 provokes many interesting questions. For example, though the first wave of the Cyber invasion fleet was destroyed, we hear nothing of the second wave. Is it possible that before the Russian warhead hit the Cyber Controlship, several of the small Cyber craft evacuated, escaping certain destruction to face uncertain survival in space? Did some indeed survive and go on to other conquests?

There are other questions which arise from Document1: what is Planet 14 to the Cybermen? Why does a race which is so apparently advanced and has presumably travelled over immense distances to get to Earth, depend on a radio beam to make its final invasion. Where, in fact, do these Cybermen come from? Some answers will be found in Documents 2 and 3: they chronicle two further invasions of Earth.

## The Quiet Invasion (Document2)

The next Cyber invasion took place in 1985. As on the first occasion, the infiltration began in secrecy in the sewer network of London. But this second invasion was quiet and small-scale – and the invaders were Cybermen from more than half a millenium in the future.

Commander Lytton was from the star system 690. Human in appearance (perhaps actually human, we do not know) his home planet was Vita 15's satellite, Riften 5. The Cybermen knew it as a place of warriors. Lytton himself was an intergalactic mercenary. He had been working for the Daleks in London when they established a time tunnel back to 1984 (see Earth document *Resurrection of the Daleks*). Doctor5 (the Doctor in his fifth reincarnation) closed the tunnel and defeated their evil intentions. Lytton, stranded in the 20th century, set up a distress call in the hope that some intergalactic intelligence would come to his aid and take him back – or rather, forward – to his own time and place.

To pay for the sophisticated electronics equipment, he had turned his hand to theft. Then, while awaiting rescue, he led a group of three men into the sewers – ostensibly to break into the vaults of a diamond bank. (At this time of Earth's history 'banks' were strongholds of money and valuables.)

But they were not alone in the sewers. A menacing black figure stalked and killed one of the crooks. Then, a section of sewer wall swung open to reveal a giant silver figure, flanked by two others. They were Cybermen, recognisable descendants of those involved in the First Invasion, but distantly so. Their appearance was altogether more streamlined, more warrior-like, more powerful. The central figure had black markings on the helmet antenna which designated the higher rank of Leader. Taking Lytton's gun, the Cyberleader demonstrated his immense physical strength as he effortlessly bent and snapped the weapon in two.

The Cybermen had set up their base at an intersection of sewer tunnels, walled off from the rest of the system. There they prepared for the culmination of their Ultimate Plan to destroy Earth. Within the Cyberbase were chambers where captured humans, or those unlucky enough to stray across the path of the black Cyberscouts, were converted into Cybermen. In this way the Cyberforces were increased.

When it appeared that they might be killed – or even worse, converted – Lytton explained that he was not from Earth. He knew the Cybermen had a ship on the dark side of the Moon: he had picked up its transmissions with his advanced communications equipment; he knew what the Cybermen planned and offered to serve their cause. The Leader decided to bring Lytton, and his

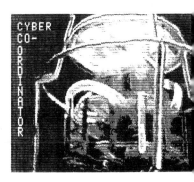

CYBER CO-ORDINATOR

PROFESSOR WATKINS        ISOBEL

LYTTON

DOCTOR 6

LYTTON

PERI

associate Griffiths, before the Cybercontroller.

The fourth member of Lytton's gang had escaped and stumbled across a strange couple who were also wandering the sewers. It was Doctor6 and his young American companion, Perpugilliam Brown – usually known as Peri. They had been drawn to Earth by Lytton's signal, thinking an alien was in need of help. Realising that 'Commander Lytton, late of the Dalek Task Force' was responsible for the distress signal, they returned to the TARDIS. But Cybermen had already discovered and requisitioned it. The Doctor was forced to set co-ordinates for the Cybermen's home planet: place, Telos; date, more than 600 years in the future.

It seemed to the Doctor that, at the stage in their future for which the TARDIS was making, the Cybermen had discovered how to travel through time – a secret which had always evaded them. But Lytton assured him that the Cybermen had merely stolen a time vessel to return to this point in their past.

Peri knew nothing of the Cybermen. During their journey to Telos, she learnt that its indigenous race had been the Cryons, a technologically advanced people who lived at sub-zero temperatures. In order to live in the warmer areas of their planet, they had become adept at building refrigerated cities. The Cybermen had discovered Telos. They were running out of power and needed to rest (see Document6) and the Cryon's refrigerated cities provided ideal 'hibernation' facilities. The Cryons were destroyed and the Cybermen adopted Telos as their own.

But as the TARDIS leaves Earth 1985 to travel through time and space towards the Telos of the advanced Cybermen's proper time-stream, we must part company with it. The story continues in Document9 and will be resumed as our CyberHistory nears its end.

Thus far, two invasions by Cybermen have remained unknown to the vast majority of people on Earth. We now consider an invasion which was to be seared into the collective Earth mind: it was talked of for centuries after.

### The Destruction of Mondas (Document3)

Even as Peri was learning something of the Cybermen's history, their original planet, Mondas, was closing in on Earth. Its intention was to plunder two resources vital to its survival: energy and humans.

Mondas had long travelled through space and its own supplies of energy were nearing exhaustion. New sources were desperately needed if the Mondasian Cybermen were to survive. Earth and Mondas had once been twin planets before Mondas had drifted away to the 'edge of space'. Earth would provide the type of energy that had

DOCTOR 1

been exhausted on Mondas.

Mondas would lock onto the energy latent within Earth and suck it dry, replenishing its own resources and exhausting those of its twin. But this proposed transference held dangers: it was possible that Mondas might be destroyed through absorbing too much energy. Before that point was reached, the Cybermen had to be prepared to destroy Earth. This would be unfortunate: an important bonus in returning to its twin was the mass-conversion of the many suitable humans available among Earth's population. However, all activity on the planet – including the Cybermen themselves – was dependant on energy drawn directly from Mondas. It was vital to renew it. Should the danger arise, the logical priority was to save the newly-energised Mondas.

It was at the end of 1986 that Earth saw the new planet. At that period in its history, Earth astronomers had found and classified nine planets. The new one was therefore seen as a tenth planet. It was discovered in an orbit between Mars and Venus when Earth spacecraft Zeus 4 was unexpectedly dragged out of its proper course under the new planet's gravitational influence.

At Earth's South pole, under the surface of an icebound continent known as Antarctica, there was a International Space Command base. Snowcap Tracking Station had been following the course of the craft and now sought to find what was pulling Zeus 4 off-course. The endeavour was complicated by the fact that, inexplicably, three people had been discovered wandering in the snowy wastes above. It was the Doctor (in his original incarnation) and two companions from London 1966: Merchant Seaman Ben Jackson, and a computer assistant, Polly. All three had been bustled unceremoniously into Snowcap and held as prisoners by the irascible head of the Station, the American General Cutler.

When the new planet was discovered to be fast approaching Earth on an oblique orbit, its land masses were seen to be a reverse image of Earth's. Senior Scientist Dr Barclay pointed out that it could not be a reflection but he was unable to provide an alternative explanation. The Doctor, however, seemed to know exactly what the planet was and what it brought: 'Before very long, I'm afraid, we must expect visitors,' he warned. True to the Doctor's prediction, the 'visitors' soon arrived.

One of the Cybermen's craft came to rest beyond where the TARDIS stood. It was entirely different from those which had invaded during the previous decade and so too were the Cybermen which now emerged. Though they were tall, bore antenna at the head and bulky units at the chest, they were closer to human form. Paradoxically, this lent to their appearance a more chilling quality: their separation from humanity was so clearly irrevocable.

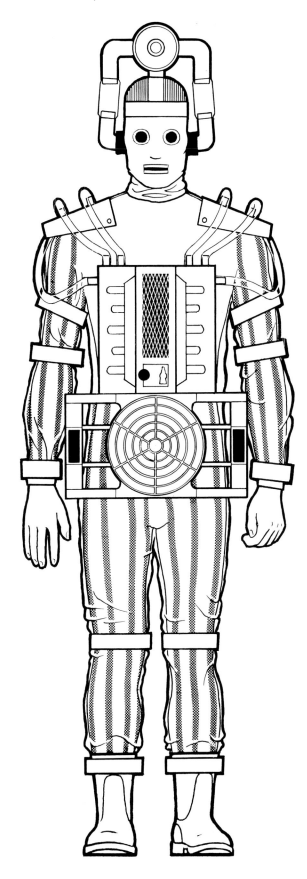

machine. Three powerful forearms rose and swiftly fell, smashing into the necks of their horrified victims. The first opposition had been overcome with effortless efficiency; it was the way these Cybermen intended to overcome the whole of Earth.

Hidden under heavy jackets taken from the bodies of their victims, the three Cybermen gained access to the base. Throwing back the jacket hoods, they revealed their alien features. A soldier instinctively raised his gun at them. Instantly, one of the Cybermen operated the dish-like weapon beneath his chest unit and a sudden pulse of light eliminated the source of danger – and the soldier's life.

One of the Cybermen spoke. The aperture that was once a mouth opened and remained unmoving as the emotionless voice emerged. Though the tone was reasonable, the content was highly disturbing to the incredulous human listeners.

Mondas was drawing the energy it needed from Earth. Earth would soon become a dead planet. Suitable humans would be able to avoid otherwise certain death on Earth by being taken to Mondas. There, they would be changed into Cybermen. Cybermen had once been exactly like humans but, to combat such weaknesses as a shortening lifespan, the scientists of Mondas had devised spare parts to replace almost all of the human body. Emotions were also considered a weakness and they were removed from the once human brain. 'It is useless to resist us. We are stronger and more efficient than you Earth people. We must be obeyed,' the Cyberman continued with logical precision. 'We have freedom from disease, protection against heat and cold – true mastery. Do you prefer to die in misery?'

The humans preferred their misery to the Cybermen's mastery and by turning the Cybermen's own weapons against them, overcame the three who had entered the base. But the Doctor – whose 'old body' was 'wearing a bit thin' – became unwell for a time and was unable to help.

Zeus 4 had disintegrated under the gravitational effect of Mondas. A relief rocket had been sent up, manned by the General's son, Lieutenant Cutler, but it too was in danger. When Snowcap technicians discovered that a fleet of two hundred and fifty Cyber spacecraft was orbiting Earth, the General decided to destroy Mondas with the Z-bomb – a weapon of total destruction sited at the polar base.

Dr Barclay knew that the radiation released could seriously effect life on Earth so, encouraged by Polly and assisted by Ben, he rendered the Z-bomb rocket inoperable. Robbed of a means to save his son's life General Cutler became unbalanced, threatening to shoot his scientists if they did not launch the Z-bomb. When more Cybermen broke into the base, the General was

Three such figures now strode purposefully towards the TARDIS where a party of Cutler's men were trying to gain access to the Doctor's

**Cyberman: Document 3 –** *cyberMondasian*

The face is swathed in plastic flesh, the human skull beneath still clearly discernible. A cap of skullbone has been removed and replaced by a metal cover – presumably to render the brain more accessible for 'adjustment'. Flesh-flaps of human ears have given way to thick antenna – tubes extending from the aural cavities on each side of the head to meet above, at a device for gathering energy beamed from Mondas – the energy which keeps them alive. The support system of their exoskeleton – a series of connected metal rings – becomes inactive without Mondasian energy, and the organic remains within, helpless. A third tube feeds directly from the lamp-like device above the head to the back of the brain, keeping it plentifully supplied with energy that is as essential to it as oxygen to a human brain.

The chest unit, even bulkier than those of the First Invasion, is a respiratory aid and might also function as kidney dialyser and artificial heart. (Polly later describes it as replacing their heart and lungs – Document 5.) It is larger, cuboid and constructed not of plasticised silvery alloy but of some transparent material that reveals flashing lights within – to each side of a central vented area – below which is a solitary control knob. Beneath hangs a detachable dish-shaped weapon – again, clumsily bulky in comparison with the cyberweapons of the First Invasion.

Most startling are the hands – human in every detail. How much more of the Cyberman body remains unchanged from its original human form? But these Cybermen are clearly far from human. Apart from obvious physical adaptations, the brain has also been ad- ▶

◀ justed to remove certain weaknesses. Entirely logical, it is scoured of human emotion. It is probably in this aspect that Mondasian Cybermen come closest to those of Planet 14. Compared with the monotonous electronic voice of early *cyberFaction*, the *cyberMondasian* have a sing-song modulation, an expression more akin to speech which emanates from human thought processes, though undoubtedly produced artificially.

POLLY

BEN

immediately eliminated. The Cybermen then ordered that the warhead be removed to the deepest part of the base, the radiation room. Polly was taken to the Cybership as a hostage until this was done.

Lieutenant Cutler had observed from his orbiting spacecraft that something strange was happening to Mondas: it was brightening up like a sun and then darkening again. The Doctor took this to be the first sign that Mondas was absorbing too much energy.

There had been mass landings of Cybermen in many other parts of Earth. At International Space Command in a European city called Geneva, Secretary-General Wigner was replaced by a Cyberman who announced, 'I am Controller of the Earth.' Since Mondas was already close to absorbing too much energy from Earth, the Controlling Cyberman ordered the 'second objective' to be implemented.

When the Doctor heard that this involved the evacuation of all Cybermen back to Mondas, he realised that they planned to use the Z-bomb, now perfectly sited deep under the Antarctic, to destroy Earth. Mondas would then be fully-energised but safe from the excessive drain from Earth which threatened at any moment to burn their planet up and which the Cybermen were otherwise powerless to stop. Before being taken hostage himself, he managed to warn Ben and the other Snowcap personnel who had relocated the Z-bomb.

Ben deduced that Cybermen must be susceptible to radiation: they had forced humans to move the warhead to the radiation room even though the operation had to be completed swiftly; yet their greater strength could have achieved this much more efficiently. By exposing them to isotope rods removed from the Snowcap nuclear reactor, all Cybermen in the base were overcome.

A second wave of Cybermen regained control but it was at this moment that Mondas reached saturation point and began to break up. As their planet cracked, melted and dispersed into space, Cybermen – dependant on energy from Mondas – collapsed and shrivelled. Secretary-General Wigner was able to announce, 'The Cyber menace has ended – all over the world.' The long journey of Mondas and the Mondasian Cybermen had come to a certain end.

For the Doctor it was a kind of ending too. Once back in the TARDIS he collapsed. Before the eyes of his two companions he underwent a physical transformation. Time Lords may undergo many bodily regenerations; the Doctor had undergone his first. He retained his extensive knowledge and 450-year-old memory but it was housed in a younger body and expressed through an alternative personality.

It was in this second embodiment, as Doctor2, that he met the Cybermen in their First Invasion and it is in this form that he will encounter them in the next three episodes of our chronology. These incidents form the Middle and part of the Later History of the Cybermen and span more than 500 years of Cyber development.

But with the details of their Early History fresh in our minds let us first use what we know thus far of the Cybermen and attempt to piece together their origins.

# Origins of the Cybermen

### Cosmological Beginnings

15 billion years ago the Universe was born.

It started with a bang. A single point had once contained everything. Suddenly it exploded. Matter spread outwards, filling the void evenly and thinly. Space-time began.

The untamed power of the Universe at last took stock of itself. Expansion slowed. Matter became less evenly spread. Billowing cosmic dust condensed into whirling constellations of suns and planets. There was a cooling, a consolidation into galaxies.

10 billion years elapsed. An ageing sun at the edge of a certain galaxy expired in an explosion outshining 10 billion stars. Cosmic cloud was compressed by the supernova and new suns were born. One of them was Sol.

As Sol became a bright yellow star it was surrounded by a disc of icy dust whose radius was 40 billion miles. Up to 300 million miles away from Sol, the ices melted and only rocky grains remained. The grains clumped together as they swept round the sun until the bodies of the planets were formed. The larger the core, the denser the atmosphere which the planet attracted from the all-pervasive gases of hydrogen and helium.

Sol was so named by a species of intelligent creatures who evolved 5 billion years later. They inhabited a planet named Earth.

Earth was watery, a warm and fertile place, one of the inner rocky planets, a mere 93 million miles away from Sol. It shared its orbit round the sun with an almost identical planet, twinned from the same condensing Matter, bearing the same life-producing elements, sharing the same climatic conditions. The twin was called Mondas. These two gems of Sol's system encircled their sun, encircling each other in the characteristic dance of double planets.

Each, in time, produced sentient humans – *homoSapiens* – who became aware of some of the larger and nearer planets in the sun system to which they belonged. Earth, for most of its history, believed itself to be the centre of a whirling Universe. Mondas did not share this delusion for as long: the unending quest for a scientific base to belief, characteristic of their later civilisation, started early and was single-mindedly pursued. Earth's progress was less consistent. Much was learned and as much forgotten in the waxing and waning of successive civilisations, in the scrabble for bare existence. Though born as twins, while Mondas grew apace, Earth dawdled.

## Prehistoric Period

The cosmological origins of the Cybermen are the least difficult to surmise. They are based on the assumptions about our own beginnings and those of many intelligent life-forms documented in the Arc. From now on our suppositions become more hazardous. For us the 'prehistoric period' is really the pre-Documentary period and is virtually impenetrable. Apart from a few tantalising clues, we must freely admit that we know nothing of this period.

But having made our ignorance quite clear, there is nothing to stop us from picking up those few poor clues and juggling. One such a clue is this: 'Mondas' was another name for Earth in one of the Ancient languages (Dr Barclay remembers this in Document3 and it is confirmed by the Cybermen). What can we make of it?

Undoubtedly, the humans of Mondas must have developed more quickly than those of Earth. Novasa suggests that Mondasian civilisation might have already been so well advanced that even at such an early stage of development, when Earth was at the hunter/gatherer stage, it had perfected some rudimentary form of inter-orbit travel in order to be able to visit its twin. Certainly there are copious references in ancient Earth texts to support the idea of visitation from another world.

In many instances these visitors would seem to have looked like Earth people but displayed great knowledge and more advanced intelligence. 'When Giants walked the Earth' is a form of an idea recurring in many early writings; it may refer to the larger than Earth-life characteristics of knowledge and stature presented by such a comparatively advanced race.

It is known that ancient Earth communities were able to perfect techniques for travelling immense distances over their largely water covered planet, visiting continents that were not to be 'discovered' until several millenia later by more advanced civilisations. Perhaps, then, Novasa's postulation is not to be ruled out and Mondasians did hop across to their twin planet thousands of years before they developed proper space travel.

## Departure of Mondas

At some indeterminate time, a cosmological event occurred of fundamental significance to the future existence of Mondas. The planet left the orbit it had shared with its twin. When and how this occurred is a point that becomes clearer through careful attention to the Documents.

Some ArcHivists have assumed that Mondas – driven by its own propulsion unit – left Earth orbit millions of years ago. But what are we told? All we know about Mondas leaving its original orbit is based on two passages from Document3: the Doctor says, 'Millions of years ago there was a twin planet to Earth – ' (he is interrupted before he can say more); and a Cyberman says, 'Aeons ago the planets were twins. Then we drifted away from you on a journey to the edge of space. Now we have returned.'

There is nothing more precise here than that Mondas and Earth shared a cosmological development some immeasurable length of time in the past. It was at an unspecified period after this that Mondas actually left its orbit.

As we shall see, it makes a great deal of sense to place this departure no more than 10 or 20 thousand years before the Return. Furthermore, the Cyberman says that they 'drifted' away from Earth. This does not sound like a premeditated act under their own control – more like the result of the cosmological event Novasa postulates and with which I concur.

The propulsion unit is mentioned only in Document2: Griffiths asks, 'How can a planet travel around – off its orbit?', to which the Doctor replies, 'Mondas had a propulsion unit – a tribute to Cyber engineering – though why they should want to push a planet through space I've no idea.' The Doctor is certainly confirming that Cybermen did have control over their planet when it returned to attack Earth; he does not indicate when the propulsion unit was first developed. For the passages not to contradict, the only sense they make is the conclusion Novasa comes to: Mondas drifted helplessly to the far reaches of the Solar system – 40 billion miles out, where the cometary cloud thins to nothing ('the edge of space') – made such technological advances during the thousands of years of that journey to perfect a way of controlling their direction and speed of travel, and so returned to their original place in the cosmos.

To imagine the Mondasians might have been capable of propelling their planet out of fixed orbit, millions of years before homoSapiens had evolved on Earth is impossible if we are to accept some kind of parity of development between what are meant to be twin planets. Moreover, if Mondas had perfected such amazing technology as to be able to leave the Solar system at a time that the Dinosaurs, say, still roamed the Earth,

### A Twin Parity?
Presumably there would have been opportunity for racial-mixing. Moreover, ancient records suggest that selected Earth people were 'taken up' to Mondas. Such cross-fertilisation might have resulted in a very similar genetic stock of homoSapiens on both planets. With the similarities of orbit, planet size, land masses, climate and evolutionary development, Mondas and Earth would thus have been true twins. As the Cyberman in Document3 makes quite clear, 'we were exactly like you once.'

Of course, as Novasa himself points out, there need not have been any kind of parity either in the pace or in the nature of development between the two planets: the same form does not necessarily imply the same development. It is quite possible that the Mondasians had reached a cul-de-sac in progress and remained thus for thousands of years before Mondas left its orbit. A successfully adapted and stable species may remain the dominant life-form of a planet for even longer, as in the case of the Dinosaurs who ruled Earth for something like 150 million years. Two things must be remembered here, however: a) the Dinosaurs in fact developed enormously during that time; b) it is the catalyst of technology which enables species, usually primates and above, to phenomenally increase the pace of their development and achievements.

then it is inconceivable that 70 million years on, Mondasians would merely have reached the stage of the (relatively) primitive Cybermen. After all that time they are more likely to have become creatures invisible to Earth perceptions (there are records of such species in the Arc – and see *Mandragora Helix*) rather than a race of metal and plastic which must be provided with a suitable radio link to invade Earth, which succumbs to radiation, gravity and gold (see Documents 3, 5 and 7), and which cannot fathom the Laws of Time. Since we have already seen the marked technological progress they make within some 600 years (between Documents 1 and 2), they would have to be the latest starters in the Universe! It is more plausible, I think, to set the departure of Mondas some time in the period after *homoSapiens* had become well established on Earth – that is, less than 40,000 years before the Return of Mondas.

There is not the space here for the elaboration of the many different cosmic phenomena that could have taken Mondas away from Earth. For that, Novasa's *CyberHistorical Postulates* provides ample technical discussion. Only two issues need to be raised.

Firstly, the Arc Hives are amply supplied with similar accounts of the transmutation of whole civilisations whose catalyst was a cosmological event: a near star going nova, a particularly intense bombardment of meteors. (The events to be related in Document4 will suggest that the Cybermen had a fundamental understanding of the significance of such phenomena.) The more plausible of such phenomena are those which might have resulted in a slow drifting away from Sol during which the Mondasians could adapt to changing climatic conditions. Interestingly, during the period of the Documents, it was known that the Moon was slowly moving away from Earth, though only at a rate of a few metres per century – Mondasians could have survived a departure a million times faster. But here we come to a another possible cause of the planet's displacement: the arrival of the Moon to become Earth's satellite. It is this possibility which introduces the second and more important issue, what Farozia has called her '14 Planet Theory'.

## The 14 Planet Theory

We know that at some stage Cybermen colonised a planet called Telos. The 14 Planet Theory starts with the common assumption that Telos cannot belong to Sol's planetary system, an assumption with which Farozia concurs given the planet's conditions: sky, cloudy and blueish; atmosphere, rarified but breathable by humans; environment, capable of evolving and supporting a humanoid species, albeit at sub-zero temperatures; if it were in the Solar system, it would have to be one of the inner planets and there is none to fit that description.

Telos is also usually thought to have been colonised as Mondas passed by on its journey. But here is a difficulty: even if we were to accept that Mondas was propelled by some device, the time it would take to drive a planet through deepest space and visit at least one other planetary system would be immense. Travelling at 100,000 miles an hour, it would take 30,000 years to reach the nearest system. Then we have to assume the existence of a suitable planet within the system as well as a return journey of 30,000 years duration. The next nearest star system is twice the distance of the first and would therefore take 60,000 years to reach – 120,000 for the round trip.

We are asked, in the conventional view, to accept that such a marathon was undertaken – and before the planet's resources were entirely drained. But what would be the meaning of 'journey to the edge of space' in this context? Furthermore, the passage of even these periods of time stretches credulity to breaking point. If, 60,000 years previously, the Mondasians were capable of such technological feats as to build planet-propelling units, how advanced would their civilisation have become by their return? The idea that Mondas colonised Telos as it passed on its journey begins to appear untenable. It is confirmed as such by the following consideration.

Mondasian Cybermen were dependant on energy beamed from Mondas and, as Document3 clearly shows, when their planet was destroyed it was inevitably the end of them too. But Document9 has the Doctor saying, 'If Mondas hadn't been destroyed, the Cybermen would never have come here [to Telos]'. We must infer that the colonisation of Telos took place *after* the destruction of Mondas but by Cybermen who had become *independent* of their home planet while it was still on its journey – Cybermen who nevertheless regarded Mondas as their home planet to be rejoined when Mondas had made its Return to plunder Earth. The failure of the Mondasian plan left these independent Cybermen dispossessed and led them finally to discover Telos.

But who were these independent Cybermen? If Mondas had developed sophisticated space travelling skills to take exploring Cybermen to other systems, or even galaxies, those Cybermen would have discovered planets of their own to colonise, relinquishing any contact with Mondas; the destruction of Mondas would not trigger the desperate search to adopt another suitable planet that is suggested by Document9. Additionally, is it not likely that Mondas would have surreptitiously sent an advance invasion fleet to conquer Earth – before bringing in a huge planet to attack it? Of course, one might consider the Cybermen of the First Invasion to be exactly that, sent from Mondas to prepare the way. But those Cybermen differ so markedly between Document1 and Document3. What is more, neither group makes reference to the other and what little is revealed of the First Invasion Cybermen implies that they come from what they call 'Planet 14'. Farozia's solution is to look for a possible temporary home for the Cybermen within the Solar system – a 'Planet 14' in fact.

The Solar system does not only consist of the Sun and the nine planets in the way that popular Earth conception imagined it at the time of Document3. It is, of course, more complex and extensive. There is, for example, the asteroid belt which was thought by many Earth cosmologists (and we have corroborative evidence in *Image of the Fendahl*) to be the remains of an ancient planet – Farozia refers to it as Asterus.

Ironically, just before the Return of Mondas, these cosmologists were engaged in feverish observation of the skies to find 'Planet 10' – not Mondas, but a body beyond Pluto – and thus explain the perturbed orbits of the outer planets. The notion, also, that the Solar system is divided into the smaller, solid inner planets and the giant, gaseous outer planets is a simplification. Pluto is a small solid body – as are many of the moons of the gaseous giants, some of which are larger than Pluto itself. It has its own moon (Charon) which is so relatively large that together they might be described as double planets. The cosmologists estimated Planet 10 itself to be four times as heavy as Earth – a dwarf compared to the giant planets of Jupiter, Saturn, Uranus and Neptune. By 20th century Earth assumptions, then, the Solar system could be said to have contained (with Mondas, Asterus and Planet 10) 12 planets.

If one includes the 'cometary cloud' of rock and ice which constantly orbits the sun and which originates many of the comets, the Solar system extends to a distance of about 1.5 light years (or 40 billion miles) from the sun. Pluto is just over 3.5 billion miles from Sol. Beyond Pluto and Planet 10, the expanse which remains under Solar influence could easily contain at least one more substantial body that may be called a planet. But this would only account for thirteen planets. And where does the Moon fit into all this?

The origin of the Moon puzzled Earth cosmologists. Moonrock is too dissimilar from Earthrock for the two planets to have formed together in space. One theory was that the Moon had formed in a different part of the Solar system and was later captured by Earth's gravitational influence. If this was the case, then as far as Mondas was concerned, the Moon was a planet in its own right: a fourteenth planet in the Solar system by what might have been Ancient Mondasian reckoning.

Farozia uses this idea to suggest how Mondas might have been moved from its orbit. She then goes on to weave it into her larger 14 Planet Theory. In *Hypotheses* she writes:

> Mondas and Earth were a double planet; they orbited round each other as they moved together round Sol. Three and a half billion miles away there was another double planet: Pluto and Charon. Significantly, in composition and size the Moon is almost indistinguishable from Mercury, suggesting that they had similar origins. What if they were formed together, were once a third double planet within the Solar system? Let us suppose that such was the case. At some stage the Moon must have been dislodged from its orbit with Mercury, to close in on Earth and Mondas. It was this event, I suggest, that pulled Mondas away from Earth on a slow but inexorable journey towards the edge of the Solar system. The path Mondas took was anything but direct, first spiralling slowly outwards (allowing Mondasians sufficient centuries to adapt to the worsening conditions on their planet) then zig-zagging across the Solar system as it came under the gravitational influences of other planets it passed on its way. In this bizarre manner, the 'journey to the edge of space' might have lasted thousands of Earth years.

The 14 Planet Theory is pure supposition. Nevertheless, given that we must surmise so much, I think such postulates are permissible – provided always that they are consistent with the facts. Farozia's theory is.

A totally literal approach equips us with the bare bones: Mondas drifting away from Sol, somehow sending out a deep space invasion fleet before itself returning to Earth under its own propulsion. It needs imaginative detail to put flesh on the bone – a hypothetical exoskeleton, if you like, within which inconsistencies (radical changes in Cyber appearance) and points of vagueness (Planet 14) may be fitted.

What follows is my attempt to put flesh on the bones: a detailed reconstruction of the un-Documented period after Mondas left its orbit – a period all the more tantalising for its transition from Mondasian to Cyberman. The reconstruction is firmly based on clues found in the Documents, and on the 14 Planet Theory.

## Journey to the Edge of Space

The Mondasians had rapidly to adapt to the severe changes that followed from moving away from their sun. The initial and most dramatic changes were those affecting the climate. The weather immediately ceased to follow age-old patterns. Storms, earthquakes, tidal waves, drought, covered the planet in chaotic profusion. Temperatures dropped and increasingly bitter

### Novasa's Scenario

This is how Novasa describes one possible scenario as Mondas moved from its shared orbit with Earth: 'There is chaos as [the Mondasians] are plunged into a frighteningly eternal Winter. Few people survive. Those who do must discover radically new ways of remaining alive. Perhaps over centuries, perhaps over millenia, they slowly rebuild a civilisation. By nature of the hostile environment, the Monadasians become motivated by logic to help make difficult decisions less agonising. They develop control over their planet's course, putting aside all other research. Only later do they explore cybernetics as they realise that the race is becoming weaker. They are thus forced to become Cybermen, proficient in some technical fields but less adept in others (e.g spaceship navigation).'

Here we seem to have an explanation of the Cybermen's seemingly incongruous need in the First Invasion – and later (see Document4) – for a radio beam to bring their fleet to Earth: space travel may have been for them a relatively undeveloped skill. We also have in outline what Farozia seeks to colour in, though she imagines much cybernetic development taking place *before* planetary drive is established.

# ANCIENT COSMOLOGY OF MONDAS

**PLANET 2**
A double planet with MERCURY. Later to be flung out of orbit to dislodge MONDAS and become EARTH'S MOON

**PLANETS 4 AND 5**
The double planet system of EARTH and MONDAS

**PLANET 7**
Named ASTERUS by ArcHivist Hegelia (and FENDAHL in Earth Document The Image of the Fendahl). Its shattered remains later become the astroid belt

**PLANET 8**
Largest of the planets of the Solar System and the only one to give out more heat than it receives from SOL. May be described as a failed star or brown dwarf

**PLANET 12**
Furthest planet from SOL known to 20th century EARTH. Strictly a double planet system – though its companion CHARON was classed as a satellite in the Ancient Cosology

**PLANET 13**
Named PENULTIMA by ArcHivist Farozia. Late 20th century EARTH suspected its existence but failed to find evidence

**PLANET 14**
Faction's base planet for several millenia as they transformed themselves from cybernetically assisted humans into true Cybermen (cyberFaction) – according to ArcHivist Farozia

Distances are given in millions of miles from the sun SOL

PLANET 14

PLANET 13 (PENTU

8

484

?260m

142m

93m

67m

2 MOON

1 MERCURY

SOL

36m

3 VENUS

4 MONDAS

5 EART

## Earth's Ideo-Logical Phase

Earth seems almost to have reached ILP by the middle of its Third Millenium AD. A school of thought embodied by the Brotherhood of Logicians had become particularly influential at this time (Document6). Even earlier, in the 21st century (Document4), the Doctor's companion Zoe had gone through a rigorous educational process – some called it brainwashing – in the School of Para-psychology. It taught that Logic, properly applied, led infallibly to Truth.

Many advanced civilisations emerge from ILP having re-affirmed that logic must be tempered by less easily defined disciplines: compassion and notions of the subtle interconnectedness of all things. The Logic/Compassion Equation usually becomes recognised as the Absolute Necessity.

We, the ArcHivists, have for long had a deep-rooted understanding of the L/C equation. The Arc Hives, and the untiring pursuit of knowledge they represent, demonstrate our dedication to the Understanding. It is to be hoped that Earth itself, should it yet remain, has now approached some semblance of it.

winters followed, one hard upon the other, until after several centuries the entire Mondasian year was an endless icy season.

To survive these climatic traumas, it is most likely that the Mondasians 'went to ground'. First utilising natural underground chambers and networks, they must gradually have perfected techniques for excavating immense subterranean living areas where life could continue almost as before. Learning to tap the vast supplies of energy available from the core of molten rock and metal deep within the planet, they found it possible to resume some kind of dignified existence. But it was not the life they knew. Only after the deepest of dark ages, perhaps thousands of years long, could they set about rediscovering their old technological prowess. Once they had achieved a kind of stability within their new, artificially created environment – had enjoyed, perhaps, a Golden Millenium of progress and comfort as underground dwellers – they could no longer ignore the deeper implications of their predicament.

Mondas was on an immense, eccentric orbit that would take it way beyond the last planet in the Solar system. On the calculation of their scientists, the Mondasians knew that the rate of drift from Sol would then gradually decrease until the turning point, the zenith of their orbit, was reached. Then Mondas would inexorably begin its return journey towards the Sun. That much was clear. What was also clear was that before they reached the outermost point of their journey all life on the planet would inevitably have come to an end. As Mondas moved further and further away from life-giving Sol, the whole Mondasian race would gradually weaken and eventually die out.

To understand the manner in which the Mondasians responded to the knowledge of that future, it is necessary to consider for a moment their cultural background.

## The Culture of Logic

Mondas had for long been a technocratic society: a society whose resources were organised and managed by technical experts for the good of all. Uninterrupted ages of scientific prowess had led to the rapid advancement of their world. Whereas its twin experienced a painfully slow rise in the level of global wealth, with one civilisation coming to prominence, vying with another, and collapsing, Mondas made steadier progress. It was able through consistent technological progress to minimise the worst excesses of poverty and deprivation and create a united world community while Earth still floundered, as it were, in the mud of the tribal battlefield.

Mondas, thus far in its history, parallels the development of several of the highly sophisticated planetary civilisations with which any visitor to the Arc Hives will be familiar. At this stage of development, the pursuit of logic as an overriding ideology can easily become established. Logic is the essence of scientific discipline and, as such, can come to be thought of not just as a useful means to an end but the end in itself. This important developmental stage has been neatly termed the Ideo-Logical Phase (ILP).

It would seem that the Ideo-Logical Phase was well underway on Mondas when it was assailed by the Great Cosmological Catastrophe that skewed its future irrevocably. Because of the need to survive in the face of potential long-term extinction they applied Pure Logic and construed their position thus:

FACT 1
Mondas is a planet which will cease to support life.

FACT 2
Survival is a logical priority – the justification of existence.

FACT 3
Mondasians are technologically adept.

FACT 4
The extent to which environment can be adapted (subterranean exploitation) has reached its limit.

CONCLUSION
Technological effort should be directed towards altering body and mind. That is, Mondasians must *adapt themselves in order to survive.*

The logic was impeccable. By technocratic consent all the resources of Mondas would be organised and managed to this end, utilising the vast expertise of the planet's many technicians for the logical good of Mondasian society as a whole. The logical imperative to be placed above all other was Survival of the Race.

So, as their planet drifted away from Sol, as generation upon generation of Mondasians became more frail and sickly, as their lifespan shortened, the science of cybernetics was developed and perfected. As limbs became useless, they were replaced by superbly efficient mechanical ones. As organs gave out, artificial substitutes were inserted which, potentially, could last for ever. As the Race, like the planet itself, became increasingly barren and fewer and fewer children were born, the quest for immortality assumed a major importance. Mondasians who underwent continuous 'cyberneticisation' discovered they had attained a form of immortal life.

But while growing numbers of Mondasians, both female and male, were thus gaining a kind of immortality, they were simultaneously giving up much of their individuality and humanity. Advances in neurological cybernetics led to the 'adjustment' of the brain to enable it to cope with the increasing demand for a ruthlessly logical point of view. The ganglia of instinctual responses, evolved during pre-human development, were hopelessly ravelled up with the more recent but illogical emotions.

Both instinct and emotion were gradually excised from the brain. They were redundant to the pursuit of pure logic. In their place were substituted artificial neuron-modules of cybernetic procedures. These encouraged actions which would ensure the survival of the race: self-fulfillment became inseparable from race-fulfillment. Increasingly sterile, and with fewer and fewer emotions to appreciate the delights of the senses, the Mondasians deemed the sexual instinct to be inappropriate and quite simply removed it. As sexless immortals intent on survival, the feminine aspects in both male and female became less valued, the masculine aspects reinforced and caricatured. Thus were the Cyber*men* born.

It was a slow birth. The full transformation of the Mondasians from 'animal organisms' (as their Cyber descendants were to classify them) into 'mechanised animates' (as Novasa terms the Cybermen) will have taken place over several thousand years. To the original human Mondasians, the first replacements of living matter by mechanical parts must have been a heady and revolutionary step. When we climb a mountain there are many points when we think the summit is near and we can go no further; but as we reach the peak there are yet more peaks ahead, other summits to scale, and our resolve to reach the top 'because it is there' takes us up and onward. So it must have been with the Mondasians. Each tampering with the human form seemed to be at the edge of the possible; yet from the vantage of that edge there always appeared ways of continuing the assault. Progress may have felt slow and uncertain, but with each glance back the heights they had reached astounded and exhilarated them and they pressed forward with new perspective and fresh determination.

## First Divergence of Species

Farozia suggests that Mondas was nearing the edge of the Solar system by the time the potential of cyberneticisation had been discovered, but before a widespread programme had been formally instituted. Understandably, there would have been considerable dissension from the idea of complete conversion for all Mondasians. But equally, she conjectures, there were those on Mondas, the hardliners, who believed that total cyberneticisation must be pursued speedily as an end in itself: to retain any vestige of humanity was no longer of logical value. The Faction, as Farozia terms these hardliners, would certainly have been in the minority, but they were fired by that blazing conviction which so often underlies the seemingly cold ideals for which logic alone is meant to have paved the way.

Naturally, the majority of Mondasians wished only to take such cybernetic measures as would ensure the survival of the race until the inevitable return to Sol. Of central importance was the moment Mondas came close to the old orbit which it had shared with Earth. By that time, Mondasian technology might have advanced to the point where the planet could be stabilised into the original position.

The Faction, however, was not prepared to relinquish their strongly held beliefs. Any notion that Mondasians could retain more than a dim memory of their former humanity during the long ages of exile was illogical and reeked of nostalgic self-delusion. What had to be embraced wholeheartedly was the realisation that neither Mondas nor its inhabitants would ever be the same again. The way of humanity was behind them now. There was no going back.

There was also a more pressing consideration which complicated the problem: the planet's energy reserves were not unlimited. It was doubtful whether they would be sufficient to support the surviving Mondasians for the rest of the journey without great austerity and much hardship. Additional energy would also be required to develop the technology for planetary propulsion, as well as to power the drive. For Mondasians, the next few thousand years would be an unremitting age of wretched waiting, torn between hope and fear.

The Faction saw a way in which Mondas could be powerful again, master of its own fate and exultant in its technological prowess: cyberneticisation must be pursued to its logical end – by which time an indestructible, immortal, fearless race would have taken the place of the faltering Mondasians. Such a race would need no special kind of environment to support it. They had lost the ability to produce offspring but this new race would propagate through the conquering and conversion of other planets. Unlike the majority, for whom it was a means to an end, survival would be an end in itself, the reason for existence. The Mondasian Cause was to Wait and Hope; the Cause of the new Race was to Survive and Conquer.

The Faction wanted to take a bold and fateful

step. Mondas was to pass close to a far planet in the Solar system, the fourteenth away from Sol. Planet 14 was cold, dark and desolate, but it represented for the Faction a place where cyberneticisation could be pursued without reservation. Resurrecting the ancient technology of Earth-hopping which had lain forgotten and unused since before the Great Catastrophe, a small group of Faction adherents, perhaps a few thousand in all, left Mondas forever in a daring leap between worlds.

They set up a new type of life. Their sacrifice, their vision, would forge a new race that would lead Mondas to found a mighty empire when at last the planet returned from the edge of space.

### The Transformation of Mondas

Mondas drifted on through the cometary cloud. Millenia passed.

Despite the departure of the hardliners, a gentle process of cyberneticisation continued. Advances were made as physiological and psychological weaknesses gradually manifested themselves. The human form was slow to disappear, yet inexorably a new race of beings was establishing itself on Mondas.

What the Faction had not flinched from predicting came to be a palpable fact. Old Mondas, Planet 4 in the Ancient Cosmology, once the rich and civilised apotheosis of technocratic humanity, had undergone a space change and was utterly transformed. It was now populated by Cybermen of the subspecies *cyberMondasian*. Mondas had become a cold, ultilitarian culture whose brilliance was solely directed towards Survival and Return.

Also transformed for them was the meaning of Return. It would not be – could never be, they gradually realised – a coming back to the old ways of the pure animal organisms they once were. Return would instead be a going forward to a new phase in their development as mechanical animates, an opportunity to reside near the centre of a rich planetary system whose resources they could usefully exploit.

Planet 5, their former twin, the richest, most temperate planet of the Solar system, would provide the greatest scope for exploitation. There was certainly copious mineral wealth to be plundered. But there was plunder more valuable still. Earth teemed with a human populace. Many would be suitable for conversion into Cybermen. The Cyber race would burgeon. It was an eminently logical process.

To aid and control the Return, their technology had been channelled towards one goal – planetary propulsion. That goal had now been reached. The Drive could only be used sparingly for fear of draining resources that were fast running out; but it would enable Mondas to take a more direct route towards Earth than the haphazard path they had helplessly followed on the outward journey: a route that could always keep Sol between them and Earth to avoid being detected until the last possible moment.

The long awaited Return was underway.

### Developments on Planet 14

There was no atmosphere on Planet 14 – it was too small to hold one. There was mineral wealth of a kind – including the metals and other raw materials necessary to the expanding cybertechnological base the Faction saw as central to their plans. But by far the most important feature of the planet was that it was geologically active. It had a molten core which the Faction could tap for their energy supplies.

The several thousand years of development which followed must have seen technological achievements to rival those of the world they left behind. Both became Cybermen with common roots and a common desire – to plunder the riches of Earth – but each was distinct from the other.

The Faction worked from the same principles of cyberneticisation. But because they had a different end in view, they diverged from the Mondasians in appearance and function. Their instincts were more radical: cyberneticisation was to them an end in itself. Humanity was an obsolescence which was to be left behind them. It did not matter to them how mechanical their appearance became. As for human tissue – the less they needed, the better. To Survive and Conquer was a war-like ethos, demanding a militaristic hierarchy: *cyberFaction* became a race whose function identified them – Controllers, Leaders, Lieutenants, Technicians, Scouts and Troops.

Once they were fully consolidated on Planet 14, several millenia after their departure from Mondas, the next logical step was to extend their influence beyond the planet. The obvious first target for conquest and colonisation was the next planet in from theirs.

Every five hundred years Planet 13 approached its closest point to Planet 14 – a distance of some seven billion miles. It afforded minimal mineral resources but was a stepping stone towards the greater riches of the other planets. It challenged *cyberFaction* to make fresh progress in a long neglected field of endeavour – space travel.

Just as these developments were reaching their peak, an observation of great significance was made by their astronomers: Mondas was on its return journey. Furthermore, it seemed that there was at least one area where *cyberMondasian*

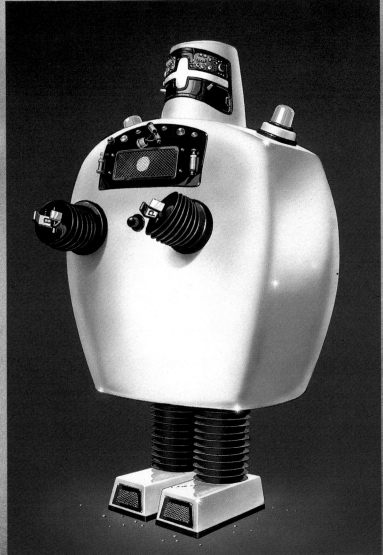

*The Wheel in Space: Document 4*
ABOVE: The Cybership
INSERT: The servo-robot

*Tomb of the Cybermen:
Document 6*
Kleig and Professor Parry stand
by the doors to the entrance
chamber of the Cybertombs. On
the far left stands the main control
panel (see over page) and to its
right is the archway leading to the
weapons testing area. On the far
right is the open hatch leading to
the tombs deep below. In the
foreground can be seen part of a
circular table embossed with four
cyber head emblems. Around the
table, not visible here, are set a
number of stools. The function of
this feature is unknown. This
viewpoint is one achieved from
near the further archway leading
to the revitalisation chamber (see
over page).

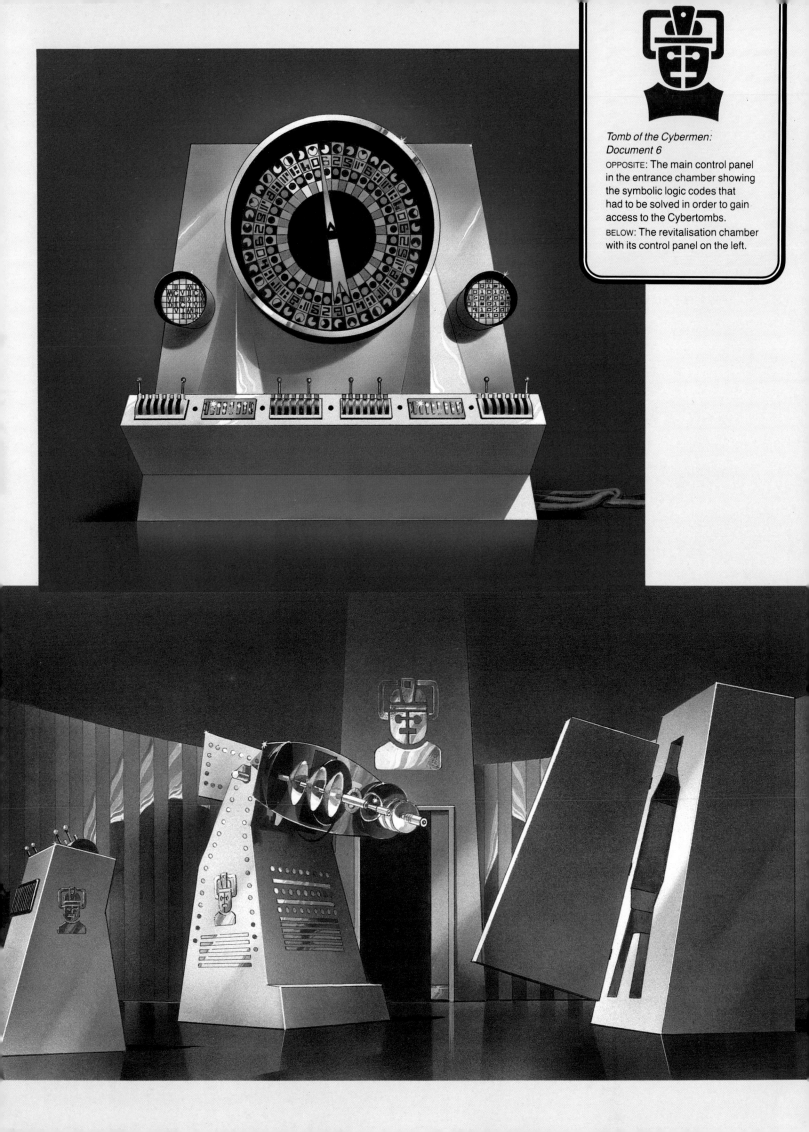

*Tomb of the Cybermen:
Document 6*

OPPOSITE: The main control panel
in the entrance chamber showing
the symbolic logic codes that
had to be solved in order to gain
access to the Cybertombs.

BELOW: The revitalisation chamber
with its control panel on the left.

technology had diverged from theirs. Mondas was no longer held within the bounds of its extended orbit, at the mercy of the gravitational influences of every planetary body it passed. The planet now appeared to possess self-propulsion devices enabling it to make its return earlier than expected. With such technology, Mondas would certainly be able to stabilise into its original orbit as, millenia before, had been the Mondasians' great hope.

Such a possibility was of fundamental importance to *cyberFaction*. Invasion of Earth for its mineral resources and billions of 'convertible' humans had always figured as the pinnacle of Cyber Conquest. They assumed, logically, that their ancient cousins on Mondas would have evolved similarly enough to seek the same spoils and resolved that if Cybermen from Planet 14 and from Mondas should join forces, the Cyber race would truly prove invincible.

Calculating that it would be some decades yet before Mondas reached its destination, *cyberFaction* reckoned that there was time enough to build up a huge invasion force to make the unprecedented voyage to Earth. It was just over twice the distance of the journey to the neighbouring planet for which they had been preparing. It would take almost a decade with their primitive space technology.

They would travel in one massive deep space ship that would transport within it hundreds of small invasion craft and itself act as the Cyber Control centre. The venture would drain the resources of their planet – the journey would be strictly one-way – but it was a risk which had to be undertaken, a logical necessity. The prize was too great to ignore. Once in possession of Planet 5, *cyberFaction* would await the arrival of their ancient world in order to join forces with it and establish the Cyber race triumphant throughout the Solar system.

### Meanwhile on Earth...

The slow climb towards global awareness on Earth continued. There was much backsliding, much forgetfulness of the valuable knowledge assimilated by previous ages. But eventually, almost two millenia after the coming of a charismatic and influential teacher whose birth was used as the basis of a new calendar, nearly 20 centuries after the Year of this Lord – or Anno Domini (AD) – the people of Earth were beginning to see themselves as belonging to a community. Phrases such as 'Global Village' and 'One World' began to be used to describe this potential unity. It was still, however, a potential that had yet to be realised.

Since audio-visual communications over the entire world had become rapid and efficient, it was no longer possible to ignore the disastrous implications of intercontinental wars, two of which had already raged during the 20th century. Stability was sought and won – but at a price. Methods were developed of bringing about total destruction to entire cities, to whole civilisations, to the world itself. No one dared use these fearful weapons of mass-annihilation yet all lived under the shadow of their threat.

Earth became deeply divided into four broad blocs: politically the East and the West were ranged against each other in what was called a 'cold war'; and in terms of wealth and resources the poor South was set against the rich North. Meanwhile, political power moved out of the hands of acknowledged leaders of the various nations and began to reside with the large international companies upon whose products the world increasingly depended.

During the 1970's AD, the Managing Director of just such a multinational firm found himself in an extremely powerful position. His name was Tobias Vaughn.

TOBIAS VAUGHN

# Middle History

As Mondas transported the Mondasians, so our History has taken us on a journey and brought us back. We have voyaged to the deepest edge of knowledge and imaginings – to the origins of the Cyber race – and, propelling ourselves with hypothesis and conjecture, have returned to our starting point the better equipped for our task. We have a clearer insight into Cyber mentality, an insight which will illumine the continuing history of the Cyber race.

Mondas and the Mondasian Cybermen were undoubtedly eradicated. But Cybermen lived on. For Mondasian Cybermen, their planet was their lifeline: the destruction of Mondas meant destruction of the *cyberMondasian* subspecies. *Cyber-Faction* were more resilient; each individual Cyberman was dependant only on its own self-contained resources, and each continued selflessly to forward the Cyber Cause – to Survive and Conquer.

When we next meet the Cybermen, their appearance is close to those of the *cyberFaction* who first invaded Earth. It will be recalled that the second wave of the invasion fleet in Document1 was never launched against Earth – and never destroyed by Zoe's well-aimed missiles. It is Farozia's contention (one I support) that many of the spacecraft of the second wave were able to evacuate the Cyber Controlship before it was destroyed by the nuclear warhead.

**Position of Wheel**
Zoe tells Jamie the position of the Wheel relative to Venus: '24,564,000 miles at perihelion and 161,350,000 at aphelion'. These figures are so close to those for Earth relative to Venus that it makes sense to imagine the Wheel in a deep orbit round Earth – perhaps half-way to the Moon. Such a position would also make sense of one of the Wheel's functions: advance weather reporting (hardly feasible if the space station were situated outside the Solar system!).

**Phases of Cyberplan**
PHASE 1: Cybermats launched as spheres attach to Wheel and penetrate its shell, causing air pressure fluctuations.

PHASE 2: Cybermen emerge from 'expanding spheres' on Silver Carrier.

PHASE 3: Hercules 208 'ionised' to deflect meteors towards Wheel.

PHASE 4: 'Teleomatic' control over Cybermats removed after bernalium is consumed, allowing them to pursue their cybermatic instincts – to search and destroy animal organisms – resulting in death of crew member.

PHASE 5: Bernalium crate brought from Silver Carrier as fuel for X-Ray laser to destroy meteors – Cybermen in crate gain access to Wheel.

PHASE 6: Cybermen take control of crew and use radio beam to guide invasion craft to Earth.

We must assume that the Cybermen who escaped did not get far: their craft was designed only for the shallows of space between Earth and Moon – based perhaps on the ancient Earth/Mondas hopping technology. Where, then, did this group seek immediate refuge? The obvious answer might be the far side of the Moon.

At the beginning of Document1, when the Cybermissile is launched against the TARDIS, the Doctor exclaims, 'That light on the Moon's surface, do you see it?' This could well be an optical illusion: an unlit Cyber Controlship would have been invisible against the Moon's dark disc. Alternatively, it may indicate that the Cybermen had set up temporary base on the Moon, a base for which the evacuee invasion craft headed. There, they might have recouped and prepared for the Return of Mondas, intending within the decade, perhaps, to join with their ancient cousins in final take-over of Earth.

**Second Divergence of Species**
The destruction of Mondas was a setback for *cyberFaction*. But since they were logical creatures, no contingency had been overlooked. For as long as there existed a community of Cybermen, no matter how small, the Cyber Cause would be continued. It is at this point, I suggest, that a second divergence within the Race was thought necessary.

The first divergence had resulted in the related but dissimilar *cyberMondasian* and *cyberFaction* subspecies. *CyberMondasian* now no longer existed and *cyberFaction* was faced with extinction. Two equally hazardous courses might lead to their continuing survival:

a) to pursue the conquest of Earth
b) to leave the Solar system and Survive through Conquest elsewhere.

The logical solution was for one group of the survivors to follow course 'a', another, course 'b'. In this way, there was the greatest chance of successful proliferation and ultimate Survival.

I would postulate that both groups, as soon as they enabled their craft to cover greater distances, initially moved away from the Moon and established themselves more productively in space, utilising the resources of other moons and asteroids within the Solar system. After several decades of intense development, a hyper-driven ship was ready. Group 'b' left the Solar system to explore and exploit other planetary systems, establishing over the next centuries their reputation as ruthless and indomitable conquerors throughout the galaxy.

Such a missing link – we might call them the

subspecies *cyberNomad* – would explain much that is mystifying in the later Documents. In Document2 we have seen (and will see in Documents 7, 8, 9 and 0) Cybermen from the future who bear generic similarities with *cyberFaction*. We do not find such similarities in the Cybermen who remained in the Solar system over the next century as they started to alter in appearance and explored extraordinary technologies in order to pursue their specific mission – to conquer Earth.

On Earth itself, the Mondasian attack had left the world shaken but perhaps more united. Though they had come close to global destruction and mass-conversion into Cybermen, it was naturally assumed that the Cyber race had now, with Mondas, ceased to exist. Many had witnessed the collapse, the shrivelling, of individual Cybermen as Mondas shattered and dispersed. Could there be more overwhelming evidence that the Cyber threat was gone for good? Most were blissfully unaware that Mondas had spawned another Cyber culture, that there had been a former invasion of Cybermen markedly different to those from Mondas and that these Cybermen were even now regrouping, consolidating and building up their resources to pursue their Cause of Survival and Conquest. The conviction that Cybermen had ceased to exist ran so deep that for some even the name faded in the memory.

By the early 21st century an active space programme was underway – though it had its detractors. Opposition, sometimes violent, came from 'pull back to Earth fanatics' and others who wanted to stop the space programme and keep 'Earth for Earth'. Nevertheless, exploration pushed outwards. Space stations were built to service and monitor the increasing space traffic. The Moon was visited and bases set up on it. Earth humans voyaged at least as far as the asteroid belt.

**Space Station W3 (Document4)**
Doctor Gemma Corwyn had lost her husband in the asteroid belt. She was second in command of a wheel-shaped space station known as W3 which was probably in orbit between Earth and Moon. It looked as though she might have to assume command of the Wheel since its Controller, Jarvis Bennett, was showing signs of being unable to cope with recent and bizarre developments.

A Phoenix IV spaceship called Silver Carrier had been discovered almost 90 million miles off-course. It was a supply ship for Service Station W5, and was apparently crewless. Jarvis wanted to use his new X-ray lasergun to 'blow it out of existence' in case it might prove a danger to them. Such zeal seemed to Gemma Corwyn excessive and she managed to dissuade him from immediately carrying out his intention. She was thus responsible for saving the lives of Doctor2 and Jamie.

They had materialised on the Silver Carrier and needed to find supplies of mercury before the TARDIS would work again. To avoid mercury poisoning, the Doctor had disengaged the Time Vector Generator, thus reducing the inside of the TARDIS to less than its outside dimensions. They had discovered no sign of life on the Silver Carrier – other than a bulky servo-robot which seemed to be controlling operations – and no mercury. A Wheel search party found them and brought them back for investigation: Jarvis suspected them of being 'pull back to Earth' saboteurs – especially after Jamie, wanting to save the TARDIS from being destroyed along with the Silver Carrier, had damaged the lasergun.

It was on this Wheel in space that the Doctor and Jamie first met Zoe. She enjoyed their company so much that, when they eventually resumed their travels in the TARDIS, she accompanied them as a stowaway. But at that first moment of seeing Jamie, she could not help being amused at his 'female garments'. Affronted, Jamie explained that as a true Great Scot he wore a kilt. Recalling the term from her considerable knowledge as the Wheel's librarian, Zoe managèd at last to suppress her amusement. As a former student of Earth's School of Parapsychology, many years of her young life had been devoted to the pursuit of pure logic and intellectual studies. With Jamie and the Doctor, she was to learn that emotions were important too – while her contact with the Cybermen was to teach her the drawbacks of single-minded devotion to logic.

When she took Jamie on a guided tour of the Wheel, thoughts of Cybermen could not have been further from her mind. In fact, like Gemma Corwyn and Jarvis Bennett himself, she had little knowledge of the Mondasian Invasion. As she said, 'Pre-century history isn't my field, you see.'

Because the Wheel carried out so many important functions, it was understandable that Jarvis should be sensitive to the phenomena that now threatened its operation. The position of the Silver Carrier was still unaccounted for; two suspected saboteurs had been uncovered; there were temporary faults in the station's system and drops in air pressure. Moreover, Zoe predicted that a star – Hercules 208 in Messia 13 – was going nova; the radiation flux would deflect meteors directly towards the Wheel. Without the X-ray laser, their only protection was the Convolute Force Field, a neutron barrier that would prove ineffective for meteors of above 200 tonnes.

The lasergun was repaired at last but a strange form of space bug was found to have consumed the Wheel's entire stock of bernalium – essential for powering the laser. Jarvis was relieved when a large crate of the mineral was discovered aboard the Silver Carrier and gave permission for it to be brought to the Wheel. But his troubles were far from over.

The dead body of a crew member was found next to a mound of solidified hyperoxide plastic. X-rays of the indestructible material revealed a space bug at its centre. The Doctor immediately recognised it as a Cybermat, a kind of cybernetic rodent which he had confronted before in the Tombs on Telos (Document6). He knew now that Cybermen were to blame for the series of unaccountable incidents. He knew also that there was some kind of invasion plan behind the apparent coincidences. It wasn't just the Wheel they were after. 'The Cybermen need to colonise,' he said. 'They must have the treasures of the Earth.'

Psychotropic drugs protected all space workers against brain control. But they did not provide a complete barrier. An adverse influence could still be identified, however, by implanted Celenski capsules and these indicated that some crew members were under Cyberhypnotic control. The Cybermen must already have found a way onto the Wheel. The Doctor hurriedly demonstrated a crude but effective method of blocking Cyberhypnosis: a metal plate and transistor taped to the back of the neck – a method he was to deploy, as we have seen, in the First Invasion.

When the Doctor learnt that bernalium had been brought into the space station from the Silver Carrier, he immediately guessed how the Cybermen might have got on board. He and Jamie went to the Hold to inspect the bernalium crate. Suddenly, they were aware that they were not alone and hid behind the crate. The tall figure of a Cyberman walked past them and out of the Hold. But they were not quite out of danger for, as the Doctor was alerting the rest of the Wheel via his radio link, two Cybermats appeared. Ordering a variable audio frequency to be put out on the communications channel, the Doctor caused the destruction of all the Cybermats on the space station.

Undetected by the Wheel, but in its vicinity, there was a large Cybership, long and narrow, encrusted with antennae at its bulbous central section. Within were many smaller craft which could only enter Earth's atmosphere by homing in on a radio beam; there was also a device, very like Vaughn's Co-ordinator, which controlled operations. The Cybermen's intended invasion of Earth was plainly similar in plan to the First Invasion.

Using extraordinary technology which the Cybermen might have developed over their period of consolidation, two spheres on board the Silver Carrier were activated and began to grow.

**Functions of Wheel**
a) radio-visual relay station for Earth
b) half-way house for deep space ships
c) space research station (e.g. interstellar flora)
d) stellar-phenomena early warning station
e) advance weather reporting for Earth.

JARVIS BENNETT EMMA CORWY

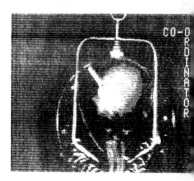
CO-ORDINATOR

**Cyberman: Document4 – later cyberFaction**
There is a direct correspondence between the Cybermen of Document1 and Document4. The differences are these: the striated blocks on each side of the head are gone; in addition to larger 'tear drop' holes at the eyes, there is also one at the mouthslit; exoskeletal supports to the limbs have become less delicate – a series of rods powered by blocks at the limb-joints; fibrillary piping extends from top and bottom of the chest units. The units themselves appear identical. In all other respects, too, the Cybermen are identical – except for one significant detail: the hands are no longer clearly ▶

five-fingered.

On first view, they might be said to be three-fingered. Closer scrutiny reveals something stranger: three fingers are being formed out of what was originally a five-fingered hand. Each of two pairs of fingers are forced together into single channels and topped with a metal cap. The thumb, similarly capped, makes up the third 'finger'. The exoskeletal powering rods no longer stop at the wrist, as with the early *cyberFaction*, but now extend to the three 'fingers'.

One explanation might be this. The *cyberMondasian* retains use of the human hand – nerves, tendons, muscles stimulated directly perhaps by a cybernetically assisted arm. Becoming independent of Mondas, *cyberFaction* evolves further from the human form and has encased the hand in armoured material which now covers the entire body. These organic remnants might now be losing their capacity to be stimulated and are being 'evolved' into the more easily synthesised, because less intricate, three-fingered variety. It seems that full five-finger synthesis is achieved by the more sophisticated *cyberNomad*.

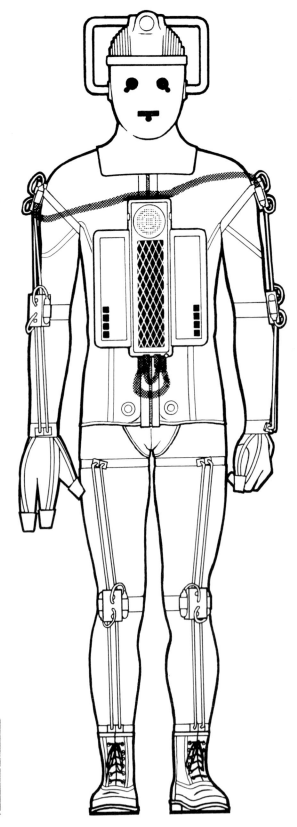

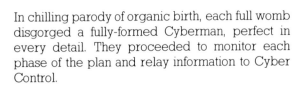
In chilling parody of organic birth, each full womb disgorged a fully-formed Cyberman, perfect in every detail. They proceeded to monitor each phase of the plan and relay information to Cyber Control.

When the monitoring Cyberman reported that all Cybermats had been destroyed by 'high current phase contrast', the Co-ordinator deduced that 'one human has knowledge beyond our predictions'. By the time they discovered it was the Doctor, he had set up a neutron forcefield round the operation room. 'The Doctor is known and recorded as an enemy', the Co-ordinator announced. 'He must be lured outside the force-field and destroyed'.

In the Power Room the Doctor was confronted by two Cybermen come to destroy him because he 'knew their ways'. He was able to electrocute one of the Cybermen but the other, having impassively observed the fate of his companion, went to open the Wheel's air-lock: the Cyber Controlship had moved close and Cybermen were space-walking across to the station.

Hurriedly fitting his Time Vector Generator to the X-ray gun to boost its power, the Doctor obliterated the Cybership, then used the force field to fling the space-walking Cybermen into the depths of space. The Cybermen were thus defeated, not only in their attack on Space Station W3, but also in their greater purpose, what the Doctor described as 'an overriding ambition to invade the Earth – plunder its mineral wealth.'

### The Moonbase (Document5)

The Doctor was again to prove a resourceful opponent in the Cybermen's next attempt to pursue their 'overriding ambition'. The scene of this encounter is set some four decades on – in 2070 AD. For 20 years or more, a dome on the Moon had housed the Gravitron, a device able to direct gravitational forces at specific areas of Earth in order to control its tides and through them to controll the weather.

In contrast to the Cybermen's attempt on Earth via the Wheel, their present approach was simple: 'We are going to take over the Gravitron and use it to destroy the surface of the Earth by changing the weather'. It would seem that after the failure of their second attempt to launch an invasion fleet at an inhabited Earth, they had decided to annihilate the opposition before setting boot on the place. Besides, we learn from Document6 that their previous defeats had left them in an impoverished state: 'Our machinery had stopped and our supply of replacements been depleted'. So, the Cybermen intended to wreak, in a matter of hours, such destruction on Earth as Mondas had endured over centuries as it moved away from the Sun.

Widespread disaster could result merely from switching the Gravitron off. Hobson, the man in charge of operations at the Moonbase, described it in these terms: 'the collapse of the gravity would

Interior of Cyber craft

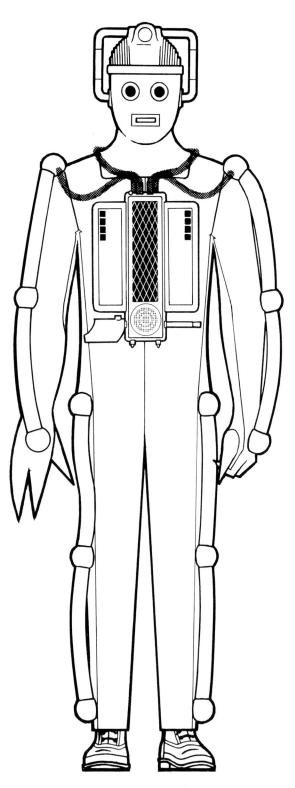

Cyberman: Document 5 –
late *cyberFaction*
These Cybermen have
evolved into a fully three-
fingered variety with a
mouthslit that opens for a
monotonous simulated
voice to emanate – a
mechanical parody of the
more human *cyberMonda-
sian* mode of speaking
(whose influence still remains in the mysterious
'moving part' behind *cyber-
Neomorph* jaw panels).
Chest units have been in-
verted and a slim weapon
neatly slotted underneath.

devastate half the globe. There'd be storms,
whirlwinds, hurricanes.' Earth was clearly vulnerable to malfunction in the Gravitron and Hobson
was understandably worried when a mystery
illness began to strike down members of his team
– some of whom subsequently vanished.

The Doctor had wandered into this situation
with companions Polly and Ben and also Jamie,
who had not long been travelling with them.
Hobson at first regarded them all with suspicion
and wanted them off the Moon. The Doctor was
himself immediately suspicious of the strange
circumstances and determined to seek the explanation. 'There are some corners of the universe
which have bred the most terrible things,' he
explained. 'Things which act against everything
we believe in. They must be fought.'

So saying, he engaged his disciplines as a
trained medical doctor ('Glasgow 1888 – Lister')
and eventually discovered that the base's supplies of sugar had been contaminated with a
neurotropic virus – an infective agent that attacked the nerves. Polly had earlier thought she might
have glimpsed in the sick bay something that
reminded her of the Cybermen. (She, Ben and the
Doctor, in their peculiar time stream, had encountered them only months before, when Mondas
had been destroyed.) The Doctor was now
convinced that Cybermen were involved – that
they had deliberately infected the base.

Hobson had been highly sceptical at Polly's first
mention of Cybermen. 'Stop this Cybermen nonsense!' he had said. 'There were Cybermen once,
every child knows that, but they were all destroyed long ago.' But Polly and the Doctor were
proved correct when Cybermen turned up in the
base itself.

The Doctor was immediately recognised by

one of them. In describing how they had gained
access to the base, its manner might have seemed
gloating, if such an attitude were not known to be
redundant in the Cybermen: 'It was very simple.
Only stupid Earth brains like yours would have
been fooled. Since we could not approach direct,
we came up under the surface and cut our way

Dating: *Moonbase* and
*Wheel*
*The Moonbase* is set in
2070 AD. We do not know
when *The Wheel In Space*
is set but Farozia places it
some 40 years before, and
Novasa some 40 years af-
ter, *The Moonbase*. It is
known from *The Mind Rob-
ber* that Zoe had read 'Kar-
kus', a comic strip of the
year 2000 AD, but in *The
War Games* she says she
was born in the 21st Cen-
tury – in which case she
would have been too young
to appreciate it at the time
of the original issue. Novasa points out, however, that
as a librarian she could
have known of it many
years later. If we assume
her to be at least 15 years
old in *Wheel*, then the
Document can be set at
any time between 2015 and
2115.

Novasa feels 'the whole
technology of the Wheel
looks more advanced than
the Moonbase', that 'it
seems far out in space,  ▶

closer to the star which goes nova'. He suggests that Zoe was born towards the end of the century and sets the Document around 2110. But he has overlooked the precise location relative to Venus given for the Wheel by Zoe herself (see entry – Position of Wheel). Moreover, the Wheel's function of advance weather reporting for Earth would suggest that the Gravitron system had not yet been deployed (2050 onwards). On balance, then, I favour Farozia's dating of Document4 at around 2028 AD, a full 50 years after the First Invasion.

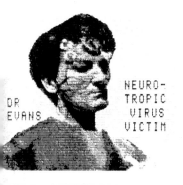

DR EVANS

NEURO-
TROPIC
VIRUS
VICTIM

### Cyber Weapon Development

It is interesting to note that the lasergun and the bazooka systems had both been very effectively used against the Cybermen (in Documents 1 and 4, respectively). Perhaps the Cybermen had taken up these ideas and developed them within their own technology.

### Cyber Inactivity Within the Solar System

The assumption that the Cybermen disappeared from the Solar system for four centuries is based on the evidence of Document6. There, a small expedition has been mounted. Its leader, Professor Parry, hints at the eccentric nature of the venture when he claims grandly, 'We are searching the

into your storeroom, contaminating your food supplies on the way.'

The Cybermen had brought with them the infected men who had disappeared from the base. They had been 'altered' (in the Cybermen's ominous phraseology) and were now under Cyber control. They were sent into the Gravitron Room to begin the destruction of Earth, not to seek revenge as Hobson suggested they were doing – having no feelings, the very concept of revenge was alien to them – but in order to eliminate all dangers to their conquest of Earth.

As with the Mondasian invasion, it was the ingenuity of Polly and Ben rather than the Doctor (who was under Cyber scrutiny) which in the first instance overcame the Cybermen. Mixing a 'Polly Cocktail' of various solvents, they managed to spray it into the chest units of all the Cybermen in the base. The Cybermen immediately collapsed and expired as the plastic of their synthetic heart/lung units dissolved. Hobson could once more take up command of the Gravitron.

The small ship in which the Cybermen had arrived was detected about three kilometres from the base. Another spacecraft was also detected, a relief ship from Earth. Although it had the weapons to 'blast the Cybermen and their spaceship to kingdom come', it was not to do so. The Cybermen, who had not fully relinquished mind control over some of the 'altered' men in the base, directed one of them, a Dr Evans, to operate the Gravitron and deflect the relief ship.

Under siege in the Moonbase, the humans still refused to give in to the Cybermen, even when two more Cybercraft landed and a bazooka-type weapon was deployed. A hole already punctured in the dome by a Cyberlaser had been stopped up with a plastic tray; the Cyberbazooka also proved ineffective since it was deflected by the force field of the Gravitron. But this gave the Doctor the idea of aiming the Gravitron at the Cybermen and their craft.

As the Cybermen approached the base for a final onslaught, they and their three ships were lifted from the Moon's surface and carried out into space. They may even have followed the fateful path to which they had condemned the relief ship for, as the Doctor and his companions returned to the TARDIS, Polly pointed out a comet-like object which glowed in the sky as it hurtled towards the Sun.

'Doctor, look! Could that be them?', she said. 'Possibly,' he replied, 'and I hope it's the last we see of them.'

For the next 400 years the people of Earth saw and heard nothing of Cybermen. The Doctor's hope seemed well founded. But they had not died out, they had merely ceased to be active within the Solar system. Why this should be is open to speculation. So let us speculate.

Thus it might have been that, in a last bid for survival, this Cyber remnant joined the Nomadic trail. The next Document in our chronology reveals what befell them. But let us for a moment dwell on the achievements of those they set out to emulate, the subspecies *cyberNomad*.

### The Vogan War

We speculated earlier that the *cyberNomad* had sought pastures new in the deeper reaches of the Galaxy. Document7 suggests that they had grown mightier and had developed a similarly mighty ambition. No longer concerned merely with vanquishing Earth, they now believed that their destiny was to become the rulers of all the cosmos'.

During the period when Earth people were enjoying respite from Cyber attentions, humans in a different part of the Galaxy were desperately fighting a Cyber war. We know nothing of the date or the location of the planetary system, or systems, where the war raged, except that it involved a planet called Voga.

The Nomads had 'evolved' somewhat since they had left the Solar system. Doctor4 describes these Cybermen as 'utterly ruthless, total machine creatures'. The Cybermen themselves claimed to be able to create a whole new army of Cyber-troops from parts which they carried with them in their ships – though this may only have been possible provided they had at their disposal suitable organic material in the shape of humanoids. Nevertheless, they made careful distinction between themselves as Cybermen and what they termed 'animal organisms'. The animal organism was less efficient. Humans were animal organisms. The logical corollary was that humans must eventually succumb to Cyber aggression. It was in this way, they believed, that Cybermen were destined to control the Galaxy.

The Cybermen fought a hard war against the humans and their other adversaries. A Cyber victory seemed inevitable. Then, from the jaws of defeat, human ingenuity snatched an unexpected reprieve. Gold – that most unreactive of metals, highly valued by humans throughout the Galaxy and long imbued with mystical powers – gold was found to be the catalyst, turning base defeat into almost unalloyed victory. It might even be said to have had a mystical power over the Cybermen for, somehow, an unexpected discovery was made: in certain forms – that of gold dust, for example – the metal devastated the Cyber mechanism. The Doctor explains its effect on Cybermen thus: 'it plates their breathing system and in effect suffocates them.' Even the Cyberleader admits that gold is 'hostile to their function'.

Voga was a planet whose heart was almost pure gold. In fact, there was more gold on Voga than in the rest of the known Galaxy. When gold was found to be inimical to Cyber function, it was the timely collaboration between humans and the humanoid Vogans that led to the almost complete destruction of the Cyber forces. The Vogans provided the gold and the humans devised the technology with which it could be turned into an effective weapon. The most celebrated of these devices was dubbed the Glittergun and (perhaps in similar fashion to the Blunderbuss of early Earth weaponry) it sprayed out deadly particles – gold dust.

But before the Cybermen were entirely vanquished, they turned their dwindling might against Voga itself. In an attempt to utterly destroy the source of their defeat by means of a massive explosion, however, the Cybermen only succeeded in vaporising part of the planet; the remaining fragment was flung out of the planetary system at such speed that it entered a space-warp. The last remaining Cybership in the once mighty *cyberNomad* fleet gave chase.

### The Colonisation of Telos

Meanwhile, another search was in progress. In their hyper-driven Controlship, the remaining Cybermen of the Solar system had finally departed and were now seeking a suitable planetary system where they could survive, grow mightier and extend the limits of conquest. But their power was running out. The search could not be continued indefinitely. At this phase of their development, Survival was more important than Conquest. It was for this reason that they became attracted to the planet Telos. The refrigerated cities built by the inhabitants of Telos – the Cryons – were ideal for the preservation of the Cybermen.

Document9 reveals the Cryons as doughty opponents of the Cybermen. This gives us some clue as to the initial difficulties the Cyber invaders might have had in establishing themselves on their newly adopted planet. What is certain, however, is that the Cryons were eventually subjugated, their cryogenic technology exploited and their race all but wiped out. The Cybermen, having conquered, now made preparation for their long-term survival.

Their physical appearance was unchanged since their involvement at the Moonbase, but this form was in itself a considerable 'evolution' from the *cyberFaction* of the First Invasion. From the moment of adopting Telos as their own planet, they can be formally recognised as a new subspecies – *cyberTelosian*. As such, these Cybermen entered a frozen limbo of suspended animation within the underground chambers. The cryogenic cities had become Cyber sarcophagi – tombs whose inhabitants rested in a living death.

Let the last word on this Middle period be left to Novasa:

The tombs were not merely a resting place for the Cybermen – they were also a trap of a very specific kind for they reasoned that one day there would be visitors to the planet. If the creatures were clever enough, they would pass certain tests inherent in penetrating the tombs and the frozen Cybermen would be re-activated. The visitors would thus have 'selected' themselves as suitable for conversion and, as Cybermen, would return to their own planet to create a new Cyber race. In this way, the Cybermen of Telos could ensure their survival. But for hundreds of years they lay in frozen sleep...

## Later History

The period we now enter – extending perhaps from the late 25th century to well into the next – is one in which Earth people gradually come to a chilling realisation: the destruction of Mondas did not signal the end of the Cyber race. On the contrary, over the previous five hundred years, Cybermen had survived and made conquests, proliferated and grown stronger.

During this Late period, the Cybermen returned to the Solar system three times. One return we have already started to explore in our discussion of Document2; it was a return to their past, before Mondas had been destroyed, and we shall be able to take up the story from where we left off. Another return was in pursuance of a mission which, by a strange quirk of fate, brought a Cyber unit to the very star system where their ancestors had originated. The third return was on a large scale with a full invasion fleet and many thousands of Cybertroops; their target was Earth and they represented probably the greatest force of Cybermen ever to be mobilised within the Solar system.

We shall also be looking at the unprecedented involvement of Cybermen in the Death Zone of Gallifrey. Though this period of Gallifreyan history is probably not concurrent with the middle of Earth's Third Millenium, it is almost certain that the Cyber units were scooped out of their time-stream during this period.

But for the moment we shall remain on Telos. The long sleep of the Cybermen in their frozen tombs is nearing its end.

### Awakening of the CyberTelosians (Document6)

The expedition party that landed on Telos at the end of the 25th century was surprisingly small-

Universe for the remains of the Cybermen.'

The 'archeological expedition' was not an official one funded by Earth authorities in a serious bid to discover what happened to its old alien enemy. It was a small-scale venture by chartered rocket and paid for by Eric Klieg, a fanatical member of the Brotherhood of Logicians whose interest in the Cybermen, like Tobias Vaughn's, was far from academic. Whatever the Professor and his colleagues may have believed at this time – and it does seem that Cybermen were commonly thought to have died out 500 years before – it is evident from other Documents (Document7 in particular) that the Cybermen were still active in certain parts of the galaxy.

### Dating: Document6

The half millenium gap (Professor: 'They've been dead for the last five hundred years') can be dated from the destruction of Mondas, on the assumption (Novasa's) that the incidents on Space Station W3 and the Moon may have been deliberately 'hushed up' – as with the First Invasion – or simply not fully publicised. Also, 'five hundred years' should not be taken too literally – it probably represents a generous rounding up or down. We can thus place Document6 in the late 25th century. Farozia, with her penchant for specific guesses, picks on the year 2486 AD – the quincentenary of the destruction of Mondas.

## Cyberman: Document 6 – late *cyberFaction*

Little visible change has taken place in the appearance of these Cybermen since Document 5. But there has been one development of major importance – the creation of a central authority figure known as the Controller (see Cybercontroller: Document 6).

PROFESSOR PARRY

VINER

KLIEG

KAFTAN

## Companion: Victoria Waterfield

Her father had been killed by Daleks (see *The Evil of the Daleks*) and so, parentless, she had joined Jamie and the Doctor in their time-travels. The Doctor knew it was the best way to heal her sadness: 'Our lives are different to everybody else's – that's the exciting thing. Nobody in the Universe can do what we're doing.'

scale. No more than a dozen strong, it had set off from Earth in a chartered spacecraft. It was piloted by Captain Hopper, Jim Callum and Ted Rogers; it was led by archeologists Professor Parry, John Viner and Peter Hayden; it was financed by Logician Eric Klieg. The only woman of the party, Kaftan, was also a Logician; she had with her a 'bodyguard' of massive strength and huge proportions called Toberman.

Somehow, the expedition knew that Telos had become the home of the Cybermen. They also knew where to find the entrance to one of the ancient refrigerated cities which had been converted into Cybertombs. No mention was made, however, of the city architects – the Cryons – and there was to be no sign of them for the duration of the archeological visit.

The TARDIS materialised on Telos just as the Great Doors of the city had been located. Doctor 2 was accompanied by Jamie and a young girl companion, Victoria Waterfield. The expedition party took them for rival archeologists and viewed them with suspicion at first. When the Doctor discovered it was the Cybermen who were the object of the party's searches, his curiosity got the better of him. He decided to assist them.

The Great Doors of the city were electrified. One of the expedition's crewmen had been killed trying to open them. When the Doctor succeeded in showing how it could be done in safety, he was accepted into the party. The Great Doors opened onto a cavernous chamber. There was a large hatch set in the metal floor and a large control panel covered with complex instrumentation. Two large archways led away from the main area. Some of the party began to explore the regions beyond. The Doctor and Klieg were more interested in opening the hatch.

The control panel was constructed to human dimensions and conveniently labelled in the kind of symbolic logic that humans would understand. But it was not immediately apparent how they should be operated. As Klieg worked at solving a mathematical sequence which might activate the controls, the Doctor warned, 'There are some things that are better left undone.'

Beyond one of the archways was what seemed to be a chamber for the revitalisation of Cybermen. It was dominated by an upright and open 'form' designed to envelop a Cyberman. When closed and activated, it would 'fire in some sort of neuro-electric potential' at the occupant. Victoria, who was measuring her tiny frame against the hugeness of the 'form', suddenly found herself momentarily trapped inside when, in the main chamber, Klieg succeeded in activating the control console. At the same time, in the area beyond the other archway, Peter Hayman fell foul of a weapons testing device and was killed.

Professor Parry decided that the expedition was putting too many lives at risk and should now be abandoned. But sabotage to the spacecraft's fuel pumps meant they would be grounded for several days. Toberman had secretly caused the damage on orders from the Logicians: Klieg knew the hatchway led to the Cybertombs and did not want to be diverted from his task now they were so close.

Klieg possessed the kind of megalomania that

had afflicted Tobias Vaughn. In Klieg's view, the Brotherhood of Logicians represented the 'greatest man-intelligence ever assembled'. But logic and intelligence were not enough. In order to carry out the kind of changes on Earth that were clearly of logical benefit to mankind, it was necessary to wield real power – power to force conformity from those who did not share the Logicians vision. It seemed the Cybermen had this power. The Logicians had financed the expedition precisely in order to find and use it.

They were exultant when the hatchway eventually swung open, responding to a logical sequence. Kaftan declared, 'Everything yields to logic – our basic assumption.'

'Yes, very,' replied the Doctor.

The party descended through the hatch to explore the warren of interconnected metal caverns in the sub-zero temperatures below. Only Victoria and Kaftan remained on ground level.

Choosing one particular tunnel at random, the underground explorers came to a massive vault whose walls sparkled silver with highly reflective material. Towering in front of them was the impressive object of their expedition – the tombs of the Cybermen. The whole party stared in awe at cells which rose above them, level upon level. In each cell, behind a frosted membrane, lurked the figure of a Cyberman in frozen stillness. Klieg spoke of it in hushed tones, scarcely concealing his malign intentions: 'Like a gigantic honeycomb – and bees waiting for the signal to rise from their winter sleep.'

On the surface, by previous arrangement with Klieg, Kaftan re-sealed the hatch. She had already drugged Victoria's drink to prevent her from interfering. It seemed to the underground party that they were trapped and might freeze to death. Under the pretence of using the tomb controls to re-open the hatch, Klieg deliberately activated the tombs themselves. As the chamber grew warmer, there were ominous signs of movement from within each cell. Then, through every membrane, a Cyberman burst forth.

They were identical in almost every detail to those Cybermen who were last seen on the Moon. Silent, slow, but with never faltering intent, the silver giants approached the fear-rooted humans. Among them – the last to be revived and emerging from a special tomb – was a giant of even mightier proportions. Cyberman in form, it had no chest pack and no antenna. Its cranium was enlarged into a bulbous dome which seemed to flicker from within as though its very thoughts were visible.

Klieg began to explain that it was he who had brought them back to life. Ignoring the Logician, the Controller (for so the Doctor termed this hugest of the creatures) declared: 'You belong to us. You shall be like us.'

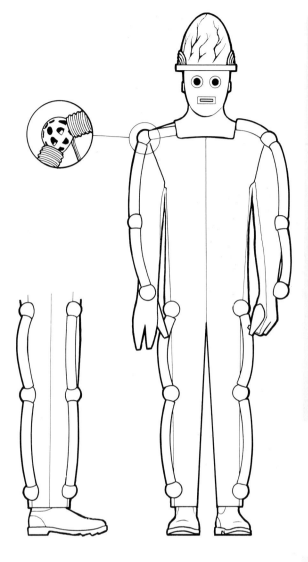

As in the past, once face to face with the Cybermen the Doctor was recognised immediately: 'Our History Computer has full details of you.'

'Ah, yes. The lunar surface,' the Doctor realised.

The Cybercontroller announced that these humans, who had proved themselves of superior intelligence, would become the first of a new race of Cybermen – a force that would return to Earth and control it. The first to be 'altered' would be Klieg: as a Logician he would make the natural leader of the new race. Fear would be eliminated from his brain.

But Victoria had woken and raised the alarm. Captain Hopper and Jim Callum came to the rescue with smoke grenades. In the confusion, all except Toberman escaped to the surface and the massive hatch was lowered once more to keep the Cybermen at bay. Klieg and Kaftan were locked into the Weapons Testing Chamber. The others spent an uncomfortable night taking it in turns to watch for signs of Cyber activity.

Reactivating their dormant Cybermats, the

**Cybercontroller:**
**Document6**
Mystery surrounds the origins of this newly-appearing central authority figure. But the roots of the Cybercontroller probably go back to the communications and planning devices of Documents 1 and 4. Certainly the Controller's enlarged cranial capacity, whose information processing activity is clearly visible, recall those earlier machines. The new development here is the augmentation of Central Processing Machine with conventional Cyberman. The powerful result is a Cyberman of increased size and strength with unquestioned authority who carries with him part, or perhaps the whole, of Cyber knowledge. – a living, mobile 'History Computer' and Cyber co-ordinator.


Over Page Professor Parry, Toberman and Doctor2 stand transfixed as they observe the awakening of the cyberTelosians.          ▶


Dating: Document7
The greatest difference of opinion amongst ArcHivists concerns the dating of *Revenge of the Cybermen*. It contains two indications of its period, both imprecise:

a) the time-travellers have recently been on the *The Ark In Space* and the Doctor states that they were now 'thousands of years before' that time;

b) the Doctor taunts the Cybermen, 'You've no home planet, no influence, nothing. You're just a pathetic bunch of tin soldiers skulking about the Galaxy in an ancient space ship.'

It has therefore been widely assumed that in *Revenge* we see the last surviving Cyberpatrol, centuries after 'a Cyber war' in     ▶

which humans 'almost wiped out' the Cybermen. Farozia dates it in this way: *The Ark In Space* tells us the Ark was put together late 29th/early 30th century (?2914), was designed to harbour Earth humans from Solar flares for '10,000 years' (?12914) and that they overslept several thousand years (?14714); if *Revenge* is set, say, 1200 years earlier then the date would be c13514. When *Earthshock* came to light, it seemed reasonable to assume that failure to stop the conference from taking place on Earth would result in the very Cyber war of which the Cybermen in *Revenge* are lone survivors.

But the difficulty is that in *Earthshock* (2526 AD) the cyberscope shows a scene from *Revenge* – an apparent anomaly (see entry – Cyberscope). But Novasa takes the cyberscope at face value and says *Revenge* must therefore be pre-2526 AD. He points out that if *Revenge* is indeed 'thousands of years before' *The Ark In Space*, then it can certainly be earlier than *Earthshock*. Moreover, 'a Cyber war' implies more than one. I agree with him and have ordered my chronology accordingly. (Also, see entry – Tardis Recognition)

**Companions: Harry and Sarah Jane**

Both from 20th century Earth, Harry Sullivan was a former UNIT medical officer and Sarah Jane Smith a journalist. Sarah Jane had joined Doctor3 several

Cybermen directed them to attack the sleeping humans. The Doctor, knowing that Cybermats – 'a kind of metalic life' – detected humans by picking up their brainwave frequencies, jammed their sensors with electrical interference. He put it this way: 'I've confused their tiny metal minds. You might almost say they've had a complete metal breakdown.'

In the Testing Chamber, Kaftan and Klieg had found parts of a Cyber weapon – a small x-ray laser – which they had reassembled. They intended to force the Cybermen to divulge a few of their secrets. Holding the rest of the party at laserpoint, they called for the Cybercontroller. The hypercranial Cyberman soon appeared, accompanied by Toberman. Kaftan's servant had been partially 'converted'. His limbs were now more powerful than before – they had been replaced by metal – and his mind was under Cyber control.

To conserve energy supplies, the Controller had sent most of the Cybermen back into their tombs. Clearly, the Controller itself was running seriously low in energy: its voice was slowing. Klieg agreed to revitalise the Controller in return for Cyber 'power devices' to aid the Logicians build a better world.

Not surprisingly, once the Controller had been recharged, the agreement was ignored: 'Cybermen do not promise. Such ideas have no value.' Now fully-powered and seemingly invincible (even bullets had no effect) the Controller ordered the reactivation of all the tombs. There was a struggle in which Kaftan was killed. Toberman's former loyalty to her penetrated his altered brain and, encouraged by the Doctor, his cyber-assisted strength was turned against the Controller. In the ensuing clash of Titans, the Controller was defeated.

Klieg, in the face of all that had happened, was still determined to take over the Cybermen's power for himself. Led on by the Doctor, he finally admitted his real ambition to be 'Master of the world.'

'Now I know you're mad,' said the Doctor. 'I just wanted to make sure.' At that moment there appeared a Cyberman, for whom any human was Enemy. Klieg was killed. The others escaped and the Doctor refroze the tombs. He had just re-set the electrification trap on the Great Doors when the Controller revived. Toberman, in a huge effort of will, closed the Doors on the Cybercontroller. The resulting electrical explosion destroyed them both – or so it appeared.

Only the Professor, Captain Hopper and his pilot remained of the original party: the Cybermen, though their plan had failed, had nevertheless exacted a terrible toll. 'That really is the end of the Cybermen, isn't it?', asked Jamie, hopefully.

'I never like to make predictions,' replied the Doctor. As the three of them made their way back to the TARDIS, they did not notice that something still moved over the dusty wastes of Telos.

It was a Cybermat.

**The Pursuit of Voga (Document7)**

Within the large fragment of Voga which had survived the massive Cyber explosion, Vogans still survived. Emerging from space-warp, they had found themselves drifting on the fringes of a planetary system which was dominated by a yellow star of medium size. Half a billion miles out from this sun was a gigantic planet that might be described as a failed star – a brown dwarf – but massive enough to radiate heat to the mini-system of its own satellites.

The sun was Sol. The planet was Jupiter. By curious coincidence, the Vogans had turned up in the very Solar system that had spawned the Cybermen. Terrified of discovery, they had remained underground in the closeness of the survival chamber which had preserved them from the effects of the Cyber attack. For centuries they cowered inside their shattered planet.

They were a humanoid race, straying little from human appearance. Their large-boned faces differed the most: a high-vaulting forehead denoted ancient intelligence; from this dome's imposing height, long tresses of hair fell back, pure white; perhaps only the deep lines to either side of the mouth suggested the generations of dark skulking that had eaten into this proud, light-loving people. Denying themselves their once lucrative trade in gold with other civilisations – avoiding, indeed, any outside contact at all – the Vogans toiled hard to survive in their subterranean world. It was the function of an elite force, the Guardians, to ensure that the secrecy of their continued survival was maintained. Over the centuries, Voga drifted in from the deeper reaches of cometary cloud and was itself caught in Jupiter's gravitational field.

Earth had now advanced to the point where the Solar system was under constant surveillance. Great Circle Freighters would make journeys beyond the Solar system which could last for decades. Sometimes their charts of the Solar system would be outdated on their return. For this reason beacons were set up whenever new objects were found in the Solar system. When Voga was discovered it was initially named Neo-Phoebus (literally, New Sun). The Nerva Beacon, a spacewheel similar to that in Document4, was put on a 30 year assignment to alert returning freighters to its presence.

Professor Kellman was the exographer or planetary surveyor aboard the Nerva Beacon. He was a specialist in Jupiter and its satellites. He landed on Neo-Phoebus to set up a Transmat station (a method of instant travel first developed on Earth in the 21st century – see *Seeds of death*), made his examinations of the new asteroid and returned to the Beacon with the unexceptional information that it was a small lifeless rock which must have drifted towards Jupiter from the void between star systems. He suggested renaming it Voga.

Kellman had deliberately misinformed his colleagues. The Vogan Guardians had immediately detected Kellman and brought him before their leader, Vorus. Though it contravened Vogan laws, Vorus had devised a bold plan to eliminate the Cybermen – who were even now searching the Galaxy for Voga. In return for limitless gold, Kellman agreed to contact the Cybermen and inform them of the whereabouts of their quarry. Vorus had secretly constructed the missile Skystriker to destroy the Cybership when it came within range.

The Cybermen were monitoring a wide range of radio frequencies in their search for Voga: they soon detected Kellman's transmissions. He persuaded them that control of the Nerva Beacon was the key to the destruction of Voga. Understanding his reason for helping them – he wanted power – they agreed that he should rule the Solar system when they had conquered it.

Using Cyber technology, Kellman unleashed in the Beacon what appeared to be an unknown form of space plague. It caused a luminous redness under the skin – along the line of the nerves – and was similar to the neurotropic virus induced by the Cybermen in the moonbase crew (Document 5). But it was Cybermats, not sugar, that carried the infection; and it swiftly led, not to coma, but to death. It decimated the Beacon's crew of fifty: only four of them remained alive, of which Kellman was of course one. Nerva Beacon was quarantined and the servicing of passing ships transfered to a nearby beacon – named Ganymede after the largest of Jupiter's satellites.

We are not told precisely during what period these events took place (for the purpose of this chronology I place it at the end of the 25th century). But we are told it was on Day 3 of the 47th week of the unknown year that Doctor 4 materialised in a sealed off section of Nerva. Two companions, Harry Sullivan and Sarah Jane Smith, materialised with him. It was fortuitous that the Doctor should have arrived at this precise moment for he knew of Voga. He explained to the Commander of the Beacon that the Planet of Gold had caused the defeat of Cybermen at the end of a war against allied human and Vogan forces.

For the Commander, mention of the Cybermen revived only dim memories. Like the archeologists of Telos, he thought they had died out centuries ago – after the destruction of Mondas. But an attack on Sarah Jane by a Cybermat soon

confirmed that Cybermen were very much alive – and were interested in the Beacon. They obviously had a human agent on board and Kellman seemed the prime suspect.

Before he was caught he managed to get a signal to the Cybership. Already within the Solar system, it now moved towards the Beacon and quickly overcame its much-reduced crew. Unlike the previous three encounters of our chronology, the Cybermen did not recognise the Doctor.

Long centuries of Cyber development in the *cyberNomad* had produced two phenomena of interest. The first was that, like the Cybermen in the Telosian tombs, they were invulnerable to the humans' hand-held weapons. The second strangely contradicted what we have come to expect of the Cybermen – there was evidence of emotion. The Vogans spoke of the 'vengeance' of the Cybermen; the Doctor said that Voga was 'hated and feared' by them.

Certainly, the voices of the Cybermen were less monotonous and electronic, particularly the voice of the Cyberleader, who was denoted by black head blocks and antenna. In fact (and it now seems natural to apply the personal pronoun) 'his' mode of speech was comparable to that of a highly-motivated human and it is significant that, for the first time, we hear a Cyberman use value judgements such as 'it is good' or 'excellent!' (a Cyber epithet which is to resound through the rest of the History).

What moved the Cybermen to seemingly vengeful action was the completion of a task they had started centuries ago in a different star system. They needed to destroy Voga utterly, to vaporise the planet so that its gold would no longer be a source of danger to them. It would be blown into sub-atomic fragments by what the Cybermen claimed to be 'the most powerful and compact devices ever invented'. These 'Cyberbombs' had been banned by an Armageddon Convention. Since 'Cybermen do not subscribe to any theory of morality in war', three bombs were to be placed in a central fissure of the planet. The Doctor, the Commander and another crewman were to deliver them personally. Any attempt at removal of the harness which attached the bombs would result in the detonation of a secondary explosion. Two Cybermen accompanied them as they transmatted to Voga.

The Cybermen were detected soon after materialising but the Vogans' weapons were totally ineffective against their old enemy. In an act of self-sacrifice, the crewman threw himself at the Cybermen, unbuckling his harness. The resulting explosion engulfed all three of them. The Doctor salvged one of the mangled Cyber chest packs and de-activated the Cyberbombs.

Denied the success of their original plan to ensure the destruction of Voga, the Cybermen

years earlier when she had stowed away on the TARDIS.

But it was not the TARDIS that brought them to the Nerva Beacon. They and the Doctor had first set foot on the Beacon thousands of years later in its history. At that stage in the future the spacewheel had been enormously enlarged into an Ark (see *The Ark In Space*). Earth was being irradiated by solar flares; to survive, humans were held in suspended animation on the Ark until the flares had subsided. Having gone on to undertake a mission for the Time Lords (see *Genesis of the Daleks*) the Doctor and his companions had now been returned to the Ark – in its original form of the Beacon – by means of a Gallifreyan Time Bracelet. The TARDIS was to be sent back in time to join them. It had not yet materialised.

SARAH JANE          HARR'

KELLMAN

TYRUM          VORUS

### Cyberman: Document 7 – late *cyberNomad*

'Evolved' from early *cyber-Faction* (First Invasion), these Cybermen retain striated head blocks and five-fingered hands but are more rugged. The slight humps on their backs might, like the Earth Camel, store extra supplies of power or, if possessing 'hydraulic muscles' as the Doctor suggests, a fluid reservoir. Hand-held weapons have been relinquished but the area to the front of the cranium bulge is the site of a sophisticated weapon: operated from the chest pack, it is capable of stunning or killing. They have an exoskeleton of thick striated piping, rather than the more delicate framework of the First Invasion – a direction in which late *cyberFaction* also appeared to be developing.

### Glittergun Technology

We might reasonably suppose that the term 'Glittergun' includes a number of different weapons based on the ingenious human technology which enabled gold particles to locate and penetrate their target. That the techniques involved were highly sophisticated would seem to be borne out by the fact that, surrounded as the Vogans were by gold, they nevertheless are unable to utilise its potential against their Cyber aggressors in Document 7. At one point, the Doctor exclaims, 'if only they knew about gold!' He cannot mean by this that the Vogans were unaware of gold's toxicity for the Cybermen – they had worked closely with humans in the Vogan War and had been pursued for centuries because of the threat gold posed to the remaining Cybermen. He must refer to Glittergun technology which had obviously been lost to them.

The difficulty of using raw

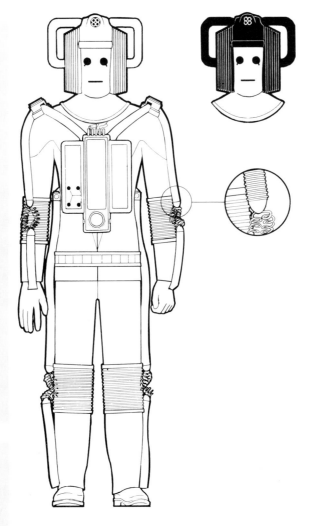

swiftly devised another. Many more Cyberbombs were brought aboard the Beacon which was to be aimed at Voga where the crust of the planet was weakest. Cyber calculations indicated that it would cause the largest explosion ever seen in the Solar system. 'It will be a magnificent spectacle', said the Cyberleader.

The Doctor and Sarah were by this time on board the Beacon. The Cybermen had left them bound together in the control room, before departing to their Cybership to observe the 'scientifically interesting' phenomenon which was about to occur. They estimated that the fireball of the explosion would extend to 1.5 million miles.

The Beacon had been put into hyper-drive and as the two time-travellers watched the Planet of Gold grow larger on the scanner in front of them, they knew they were heading for 'the biggest bang in history'. This was regardless of whether they struck Voga, for Vorus's Skystriker missile had been launched and was heading towards the Beacon.

The Commander and Harry, under the Doctor's guidance, diverted Skystriker's course and aimed it at the Cybership. Before the Cybermen had time to take evasive action, the missile had struck.

The huge craft was obliterated. Harry Sullivan sighed with relief. 'That's the end of your Cybermen,' he said.

Tyrum, the Chief Councillor of Voga, agreed: 'Never again will they be a threat to Voga.' But Sarah Jane and the Doctor were not yet safe: the Beacon's course had been locked-on by the Cybermen and it was still heading at hyper-driven speed towards Voga.

Utilising a handy rope trick he had picked up from Houdini, a 19th century Earth escapologist, the Doctor freed himself just in time to set up a manual override to stop the Beacon from crashing into the planet. The rocky surface spun beneath them as the spacewheel zipped round Voga at incredible speed. At last it broke away from the planet's dizzying grip and settled into a safer and more stable orbit. Preserved from alien destruction by the non-human Doctor, the Beacon would in future millenia become an Ark of refuge to preserve the lives of millions of Earth people.

## Proliferating Cybermen

The Skystriker missile had destroyed the last of the *cyberNomad* subspecies. Blind pursuance of deep rooted cybernetic instincts had, as human emotion sometimes can, consumed the pursuer. It is often said we kill the thing we love; these Cybermen, who sought nothing above their own survival, brought about their own destruction through too zealous a seeking of that end. Revenge had claimed the avenger as its victim.

But if this History teaches us nothing else, it tells us one thing quite clearly: complacency over Cybermen is misplaced. One line of the Cyber race may have ended but other subspecies continued to survive and conquer. We need only think of the Cyberleader's boast to know that, like an infectious disease, the Cybermen would be hard to eradicate: 'We have enough parts in our ship to build an entirely new army and this time, Doctor, it will be invincible.'

The Cyberleader's ship – and its potential for creating new Cybermen – was no longer a source of danger. But the threat could not be discounted because of that. How many other battalions of Nomads roamed the Galaxy? More to the point, how many had the capability of reproducing themselves?

By the middle of the Third Millenium the people of Earth had not only firmly established themselves within their own Solar system. They had also gained a foothold on planets in other star systems. Farozia thinks that, in a similar process, *cyberNomad* had proliferated.

She finds evidence in our final three Documents to suppose that the influences of two subspecies had come together. Out of the union had been forged a new, indomitable Cyberman, a subspecies advanced to a breathtaking degree of sophistication – a leap of 'evolution'. She dubbed them the Ultimate Cybermen. I should like to classify them as *cyberNeomorph* – new-fashioned Cybermen.

## The Forging of a New Race

As commonly happens once a connection is made, it seems so clear. But it needed Farozia's insight to help us see the obvious.

The new Cyberman had been formed from two differing Cyber subspecies. One was *cyberNomad* – of a type probably less advanced than the Cybermen involved in the Vogan war. The other was *cyberTelosian* with its Cybercontroller as the catalyst.

Farozia postulates that one of the proliferated and successful groups of Nomads came to Telos. They revived and reconstructed the Cybercontroller and developed a new form of exoshell that incorporated the most efficient aspects of Nomad and Telosian design. It was based on the less encumbered technology of the Cybercontroller.

The Tombs were reactivated and the Telosian Cybermen within, as well as their Nomadic liberators, were converted to the new form. The energy sources of Telos were opened up for

gold as a weapon is demonstrated soon after. Armed with handfuls of gold dust, the Doctor and his friends still fail to overcome the two Cybermen they attack. Similarly, though in Document8 Doctor5 actually succeeds in scraping the edge of Adric's gold badge against the Cyberleader's vent grille, this assault serves only to weaken and confuse the Cyberman; it is the nine blasts from his own gun that actually destroy him.

### The Neomorph Hypothesis

Farozia's hypothesis, accounting for how the Neomorph Cybermen may have been created, runs thus. We know little of almost five centuries of *cyberNomad* activity. From the first part of this period we know nothing – that is, from the time they leave the Solar system in the late 20th century until they turn up in an advanced form in another star system in the Vogan War. We placed the episode of the pursuit of Voga (Document7) in the late 25th century. The Vogans had lived underground for centuries. We may assume therefore that the Vogan War had been fought during the 22nd century. That would allow up to two hundred years (from c1990 to c2190) for *cyberNomad* to establish themselves and proliferate – time enough, Farozia suggests, to spawn several divergent groups. One group became involved in the Vogan War and the subsequent hounding of Voga. Another might well have gone on to the conquest of other planets in the Galaxy.

Here we come to the crux of her speculation. Suppose that, after the Tombs had been refrozen by the Doctor, this successful group of Cybermen came somehow into contact with Telos. We know from Document9 that the Cyber- ▶

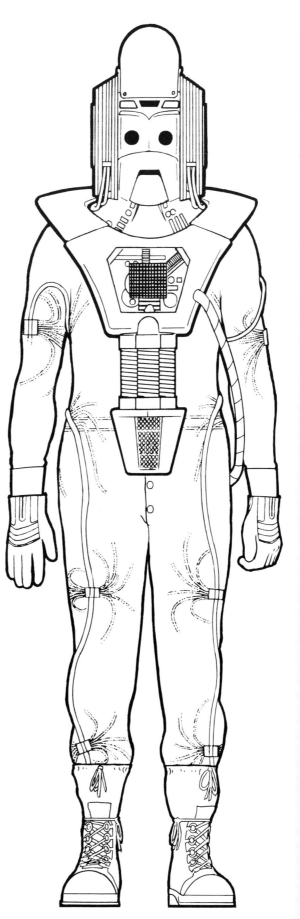

**Cybercontroller: Document9**

◄ controller was not destroyed, 'merely damaged'. Perhaps he himself had activated a radio signal designed to attract the attention of any Cyber group which may have successfully proliferated during the five centuries of *cyberTelosian* sleep.

### Cyber Emotion

It could not actually be emotion which the Cybermen seem to display. Cyber development is solidly based in logic; emotion is entirely alien to them. Document1 shows it to be as hostile to their function as radiation, gravity or gold.

Emotion is an instinctive response as opposed to a rational one. In an emotional response, one is not precisely aware of the reasons for one's behaviour; but a rational response, by its very definition, implies that the reasons for it have been thought out beforehand. It is significant that the words 'emotion' and 'motivate' have the same root, meaning 'to move'. Over centuries of cybernetic development, the aims which motivated the Cybermen – the very rational goals of Survival and Conquest – had become, through constant use and the need for swift decision making, an almost instinctive response in itself.

Reasoned behaviour proceeds from one step to the next in logical progression. If the process is cybernetically controlled (which in the Cybermen it clearly is) there are guiding principles or directives which steer the decision making towards the target. The target for the Cybermen is Survival – it can be described as their intent or directive. Survival motivates them. Their behaviour depends on what fits in best with their ultimate intent, Survival. When their intentions are

Cyber exploitation. Telos became what Mondas failed to be – the centre of a flourishing Cyber Empire.

Colonial expansion was followed by periods of consolidation: as conquests were made and humanoid races converted, vast armies were stored in the refrigerated cities of Telos. They would soon be powerful enough to unleash an attack of unprecedented effectiveness on Earth.

It was perhaps while building up their forces to achieve this long-standing ambition that three *cyberNeomorph* patrols went missing. Cyber Control could discover no final explanation. We are more fortunate. Document0 tells the full story. It is a story quite separate from the chronological development of the other Documents. The reader who is keen to follow that development may immediately move on to the events of Document8. But those who wish to delay the fast-approaching climax of our History will gain a richer insight into the nature of the *cyberNeomorph*.

### Cybermen on Gallifrey (Document0)

At the dark centre of the mountains of Gallifrey is a bleak and sinister landscape. High, inaccessible to the uninitiated, barren and unmistakably a place of ancient evil, it is the Death Zone.

The Master had called it 'the black secret at the centre of your Time Lord paradise.' The Master was a ruthlessly evil Time Lord renegade. He had been summoned by Gallifrey's High Council to aid his greatest enemy – another renegade Time Lord – the Doctor.

The Death Zone had become mysteriously reactivated. All regenerations of the Doctor had simultaneously disappeared from their respective time-streams. Time-traces of all but one of his selves (Doctor4 was trapped in a time-eddy) converged at the Zone. It was evident that they had been brought to the Death Zone by means of the Time-Scoop, the use of which had long been banned.

It was the wish of the Lord High President Borusa and the others of the Council that the Master should put his determined cunning to good use. He was to brave the dangers of the Death Zone to find the Doctors. In return he would receive full pardon for his crimes, and a complete new life cycle. The irony of the situation appealed to the Master. He accepted.

When Doctor2 and the Brigadier had found themselves in a strange, dark wilderness, it was the sight of the Dark Tower that told him where he was. Ashamed for the Time Lords' past, he explained, 'My Time Lord ancestors had tremendous powers which they misused disgracefully. They set up this place, the Death Zone – walled it with an impenetrable forcefield. Then

they kidnapped other beings and set them down here.'

There was one man whose name was forever connected with the Death Zone – Rassilon: 'the greatest single figure in Time Lord history'. It was he who ended the Game of Death that until his time had been played in the Zone. He had lived in the distant past of Gallifreyan history and was buried within the Death Zone in the Dark Tower.

The Doctor had a feeling that Rassilon himself might have brought them to the Zone. Though the official history portrayed him as a noble figure, there were many rumours and legends to the contrary. Some said that, because of his cruelty, he was bound in the Tower in eternal sleep. No one knew how extensive his powers were. They might be playing the Game of Rassilon at that very moment. If that was so, there were other players in the Game: the dim figure of a Cyberman could be made out through the mist. From a broken wall a silver arm emerged to grab the Brigadier. He and the Doctor hurried towards the comparative safety of the Dark Tower and Rassilon's Tomb.

Two other Doctors and their companions found themselves unexpectedly in the Death Zone. Doctor3 had met up with Sarah Jane; they soon discovered that a patrol of Cybermen was pursuing them as they climbed the mountains which rose by the Tower. The original Doctor and his 'grandaughter', Susan, had been re-united, too; when they came across the TARDIS, Doctor1 met himself, as it were, in the person of Doctor5.

In his fifth incarnation, the Doctor had felt himself diminished as each of the other Doctors had been taken out of time. He had come in the TARDIS to this place of 'nowhere and no-time' with companions Tegan and Turlough to 'find his other selves'. Tegan was an assured young Australian woman, brave and spirited, from 1980's Earth; Turlough was an altogether more mysterious non-Earth character but nevertheless resourceful and firmly on the side of his fellow travellers. After introductions of a somewhat confusing nature, Doctor5 and Doctor1 decided to follow separate paths towards the tomb.

The three patrols of Cybermen who now found themselves in the Death Zone had also been time-scooped. How they had materialised at this place was unknown to them. Nevertheless, their cybernetic conditioning immediately launched them into action. They would pursue their Cause of Survival and Conquest, destroying anyone or anything that got in the way.

A Cyberscout had located the Master and Doctor5. The Master was trying to persuade his old enemy that he had been sent by the High Council to find him. The Doctor was inclined to disbelieve him, especially when a patrol of Cybermen approached. He escaped using the Master's recall device and was transmatted to the

Council Conference Room in the Capitol. There, he told President Borusa of his suspicions that it was an important Time Lord who was responsible for reviving the Game.

The Cybermen had located him surprisingly quickly in the Death Zone: they must have had help. Within the recall device given to the Master by, the Castellan, a High Council member, the Doctor found a transmitter beacon. It was this that had alerted the Cybermen to his presence. The Castellan was immediately arrested but shot dead in an apparent escape bid.

The Master, now a prisoner of the Cybermen, persuaded them that he could be of help. Beginning to realise that there was more going on than a simple revival of the Game, he told them that all the creatures in the Zone had been brought there to destroy each other. With his help they could take control of the Tower – stronghold of their enemies the Doctors.

The Cyberleader decided to use the Master to get into the Tower, then destroy him, since 'promises to aliens have no validity.' One Cyberpatrol had already been sent to follow two unknown aliens; now they were known to be the third incarnation of the Doctor and his companion, they must be captured and interrogated. Another Cyberpatrol was dispatched to destroy the TARDIS. The third patrol would accompany the Master to the Tower.

As they climbed up the steep mountain face, Sarah Jane and Doctor3 came to a rocky ledge. She thought they had shaken off their pursuers. 'They don't get tired,' the Doctor warned her, 'and they never give up.' Images of Voga came into her mind. 'No, I remember,' she said.

At that moment, a grey faceless android seemed to materialise before them. The Doctor recognised it as 'a Raston Warrior Robot – the most perfect killing machine ever devised.' Its deadly armaments were built in and its sensors detected any movement as hostile. As they froze to avoid detection, a Cyberscout appeared on the ledge.

Instantly, the Warrior Robot lifted an arm. A sharp lance zipped from its fingers and embedded itself in the Cyberscout's venting unit. Razor-edged discs followed hard behind, slicing away the Cyber head.

Three more Cybermen appeared. One of them, the Patrol Leader, immediately sensed danger and held back. The other two, at the sight of the headless, smouldering body of the Cyberscout raised their blaster-guns in anticipation of attack. But the Robot was too swift for them. One lance, with deadly accuracy, tore through a Cyber chest. As the other Cyberman swung round to face its attacker, a disc sliced away the blaster-gun – along with the arm that held it.

The main body of the patrol now closed in to eliminate this sudden source of danger. Five Cybermen saw their quarry and prepared to blast it out of existence. The Robot vanished with a leap and reappeared behind them. As they turned, five lances shot towards them in rapid succession. A sixth sought out the Leader and impaled him in the arm.

A playful killer, the Raston Robot teased out the Leader's final destruction. Pulled round by the force of the spear, the Leader exposed himself to the lacerating devastation of a disc. Cutting into the armoured exoshell, it remained half-embedded in the the Leader's side. An explosion shorted circuits and shuddered through the convulsing Cyber body. The Leader rasped and rattled. There issued from his mouthpiece a liquid, whitish-grey and thick.

As the Robot dallied among the smoking, broken remains, the Doctor and Sarah Jane made a dazed but hurried departure. With borrowed Raston rope and javelins they improvised a rope bridge from a high mountain crag and entered the Tower from above. Having been driven into a cave by a Yeti, Doctor2 and the Brigadier discovered a way into the Tower from below. The original Doctor, accompanied by Tegan, gained access via the main door by the simple expedient of pulling on the bell-rope.

The Cyber threat to the Doctors had not ended. Outside the TARDIS, a Cyberpatrol busied itself setting up a large explosive device. Inside the Tower, the Master with his Cyberguard was close behind Doctor1 and Tegan. Warning them to hide from his 'suspicious allies', the Master put on a diabolical display as he demonstrated the evil cunning of his Time Lord ancestors.

Before them was a area of floor covered in alternate squares of red and white. Beyond it were the deeper reaches of the Tower. The Cyberleader was cautious about crossing this oddly-marked area but, after the Master had himself walked over it and back, the Cyberlieutenant was ordered to take the patrol across.

The five Cybermen slowly strode towards the other side. As the Cyberlieutenant reached the fifth row, jagged lines of intense green light came flashing down. As each Cyberman was struck, it exploded into flame and collapsed to the floor. The Lieutenant struggled back through the bodies of his men, only to expire, smouldering, at the feet of the Master.

Surreptitiously picking up the Lieutenant's gun, the Master promised to show the Leader the safe route across the board. The Leader concentrated on which squares the Master set his feet: as soon as he was safely across he would destroy this troublesome alien the Master –

A flash of blaster-gun. A searing wrench in abdominal tubes. The Master had turned and fired. The Cyberleader groaned in disbelief as his

threatened or thwarted, Cybermen always react logically. It is evident, however, that at the stage of development we see here, there is a certain, shall we say, intensity of reaction. It is that intensity which can appear comparable with emotion.

To say that these more advanced Cybermen (later *cyberNomad* and *cyberNeomorph*) possess emotion is misleading, an approximation. Closer to the truth is the statement that their first priority is logical behaviour, behaviour directed towards Conquest and Survival; and that what appears to be emotion – anger, revenge, hate, pride – is merely a necessary procedure for achieving what reason demanded. It is not emotion that moves the Cybermen but logical imperatives.

### TARDIS Recognition
Apart from Documents 0 and 8, the TARDIS (in its police box form) rather eludes the Cybermen:

Document1 – TARDIS invisible.

Document2 – assumes various shapes but not that of police box.

Document3 – seen by the *cyberMondasian*, none of whom survive.

Document4 – remains undetected by Cybermen on board Silver Carrier.

Document5 – hidden in a Mooncrater.

Document6 – remains on surface of Telos.

Document7 – arrives on ▶

◄ Nerva Beacon only after destruction of Cybermen. Document9 – becomes police box immediately prior to destruction of Cybermen.

So how is it, Farozia asks, that the Cyberleader in Document8 recognises the TARDIS as the blue police box? She sees this as an anomaly – like the cyberscope showing records of *Revenge* which she places last in her ordering of the Documents (see entry – Dating: *Revenge*). My response is this: a) Document1 begins with the TARDIS in its police box form under attack by Cybermen and we later learn that they know of the Doctor's 'machine', so even if the police box is not immediately associated with the Doctor, we know that it is in the records of the Cybermen; and b) presumably due to that record, they recognise it in *The Five Doctors*, something that Farozia does not question. It is quite clear from *Earthshock* that information about the TARDIS in its police box form is readily available from Cyber records and is displayed, along with previous encounters with the Doctors, on the cyberscope (see entry – Cyberscope).

**Cyberleader: Document0**
The Cyberleader who deals with the Master is a creation of immense intelligence and ruthless logic, the apotheosis of the cybernetic phenomenon whose progress we have noted. It

cybernetic system malfunctioned. Unsupported by his exoshell, he fell to the chequered floor and lay quite still.

In a High vaulted hall of the Tower lay the Tomb of Rassilon. Around the sides of the stone sepulchre were carved a series of faces. One uncarved space remained. As the three Doctors arrived, they began to decipher an Ancient Gallifreyan inscription:

This is the Tomb of Rassilon where Rassilon lies in eternal sleep. Any who have passed thus far have overcome many dangers and shown great courage and determination. To lose is to win. And he who wins shall lose. Whoever takes the ring from Rassilon's hand and puts it on shall have the reward he seeks – immortality.

In the Capitol, Doctor5 had stumbled on a secret chamber – the Control Room for the Ancient Game of Death. There he discovered the true identity of the Player of the Game: the Lord High President Borusa himself. His goal in sight, Borusa divulged his long held ambition. He sought immortality – the reward offered to the winner of the Game – that he might be President Eternal and rule forever. Because the Game held many dangers and traps, he had made use of the Doctors' combined ingenuity to penetrate the Zone and Tower. Provided with companions to help and old enemies to fight, they had played 'a game within a Game'.

Around the TARDIS, the remaining Cyberpatrol had completed the setting up of the bomb. 'All is prepared,' said the Cyberlieutenant.

'Excellent!' said the Leader. A churning noise started to come from the time-machine. If the TARDIS was about to take off, they must act quickly. 'Detonate!' ordered the Leader. A huge sheet of flame engulfed the time-machine. When it died down there was nothing to be seen. The patrol of Cybermen was left bewildered by an unfinished task that could not be completed.

The TARDIS materialised by the side of Rassilon's Tomb. Doctor3 had reversed the polarity of the neutron forcefield, allowing the TARDIS's pre-set controls to bring it to the Tower. Borusa had also appeared, transmatted with Doctor5 from the Capitol.

The Image of Rassilon manifested itself. The Lord President demanded immortality. 'Be very sure,' warned the Image.

'I am sure,' claimed Borusa. He put on the ring of Rassilon.

'Others have come to claim immortality through the ages. It was given to them – as it shall be given to you.' Carved in the sepulchre, the faces of stone were suddenly revealed to have living, haunted eyes. 'Your place is prepared, Lord President Borusa.'

Borusa vanished and in the space reserved for it an effigy appeared. The Lord President had won his prize. He had been immortalised alongside previous seekers of eternal life. Trapped in a living death, only his eyes cried out with horror at his fate.

## Onslaught on Earth (Document8)

Once the Neomorph Cybermen had established themselves on Telos and built up sufficient forces, their attention turned to the conquest of Earth. The Cybermen in their new, indomitable form at last had a secure and powerful base from which to attack. Earth had colonised other planets and spread its insidious humanity to distant parts of the Galaxy. Since they no longer needed it as an adopted home, there was nothing to stop the Cybermen from utterly destroying Earth, before systematically increasing their Cyber forces with converted human colonists.

There was another reason why the time was ripe to destroy Earth. Over the forty years or so that had passed since Cybermen had suddenly reappeared in the Solar system, Earth people had been alerted to the fact that their old enemy still survived in parts of the Galaxy. When reports started to get through of the activities of a new, more deadly Cyberman, it seemed that action was needed on a Galactic scale to counter the *cyberNeomorph* threat. Discussion took place between colonised planets and moons within the Solar system and civilisations in other star systems. Attack was thought to be the most appropriate means of defence against the Cybermen. So, in the year 2526 AD an interstellar conference took place on Earth under conditions of the utmost security. The leaders of many powerful planets came to sign a pact uniting their military forces in a war against the Cyber race.

Cyber intelligence had managed to discover plans for the conference. Not even the might of the Cyber race could withstand the onslaught of a combined interstellar force. An offensive had immediately to be launched against the conference itself: 'It will be a great psychological victory,' the Cyberleader was later to declare. 'The strength and might of the Cyber race will be confirmed.'

The Cybermen planned a massive pre-emptive onslaught on Earth. First, a bomb was secretly planted within one of the planet's cave systems; guarded by two primitive androids against interference, it would be powerful enough to make life intolerable for those few who survived its impact. Second, a large interstellar merchant freighter was unwittingly to transport a vast Cyberarmy through the 'red alert' security screen thrown around Earth; once on the planet, the Cybertroops would eliminate those few who survived the bomb. Third, a fleet of Cyberships were to hold off in deep space until the destruction of Earth; it would then move in to make conquest of the rest of the Solar system. The plan was on such a scale as to dwarf the previous invasions of the Cybermen.

By chance, the cave system where the Cyberbomb had been set up was discovered to be rich in fossils. Well-preserved bones of a supremely adapted Earth species were of particular interest. The reptilian Dinosaurs had existed for more than a hundred million years on the planet. Then, 65 million years before *homoSapiens* evolved, the Dinosaurs had abruptly become extinct – vanquished, it was thought, by the impact of a massive meteor.

As an exploratory party of scientists approached the site of the bomb, the two android guards killed seven members of the team. Troopers were also attacked. The androids' built-in weapons reduced the victims to slimy puddles. Also built-in to the androids was a monitoring device which relayed three-dimensional visual information to Cyber Control (secreted on the freighter). The Cyberleader watched as the troopers, led by Lieutenant Scott but advised by an unknown civilian, concentrated their fire and destroyed the androids.

The civilian was the Doctor, not long regenerated into his fifth incarnation. In his own timestream, he had not yet been time-scooped to Gallifrey and had yet to encounter the Cybermen in their new form. With him were companions Tegan, Nyssa and Adric. Tegan we have met. The other two were youths with brilliant non-Earth minds: the girl Nyssa, quiet and gentle, specialised in bioelectronics; the boy Adric, difficult and immature, was an incisive mathematician and would before long entirely redeem his less attractive qualities.

The Cyberleader decided to explode the bomb. The freighter had reached the space station security check: clearance would soon be given for it to go straight on to deliver its cargo. Cybermen were now ready to proceed towards the destruction of Earth. But someone was interfering with the bomb mechanism – had succeeded in deactivating it – a task impossible for an 'Earthling': Cyber technology was too advanced. Then, the Leader spotted an object he recognised – a TARDIS in the form of a blue police box. Its owner called himself the Doctor. Through several regenerations he had been a source of interference in the plans of the Cybermen. The Leader ran through visual files of the incarnations known from previous encounters: Doctor1 at the return of Mondas, Doctor2 in the Space Wheel and Doctor4 during the pursuit of Voga. None of them matched any of the people in the cave. The Leader deduced that the Doctor

must have regenerated again.

The Doctor had meanwhile traced the androids' signal to sector 16 – deep space. Using the TARDIS, he and his companions (including Scott and his troopers) arrived on the freighter. The gloomy Hold where they had landed was filled with thousands upon thousands of cargo silos. The Doctor and Adric decided to investigate.

The Cybermen had a human agent on board the freighter – a crewman called Ringway. He was ordered by the Leader to apprehend the intruders and use them as scapegoats. Two other crewmen had been patrolling the dark vastness of the Hold. They were uneasy in their task: recently three of their colleagues had mysteriously gone missing.

Suddenly, the Doctor and Adric heard terrible screams. They ran to where the two crewmen lay dead in a battered heap. Ringway arrived at the scene a moment later and accused them of the deaths. Observing the prisoners on his scanner as they were taken to the Captain on the bridge, the Leader deduced that the tall figure with fair hair was the Doctor: 'even under the threat of death, he has the arrogance of a Time Lord'. He was to be captured alive and made to suffer for the Cybermen's past defeats.

The time was right for the Cybermen to take control of the freighter. Electrical power was redirected from the ship's hyper-drive demands. It surged into six of the silos. In each, a Cyberman came to life and broke through the silo wall. The Cyberleader's personal guard had been reactivated.

Power loss had been detected on the Bridge. The Captain, a hard-bitten woman determined to claim her bonus for getting her cargo through to Earth on time, was at first convinced that the intruders were responsible. But she realised she was wrong when monitors showed movement in the Hold – a phalanx of marching silver figures. To the Doctor they were immediately recognisable but he had never before seen them in this ominous form. They were clearly advanced Cybermen – and they were about to attack the Bridge.

Even the powerful ray-weapons of the crewmen had no effect on these creatures as they drew near to the Bridge Control Room. Before the room could be isolated with its armoured shutters, Ringway revealed his duplicity and held them all at gunpoint to await the arrival of his masters. Just as the first Cybermen reached the Bridge, however, Ringway was overpowered. The two metal doors slid into place and for a time kept the small group of Cybermen at bay.

It was not long before the Cybermen were attacking one of the shutters with a 'thermal lance'. The dense metal of the door glowed red-hot, then white-hot as its molecular structure broke down.

is interesting and significant, I think, that the more refined and subtle the process to replace human functioning, the closer cybernetic functioning comes to a parody of human characteristics. A deep malignity seems to ooze from every inflection of his voice, though it reflects only cold calculation – intense and logical pursuit of the Cyber Cause (see entry – Cyber Emotion). Bodily gestures appear to betray an exultation in his extraordinary power – a thrusting finger, a closing fist – but in reality they are simply an effective signalling of cybernetic intention and brute strength. (Also, see entry – Cyberleader: Recurrent 'Persona')

## Cyberscope

The cyberscope is at the centre of one of the most furious debates concerning the dating of the Cyber-Documents (see entry – Dating: Document7). To me, it seems quite plain that the cyberscope is no more than a useful piece of 3-D projection equipment. As well as relaying live action from the androids' visual monitoring system, it can also display information from the Cybermen's 'history computer' whose records seem to stretch back for centuries and which has, on at least four previous occasions (Documents 1, 4, 5 and 6), enabled them to recognise their arch-adversary.

Some ArcHivists, however, see the cyberscope as something altogether more remarkable, including Farozia who suggests it may possess the facility to probe minds, enabling them to see their future in the Doctor's memories. The Cybermen have many times demonstrated their ability to control human minds (Documents 1, 2, 4, 5, 6, and 9) and so this pos- ▶

◄ sibility cannot be dis-
counted.

Less plausible is an
alternative suggestion that
the *Earthshock* Cybermen
had some ability in time-
travelling or 'temporal projection' (ArcHivist Al-
stevena). It is clearly evident from Document9
alone that the Cybermen do
not understand even the
principles of time-travel.

**Cyberman: Documents 8,
9, 0 – *cyberNeomorph***

Instead of the Cyber chest
pack (which the *cyberTelosian* Controller did not
need) an elegant armoured
unit protects the torso; its
sleek lines contain all that is
necessary to independent
functioning. Instead of a
mass of flimsy pipes, one
sturdy tube leads from the
torso-unit, feeding and
controlling the rest of the
Cyber body. Instead of a
framework of rods or tubes,
a sophisticated exoshell
ensures optimum support
and control – the former exoskeletons seem clumsy by
comparison. The face has
become more fearsome
and cranial capacity is larger; refined Nomad head
blocks support Telosian-
type antenna. Finally, new
weapons which emit lethal,
blasting rays are carried in
hands that are powerfully
five-fingered. Thus Cybermen created the Neomorph
in their own, perfected image.

Once it was soft enough, the Cyberleader
ordered one of his men to break through.

But the Doctor was ready. He had adapted the
freighter's antimatter container to re-stabilise the
molecular structure of the door. As the Cyberman
strode through, the metal of the shutter resumed
its hardness. The intruding Cyberman was instantly immobilised – permanently fixed into the
structure of the door.

In the Hold, Scott's small party of troopers
managed to disable a couple of Cyberguards by
concentrating their fire. Tegan put an end to one
of them by using its own gun against it, but the
other managed to stumble away. Leaving a slimy
green trail of internal fluid, it reached the Cyberleader on the Bridge before collapsing. The
Leader quickly deduced that their agent Ringway
had lied about the level of Earthling resistance on
the freighter. He ordered further Cybermen to be
re-activated to serve as reinforcements.

Cyber charges had now been set up to destroy
the other shutter. At the Leader's command, a
hole was blown in the armoured shutter and
seven Cybermen strode slowly through. Last to
enter was the Cyberleader.

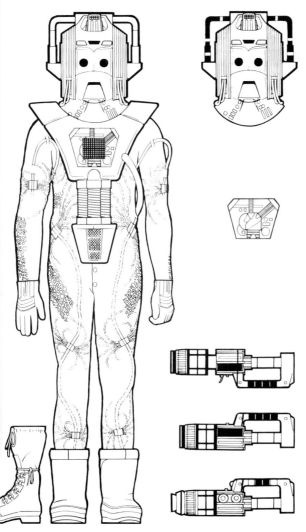

Tall, with powerful bearing and a voice whose
cadence only sometimes revealed he was more
machine than man, he bore striking similarity to
the Leader who first interrogated the Master on
Gallifrey and was destroyed by him on the
death-board of squares. Though in his own form
he had never before met the Doctor, it was with
the collective memory of the Cyber race that the
Leader approached the 'meddlesome' Time Lord.
Behind the transparent lower panel of his helmet
something soft and silver moved. 'So, we meet
again, Doctor,' he purred.

Ringway was quickly and dispassionately killed. Surprise and horror mixed in his open eyes as
he fell dead to the ground. 'He deceived us,'
explained the Leader.

Noting the Doctor's 'fondness for Earth', the
Leader disclosed their intention to destroy it.
'Now you will see our strength,' he promised.
Down in the Hold, re-activation was continuing.
Silo after silo burst open under the mighty fists of
emerging Cybertroops. Patrol after patrol, each
headed by a Leader of its own, marched resolute-
ly along the gloomy corridors. Monitor after
monitor on the Bridge revealed the awesome
threat. 'My army awakes, Doctor,' announced the
triumphant Cyberleader.

Locking-off fixed co-ordinates for the freighter's
destination, the Cybermen turned the spaceship
into a flying bomb – and one that had direct
clearance through to Earth. This contingency plan
– necessary because the Doctor had de-activated
the original bomb on Earth – meant that the newly
activated Cybertroops had now to evacuate and
join the main Cyberfleet. The Leader chose to use
the TARDIS to observe the freighter's destructive
collision with Earth.

Tegan had been captured and was now
brought before the Leader. Recognising that the
Doctor had 'affection' for her, he coldly demonstrated the weakness that such emotions imply.
Threatening to kill her, he forced his discomfited
adversary to leave Adric behind with the Captain
on the Bridge.

The Doctor and Tegan were taken to the
TARDIS. There, the Doctor was made to pilot the
craft and shadow the freighter. Two Cyberguards
were left on the Bridge; they would observe and
learn from their prisoners' growing terror. It was
scientific research: 'if we are to fight Earthlings, it
is better that we understand their weaknesses.'

Scott and his troopers were still on the freighter. They surprised and overcame the Cybermen
guarding the Captain and Adric. But the freighter
remained locked-on to the crash-course towards
Earth. Propelled at hyper-speed, it was fast
approaching its destination. Three logic codes
had to be solved before the freighter could again
be controlled from the Bridge. Even Adric's
mathematical prowess – attested to by a gold-

edged badge which the Doctor had earlier pocketed to avoid detection by the Cybermen – was severely stretched by the task. He managed quite quickly to solve the first logic code but because of the unpredictable effect of the cyber-technology overriding the freighter's computer, this succeeded only in pushing the ship into time-warp. As it spiralled backwards in time, the TARDIS was made to follow.

The Doctor realised that the spatial locked-on co-ordinates remained relative to Earth. The Cyberleader found this information gratifying: 'Excellent news, Doctor. Earth will be destroyed. It will never exist as you have known it.' But the Doctor disagreed. They had travelled back in time 65 million years. Was the massive disruption which ended the Dinosaurs in fact caused, not by a meteor, but by the freighter? It was the inevitable conclusion.

Over the radio transmitter, which the Leader had wrested from Nyssa, came Scott's voice: everyone had left the freighter in an escape pod – except for Adric who was still desperately trying to crack the final logic code. The Cyberleader knew now his mission had failed but he was determined to succeed for the Cyber race in another regard. Casually crushing the radio transmitter in a mighty fist, he turned to the Doctor. 'You will not enjoy the victory,' he said and raised his weapon to the Doctor's head. The Time-Lord's meddling in Cyber affairs would soon be ended for ever. 'I shall now kill you, Doctor,' he said.

Before he could shoot, the intrepid Tegan had grasped him from behind. Her tiny frame was quickly flung off as the Leader twisted round but the Doctor had already thrown himself on the Leader and was rubbing the soft gold of Adric's badge into the chest venting unit. Particles of deadly gold reacted with the Cyber mechanism. The Cyberman uttered cries of electronic alarm. Disoriented, he spun around, shooting wildly. The Doctor wrenched the gun from the Leader's loosened grip and shot point-blank into the already weakened chest unit. Another cry in parody of pain, another blast of Cyber ray into the slowly sinking form. A groaning sigh. A dying fall. A final blast. And the Cyberman lay still.

A sudden explosion shattered the prostrate figure. The Cyberleader had now been utterly destroyed.

'Look!' shouted Tegan. On the scanner, the freighter was glowing. It had started to enter the atmosphere of Earth. The glow grew brighter and the freighter burst like a star as it plummeted towards Earth. At the Doctor's feet the remains of Adric's badge glinted dully in the silent room.

## Departure from Telos (Document 9)

Document 9 makes up the second part of what was originally, with Document 2, a single piece. We told the earlier part of the story near the beginning of our *History*. In that account, a patrol of Cybermen from the future (we have termed them *cyberNeomorph*) led by the Cyberleader-type that has become familiar to us, infiltrated the sewers of London a year before the return of Mondas. The reason for that brief appearance on Earth in 1985 AD is revealed by this final episode of CyberHistory.

We do not know what happened to the main Cyberfleet when one of its Leaders disappeared forever into the past. He was to have led a force of Cybermen to deal with survivors of the pre-emptive strike on Earth. As we have seen, the strike was 'diverted' so that it actually occurred during the pre-history of the planet – an established event for 26th century Earth. The irony for the Cybermen is that it may have been this event which enabled *homoSapiens* to become the planet's dominant species.

We may assume that agreement was reached to join forces against the Cybermen, that a Cyber war began in the Solar system – with a battle between the main Cyberfleet and human forces – which extended to other parts of the Galaxy and which eventually overcame the Cyber race. Document 9 depicts Telos before Galactic forces have made a significant attack on the planet. But the desperation of their Final Plan implies that they can foresee the extinction of the Cyber race.

The Cybermen were preparing to abandon Telos. One reason for this may have been the threat of imminent attack. Another reason is more certain: the Cryons had not been totally wiped out; pockets of them had become resistance fighters and were sabotaging the refrigerated cells in which, to conserve energy, many Cybermen were stored until needed. All the Cybermen were required for departure but the interference of the Cryons had damaged the effectiveness of the refrigeration plants. Some Cybermen rotted in their cells. Others went 'rogue', bursting out to wander destructively over the different levels of the 'tombs' – a term which was becoming more and more apt.

Above ground, there were groups at work laying explosive charges. It was the Cybermen's intention, when they left, to destroy the surface of the planet. This would wipe out the Cryons for good – as well as providing useful experimental data for the effects of such explosions on the atmosphere. The work parties were made up of captured aliens. Among them were some of the humanoid crew of the recently captured timeship which the Cyberpatrol had used to get back to Earth 1985. Like other captured aliens, most of the timeship's crew and passengers had been turned into Cybermen but two called Bates and Stratton were among the 'rejects', those for whom the conditioning process did not always work: their

### Cyberleader: Recurrent 'Persona'

A recognisable Cyber-leader-type recurs in Documents 2, 8, 9 and 0, though he is often clearly seen to be destroyed. The apparent resurrection of the familiar Cyberleader 'persona' is an interesting phenomenon. It might be explained thus: the living organic core of each of these more 'personalised' Cyberleaders have been adjusted in line with a cybernetic blueprint whose software contains a continually updated memory of Cyberhistory – its achievements and its enemies – and whose mechanical hardware is at the forefront of cybertechnology.

We witness in the figure of this Cyberleader one of the high points of efficiency and success for Cyber development (see entry – Cyberleader: *The Five Doctors*). Ruthlessly intelligent, with incredible strength and agility, possessing far-reaching memory of the collective Cyber race, he is a formidable personal counterpart to the Doctor: a cybernetic match to the devious ingenuity of the Cybermen's greatest opponent.

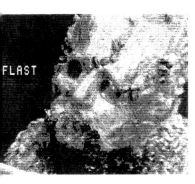

## The Cryon Inconsistency

For a crogenic species to evolve, it would seem necessary for Telos to sustain temperatures well below zero. Why then did the Cryons have to construct refrigerated cities? How is it, in other words, that the temperature of Telos, which once gave life to the Cryons, now threatened their very existence?

It is useful to turn to Novasa for help. He suggests that, like the Mondasians, the Cryons had soon become an advanced society. He goes on to sketch the possibility of even closer parallels with the fate of Mondas: 'Short-sighted ecological exploitation so alters the density of their atmosphere that the heat generated by their technological processes can no longer escape. Slowly, the temperature of those parts of their world where activity was greatest rises to between 10 and 15 degrees above zero. Then comes a dramatic cataclysm. Vastial, a common mineral on Telos and inert at lower temperatures, is unstable above 10 degrees and at 15 degrees spontaneously combusts. There is wholescale devastation of densely-populated areas and atmospheric temperature is further increased. There still remain sub-zero areas of Telos where vastial is stable but they are desolate. These advanced creatures prefer to create more suitable artificial habitats. They construct refrigerated vaults underground and gradually come to accept this profound change in

limbs had been replaced by cybernetic counterparts but their minds were largely unaffected.

Bates had a plan. If three of them could make a break for it, decapitating a Cyberguard on the way, the cleaned out head could be used to disguise one of them as a Cyberman. As prisoners and escort, they might be able to gain entry to Cyber Control and recapture their ship. In the event, only Bates and Stratton got away and the large timeship needed at least three to pilot it. They nevertheless headed for Cyber Control.

When the TARDIS landed on Telos, it materialised in the tombs themselves instead of Cyber Control: the Doctor had distorted the navigational controls by a fraction. The tombs reeked of decay. The Cyberleader's immediate priority was to get the Doctor to the Cybercontroller, many levels above. Suddenly, a rogue Cyberman smashed through a cell door. The Cyberleader swiftly dealt it a deadly blow to its main supply tube, but in the confusion all except the Doctor escaped.

Peri was found by Cryon guerrillas and taken to their hideout. Dressed in simple, close-cut, insulated suits, they were similar in shape and size to the human female they caressed and found so beautiful but in other respects they seemed more creatures of the sea. The large and hairless cranium was smooth and shiny as polished silica; humanoid facial features gave way to big, fish-like

eyes; matted fibres of delicate transparency grew from the upper lip. The hand's five fingers were thin and long, constantly undulating like the tendrils of a sea anemone.

From these gentle but dedicated survivors, Peri discovered the awful extent of the Cybermen's intentions. The patrol she had met on Earth in 1985 was but a test run for the Ultimate Plan. The Cybermen were to use the captured timeship – and now the TARDIS as well – to return to what had been the destruction of Mondas. Halley's comet was then close to Earth. Once Mondas had re-energised itself, the Cybermen planned to divert the comet so that it would smash into Earth. Mondas would be saved from absorbing too much energy. In contrast to established history, the original Cyber planet would continue to exist. History would move along a new path – with Cybermen triumphant.

In Cyber Control, the Doctor was learning of the Cyber plan, too. He had been placed in a refrigerated chamber with a Cryon called Flast. When she revealed how the Cybermen intended to alter established history, he realised that the Time Lords had probably manoeuvred him into the situation so that he could act as their agent. It was up to him to stop such gross violation of the Laws of Time.

The room was packed with vastial, the highly

explosive mineral that was safe at sub-zero temperatures. With a small quantity of it, he disabled the Cybermen guarding the door and made his escape, leaving his thermal lance with Flast. She could not leave the protection of the refrigerated room: in higher temperatures she would boil.

The surviving Cryons had dedicated their lives to the destruction of the Cybermen. Ironically, they knew that if they allowed the Cybermen to leave, Mondas might not be destroyed; those who were now their oppressors might never, in the unfolding of a new history, need to come to Telos at all and the Cryons might never have to suffer in the way they had. But the Cryons had accepted their fate. Besides, the Cybermen intended that no Cryon should survive when they left Telos. It was essential for the Cryons to block that departure. Flast now prepared to sacrifice her own life in the cause of preserving the Cryon race. She buried the thermal lance in a box of vastial. Soon the entire supply would be detonated. Cyber Control would be annihilated and with it, the Cybercontroller.

The Doctor hurried back to the TARDIS. On the way he was met by Peri and the other Cryons. He was just about to take her with him when she told him about Lytton's part in the affair. Commander Lytton had been working for the Cryons. They had picked up his distress signal and bought his services as an intergalactic mercenary. He had come to Telos with his unsuspecting accomplice Griffiths to join Bates and Stratton and help recapture their time vessel. The plan had seemed to be working but Cyber Control had known of it all along and observed with clinical interest as the humanoids drew closer to their ship. Lytton was captured and tortured until he divulged the plan in detail. The three who remained were allowed to reach the very door that separated them from the timeship. Then, the experiment was ended and its victims killed. Only Lytton had been kept alive. He would make a useful Cyberman.

The Doctor and Peri took the TARDIS into the heart of Cyber Control. They found Lytton wired-in to a conversion unit. Though he still had his own limbs, his brain and voice were already affected. In his chest had been implanted the internal replacement units for heart and lungs. The Doctor rushed to find something, anything, to help release him quickly. On a nearby console was some sharp instrument. He grabbed it and ran back to Lytton whose partly converted voice begged for a different kind of release: 'Please, Doctor, kill me!'.

Another voice rang out, this one fully cybernetic. 'Move away from him, Doctor.' The massive figure of the Cybercontroller lurched towards them. The Doctor placed the sharp instrument in Lytton's hand. 'Emotion is a weakness,' announced the Cybercontroller as he came closer. 'It brought

you back for your friend and it will cost you your life.'

Lytton lunged with the sharp blade. Green liquid spurted from a punctured tube. Stung, the Controller felled his attacker with flailing blows. At the door appeared the Cyberleader, followed close by his Lieutenant. But the Doctor acted quickly. He retrieved the Controller's fallen weapon and fired. Caught at the shoulder, the Cyberleader swung round into the Lieutenant whose gun went off point-blank into his Leader's body. Another shot from the Doctor brought both Cybermen to the floor.

The Controller was almost on top of him. Arms still swinging wildly, he knocked the Doctor off balance. But before he could smash the Time Lord into oblivion, the gun went off. The Controller tottered – and fell.

Peri emerged. The Doctor was bending over Lytton's prostrate form. She knew he could do nothing more for Lytton. She gently persuaded the Doctor back into the TARDIS. The blue police box dematerialised not a moment too soon. A vast explosion ripped through Cyber Control. The Cybermen of Telos had met a sudden end.

The Cybermen's 'departure' from Telos could not have been more final. The planet belonged once more to the Cryons. In the teeth of Cyber conquest, it was the Cryons who survived.

# Epilogue

If the Cybermen on Telos were really the last of the Cyber race, then our *History* might seem to have reached a satisfying conclusion. But we have no way of knowing whether the Neomorphs on Telos were the sole surviving Cybermen in the Galaxy or whether there had been a wider proliferation of subspecies over the centuries. In the end, the CyberDocuments tell us so very little. Yet they alone have led us to surmise an evolution and proliferation that has encompassed a diversity of subspecies. Here is a summary of what we have surmised.

Subspecies *cyberMondasian* and *cyberFaction* developed in parallel before Mondas returned to Earth. After the planet's destruction, a *cyberFaction* group remained in the Solar system while another group split away to become *cyberNomad* and explore other star systems, splitting over the centuries into several diverse groups.

Meanwhile, *cyberFaction* underwent gradual change, left the Solar system and, finding the planet that met its requirements, became *cyberTelosian* and entered centuries of hibernation.

One of the *cyberNomad* groups evolved into 'total machine creatures' before becoming extinct

their environment.'

There is an echo here of the changes the Mondasians themselves had to undergo. Like them, too, the Cryons probably became parthenogenic (two sexes were not needed for the procreation of offspring) but the race was predominantly feminine by nature, as opposed to the predominantly masculine Cyber 'men'. Nonetheless, there are hints in Document9 (in which, we shall see, they play a significant role) that, unlike the Cybermen, the Cryons are not unaware of the delights of sexuality.

CYBER CONVERSION PROCESS

## Return To Mondas

It is a thought-provoking idea that the Cyberleader, in following the freighter as it regressed 65 million years into Earth's past, was also returning to the site of his race's own origins. It is very likely that when the freighter re-materialised, the planet Mondas would have been close by. This notion has led some ArchIvists (notably Drews-killia) ingeniously to suggest that it was the freighter's tremendous explosion which dislodged Mondas from its orbit and sent it on the journey to the edge of space. An irony indeed, if such was the case. (But see Origins subsection of the *History* for objections to this view.)

in an attempt to destroy Voga. Others may have developed successfully in different star systems, possibly even different galaxies – the permutations are as inexhaustible as one's imagination.

We have imagined one such group being summoned to Telos and creating the new subspecies *cyberNeomorph* which launched a massive attack against Earth. It was only the combined might of interstellar confederacy closing from without, and the Cryons' devastating sabotage from within, which brought about the destruction of the *cyberNeomorph*.

Somewhere, somehow, Cybermen might still survive. Their shadow falls wherever logic is untempered by humanity.

We have travelled far. From a handful of CyberDocuments we have spun a tale that has stretched back to the beginnings of existence, that spans the breadth of galaxies, that penetrates to the heart of humanity and its antithesis, the Cybermen. It is one of many tales that may be drawn from the Documents.

What I have done is to take up the isolated fragments of Cyber knowledge and piece them together in a way that makes sense to me. There are other ways the tale can be told. We must not cease discovering the ways. And the end of our exploration will be to arrive at the place where we began – the CyberDocuments. But we shall know them better.

I take up the fragments and scatter them again. It is your turn to pick up the pieces.

### A Late Note

Since preparing this history, a further CyberDocument has been discovered. Research chroniclers at the Cyber Hive are even now decoding and analysing it.

Until their task is finished, we cannot, of course, attempt to fit this new fragment into the larger pattern. However, the dating of the Document is interesting for it is consistent with a phenomenon which has so far remained unexamined. I have called it the Nexus Phenomenon.

Briefly, the Nexus Phenomenon Theory goes as follows. There appear to be two eras of Earth history, each less than a hundred years in duration, where Cyber activity is concentrated. The First Nexus is from around 1978 AD to 2070 AD (Documents 1-5); the Second Nexus is from around 2486 AD to 2530 AD (Documents 6-9). Why this should be so is not clear (though it should prove a fruitful area of research – an idea which I throw open to other ArcHivists). But as if to confirm the Theory, the newly discovered CyberDocument fits neatly into the First Nexus.

Nevertheless, what is finally most revealing and chilling about the new Document is the further evidence it seems to provide that the Cybermen have indeed proliferated widely through the Galaxy. When this most recent CyberDocument has been made available for universal perusal, it will have certain effect. The hope that Cybermen have entirely vanished from our Galaxy will be seen to be fragile in the extreme. As fragile, indeed, as the humanity which Cybermen seek to crush.

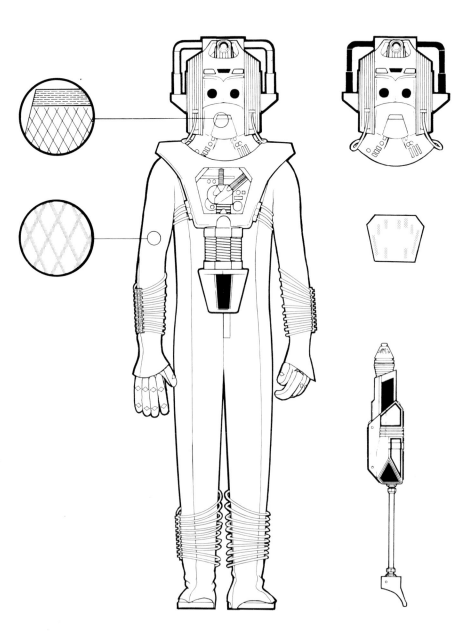

# PROGRAM
## THE CYBERMEN ON TV

Based on original material by Adrian Rigelsford

Revised and with additional material by
David Banks

'You could escape from the Daleks quite easily. But the Cybermen were different. They never gave up. Nothing could stop them.'

Innes Lloyd, DOCTOR WHO producer 1966-68

## Introduction

Some years ago, a mass purge took place in the vaults of the BBC film archives. Many episodes of classic black-and-white television serials were destroyed in order to make way for the new colour programmes. *Doctor Who* was affected badly. Well over one hundred episodes – mainly from the Patrick Troughton era – were junked. The early Cyberman stories did not escape the devastation. *The Tenth Planet*, *The Moonbase*, *The Wheel In Space* and *The Invasion* are all now incomplete. Nothing at all remains of *Tomb of the Cybermen*. Thankfully, the four other Cyberman stories remain intact.

This section, *Program*, covers the production of all the Cyberman stories – regardless of whether they are still in existence – including the 'guest' appearances Cybermen have made in other *Doctor Who* adventures. Fortunately, our information has not had to depend solely on the incomplete film archives. It has come mainly from the people who were involved in making the programmes.

The work of these writers, designers, producers, directors and actors goes back as far as 1966 and trying to locate them has been no easy task. Sadly, some are no longer with us – the list includes: Kit Pedler, co-creator of the Cybermen; William Hartnell, the first Doctor; Richard Hurndall, who recreated the first Doctor in *The Five Doctors*; Patrick Troughton, the second Doctor; Douglas Camfield, director of *The Invasion*; David Whitaker who wrote *The Wheel In Space*; Robert Holmes, co-author of *Revenge of the Cybermen*; and Ian Marter, who played Harry Sullivan and wrote several novelisations of *Doctor Who* scripts.

But there are many whose vivid recollections make up the bulk of this section. They are (in alphabetical order):

| | |
|---|---|
| David Banks | Martin Bower |
| Michael E Briant | Peter Bryant |
| Nicola Bryant | Dinah Collin |
| Nicholas Courtney | Michael Craze |
| Gerry Davis | Chris D'Oyly John |
| Pat Gorman | Richard Gregory |
| Peter Grimwade | Peter Halliday |
| Mark Hardy | Peter Hawkins |
| William Kenton | Richard Kerley |
| Michael Kilgarriff | Innes Lloyd |
| Derek Martinus | Peter Moffatt |
| John Nathan-Turner | Brian Orrell |
| Charlie Pemberton | Victor Pemberton |
| Sandra Reid | Eric Saward |
| Roy Skelton | Tristan de Vere Cole |
| Hans de Vries | |

Kit Pedler and Gerry Davis
The men behind the Cybermen

There are times, of course, when they recall the same event somewhat differently: after all, some of these events took place up to twenty-one years ago. But it is only from their recollections that we can begin to piece together how the programmes were made: they are the people who have brought the Cybermen to our TV screens.

Perhaps Sandra Reid provides the best introduction for *Program* when she says, 'I'm really excited by the prospect of a book on the Cybermen and thrilled that you were able to get in touch with me. It's given me a great kick-along to think that something we did all that long time ago has actually carried through over two decades. So much has happened since, it's not all that easy to recall the people I worked with and the incidents that took place. It's a bit like revisiting the scene of the crime twenty years later! It's a sobering thought that when I worked on this series, Steven Spielberg and George Lucas were only the boys next door – no one had ever heard of them outside their own street. That made me realise quite how long ago it all started'

## How it all Started

Television first gave its viewers a taste of science fiction in 1953 when Nigel Kneale's classic serial *The Quatermass Experiment* was broadcast during the icy winter of that year. There had been plenty of low budget films dealing with the subject of alien invasions of our planet. But such tales had never been brought into 'your own front room' before. The public was gripped by each of the six frightening thirty-minute episodes. *The Quatermass Experiment* had set the scene. Alien menace from space was to be the subject of many memorable TV productions over the next thirty years.

Two sequels written by Kneale followed quickly: *Quatermass II* and *Quatermass and the Pit*. Then there was Orwell's *1984* with Peter Cushing, and Fred Hoyle's unusual *A For Andromeda* with Julie Christie and Peter Halliday. In the summer of

1963, Sydney Newman and Donald Wilson devised a format for a TV series that would essentially be science fiction for children. They gave the job of producing it to a former colleague of Newman's from his days at ATV. It was Verity Lambert's first job as producer and her task was to find someone to play the mysterious 'Doctor Who' of the title.

The rest is history – how she managed to persuade the actor William Hartnell to take on a sympathetic role after years of playing army sergeants and crooks, how the series started on the same day that the American President was assassinated, how cynics at the BBC thought it would not run for more than five weeks and how, after the Daleks first appeared, the series was destined to go on longer than anyone had dared to contemplate.

After two years, having established herself as a producer, Verity Lambert decided to move on to other productions. Her successor, John Wiles, left the series after only four stories. Script editor Donald Tosh left too and was replaced by one of the BBC's in-house script writers – Gerry Davis. The new producer was Innes Lloyd.

He came to *Doctor Who* reluctantly: 'I wasn't really interested in the mechanics of science fiction unless you could relate it to reality in some way.' He had spent several years working with the Outside Broadcast Unit at the BBC, successfully handling the coverage for *The Eurovision Song Contest* and *Wimbledon*. Producing *Doctor Who* was an ideal opportunity to explore the field of television drama.

*Doctor Who* was going through a particularly bad phase. The public seemed to have lost interest in the adventures of the good Doctor. Viewing figures were declining and even the novelty of the Daleks had worn off. Innes Lloyd set about reshaping the series with several innovative ideas.

One change was a move away from Earth-based historical stories because of the monumental disaster called *The Gunfighters* – possibly the worst story in the programme's history. Another change was the introduction of some new travelling companions for the Doctor. Ben Jackson (Michael Craze) and Polly (Anneke Wills) were introduced in *The War Machines*. As fictional representatives of the 'swinging sixties', it was hoped they would encourage teenagers to watch what was widely regarded up to that time as just a children's serial.

By the end of the third season, Lloyd had produced four stories. He was greatly assisted in this by the programme's script editor, Gerry Davis.

'Gerry was an excellent script editor,' says Lloyd. 'He could probe people's minds to see their line of thinking and then talk to them in their own language. He didn't just want them to write a story

for him. He wanted to understand the way they wrote a story. The ideas, the characters, their motives, he knew inside out.'

Lloyd and Davis had worked fast to introduce the realism they wanted. But the peak of their work came with the final story of that season, *The War Machines*, the first story that Lloyd was happy with. It achieved a plausibility by bringing more science fact than science fiction into its plotline; and it marked the first contribution to *Doctor Who* by Kit Pedler, a doctor who was to become co-creator of the Cybermen.

To ensure that the science fiction of the plotlines had a plausible element, Lloyd decided to bring a scientific adviser into the production team. Davis recalls, 'To me fell the rare pleasure of meeting such scientific luminaries as Patrick Moore, Professor Lethbridge, and even Dr Alex Comfort (in pre sex-manual days). I tried to gauge the flexibility of their response to fictional situations by asking what would happen if, say, a vast asteroid comes on collision course with Earth. "Utterly impossible!" was Patrick Moore's dismissive reaction.'

Lloyd takes up the story: 'I went back to the Outside Broadcast Unit, where I'd worked previously, and I talked with my old chums who did all the medicine and science there and I said, "Do you know of any scientists who might have an imaginative mind?" and they said, "Well, there's a guy called Kit Pedler." So I thought I had better meet Kit.'

After a brief meeting, Pedler was invited to come to the production office and be interviewed by Gerry Davis.

From the window of Davis's office at Union House there was a clear view of the recently constructed GPO Tower. It was new and looked almost alien. He would throw out the question, 'If an evil power had control of the Post Office Tower, how would it invade London?' Generally, the answers he got were either totally impractical – because such a story could not be made on the show's tight budget – or they were just too weak for a *Doctor Who* story.

Pedler's idea was different. He quite logically pointed out that the instigator would probably be a rogue computer, housed at the top of the Tower, and would use some form of war machine as a spearhead for an invasion. Davis loved the idea and asked Pedler to write a script around it. Lloyd recalls:

'Kit was nervous about writing. He'd never done anything like it before. It was a totally new area to him. His knowledge and understanding of science – and how he could twist facts into plausible science fiction – was the main element that came to light while he was with us.'

Pat Dunlop, one of the BBC in-house writers, was given the job of helping Pedler develop the concept into a workable plotline. Ian Stuart Black then took over and wrote the script with Pedler,

Sandra Reid

adding the odd scene now and again. Together they produced *The War Machines*. Director Michael Ferguson turned the story into one of the successes of the season. For Lloyd, there was no doubt that the right person had been found for the job and that he was also a very special person:

'Kit was a very passionate man. Not only did he love life, but also everything around him. He hated to see people who could not live life to the full – which is probably why he became a doctor. If Kit was still alive today, I'm sure he would be out there leading Greenpeace into battle. He was a strong supporter of such things. He just wanted pollution to stop and the Earth to be given its chance to grow again.'

'He created a great furore in a supermarket once,' recalls Sandra Reid. 'He was very upset about the amount of packaging that was put on consumer goods, so to show his outrage and indignation he removed all the packaging from everything he'd bought and dumped it all on the checkout. There was a great hoo-ha about it. If I remember rightly, he was charged with something or other by the police. But that was his stand against having to pay so much just for packaging – and he had a point there, I think. He was an awfully pleasant man, very friendly, very interesting to talk to – although, I suppose, perhaps a little scientific. Unless you were tuned into that kind of thing, he wasn't all that easy to follow.'

After the success of *The War Machines* Lloyd asked Kit Pedler to submit ideas for a possible future script. 'Kit came back with several story-lines,' remembers Gerry Davis. 'They were all based upon familiar sci-fi themes which had been already aired in one way or another on the programme – including one about a race of "Star Monks" inhabiting a twin planet of Earth's. I gently rejected them and asked him what his main phobias as a doctor were. "Dehumanising medicine" was his answer – and it led us to a race of beings who had carried Cybernetics to its logical conclusion and become "Cybermen". We developed the "Star Monks" story and *The Tenth Planet* was born.'

### *The Tenth Planet*: Birth of the Cybermen

The title for Pedler's second *Doctor Who* story came from his wife. She pointed out that if we discovered another planet in the solar system it would become known as the 'tenth planet'. Lloyd approved of the title and arranged for the story to be the first of the next season. But an unexpected problem changed his plans dramatically.

William Hartnell had been playing the Doctor for three years. The exhausting work schedule had taken its toll on him and his health was growing steadily worse. He wished to leave the series. If the programme was to continue after Hartnell left, it would mean another actor taking on the role of the Doctor. Could the public be persuaded that it was the same character?

Season Four was quickly re-scheduled. *The Tenth Planet* would be broadcast as the second story of the season and would include the changeover of the Doctors. Gerry Davis thought the changeover might be arranged by having the Doctor die and come back to life as a different man. Innes Lloyd extended the idea and imagined the Doctor's body rejuvenating. As for the actor to replace Hartnell, Patrick Troughton was eventually chosen from a list which included Ron Moody and (now Sir) Michael Hordern.

All that remained was for *The Tenth Planet* to be written. At first, as with *The War Machines*, Pedler was to be assisted by Pat Dunlop. But very early on Gerry Davis stepped in and the now famous writing partnership with Kit Pedler began in earnest.

Innes Lloyd could see that they worked well together: 'There was total understanding between them. Their minds worked along the same tracks.'

The script was only just finished in time to allow the director to complete his pre-production work. The task of directing this important story was given to Derek Martinus, who had worked on two stories in the previous season, *Galaxy Four* and *Mission to the Unknown*. His reputation was excellent and his earlier *Doctor Who* work meant that he was better placed to handle the fraught schedule.

'Hartnell was very ill at that time,' recalls Martinus. 'In fact we had to use a double for him for most of the story. It was obvious he wouldn't be able to carry on much longer so it was a good thing that they brought Pat in when they did. The Cybermen were a good way of letting the First Doctor bow out gracefully.'

Having got a script and director, Lloyd knew that the success of *The Tenth Planet* would hinge on what these new monsters, the Cybermen, were to look like. That was the job of the costume designer.

'We had a wonderful costume designer called Sandra Reid,' remembers Innes Lloyd. 'She worked wonders on the peanut tight budget we had. Each story required a different set of elaborate monsters and she produced weird and amazing creatures with money that was scarce. Most of the aliens were held together with glue and sellotape. In fact I think most things on *Doctor Who* were done with sellotape in those days.'

Though she was to be with the programme for the next two seasons, Sandra had not previously worked on *Doctor Who*. 'That first story was interesting and different for me,' she says, 'because I'd never done any science fiction before. I felt quite uncomfortable about it, though it was a thrill to be given *Doctor Who* to do. Daphne Dare had worked on it before me and thoroughly enjoyed it. I used to share an office with her and the mantle fell on me when she was taken off *Doctor Who* to work on something else. We were actually labelled "costume supervisors" at that time. It was before the days when the nomenclature went all upmarket and we all became "designers".

'Lovely Innes Lloyd was the producer – he was an absolute delight to work with. The director was Derek Martinus. He was a very enthusiastic guy and very excited about the prospect of doing the

Cybermen. He talked a lot about Kit Pedler – filled us in on Kit's background: what he was, what he was interested in, and generally gave him a great "promo" before we met him. In those days, cybernetics was virtually unheard of by people like me. Nowadays, we take it very much as an increasing part of our lives, but then it was something very new to think that parts of our body could be replaced by machines.'

It was up to her to create for the TV screen the

**Drawings of Cybermen by Sandra Reid**
BELOW RIGHT Original design sketch (1966)
BELOW LEFT *Tenth Planet* Cyberman drawn from memory (1986)

Cyberman MK I    Tynan '86

Cybermen.
Practical)

Peter Kindred
2591

S Reid

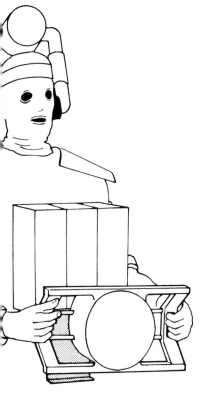

monsters of Kit Pedler's imagination, visualised by him in his notes as 'tall, slim, with one-piece, close-fitting, silver-mesh uniforms.'

'Their faces and heads,' he goes on, 'are normal but under the hair on the head is a shining metal plate stretching from centre hairline to occiput. (This could be disguised with a hat.) Their faces are all rather alike – angular and, by normal definitions, good-looking. On the front of their trunks is a computer-like unit consisting of switches, two rows of lights and a short movable proboscis. They all carry exotic side arms. At the elbow and shoulder joints there are small ram-like cylinders acting over the joints themselves. Instead of flesh there is a transparent arm-shaped forearm covering, containing shining rods and lights but there is a normal hand at the end of it.'

Such sophistication was impossible to achieve on the budget which Sandra Reid had been allotted. Nonetheless, she is characteristically self-deprecating about her achievement: 'I was rather put to the test in designing the original Cybermen costume. In retrospect, I think I did a rather poor job on it. If I had to do it now, of course, it would be a completely different kettle of fish because I'm that much more experienced and there are a lot of materials available now which were unheard of in those days.'

Actor Michael Craze (who was playing Ben, one of the Doctor's companions) recalls little about those early Cybermen. But what he does remember tends to corroborate Sandra Reid: 'I remember how cumbersome the Cybermen first were – and rather shoddily made. Sellotape was used to stick them up. They had trouble with the lighting effects and selecting the right voice modifier for the final voice took some time. But I thought they were rather lovable monsters!'

After making several test costumes a design was finally reached which both director and producer agreed on – mainly because time was running out. Filming for the story had to begin.

To portray his Cybermen, Martinus chose actors who were all over six foot tall. The costumes had to be fitted together on their bodies in several layers. The main part of the costume was a thick, stretchy body-stocking. It covered everything except the hands – they remained uncovered in accordance with Pedler's description. Three holes were cut in the head covering, two for the eyes and one for the mouth. Two layers of thin black gauze were sewn over the holes on the inside with a circular layer of white cloth on the outside. These three holes formed the somewhat restricted apertures through which the actor could see and breathe.

To make the costume look more robotic, a thick polythene suit was put over the cloth. Incorporated into this was a series of thick plastic ribs which were spaced down the arms and legs and

over the chest to give the impression of a mechanical exoskeleton.

Derek Martinus believed this initial attempt to embody Pedler's Cybermen was effective to look at but difficult to work with. 'That first Cyberman story,' he confesses, 'was hell to do. The costumes were good – they'd turned out better than we thought they would. But under the studio lighting they practically boiled alive in their suits. It was up to either me or the PA [Edwina Verner, who was married to Michael Craze] to run through the snow and pick them up.'

Sandra Reid adds, 'It was rather hot weather. It was September but it was still warm. The heat in the film studios at Ealing was pretty nasty – and it was supposed to be at the South Pole! There's a very funny photo of Derek and Edwina pulling a Cyberman up off the ground out of all this polystyrene snow – the poor Cybermen kept falling over. The heat and the great things they carried on their fronts were too much for them.'

These 'great things they carried on their fronts' were the chest units, the heaviest part of the costume. They contained large battery packs to power the coloured flashing lights of the unit and were supported by metal epaulettes clamped on to the shoulders and front of the chest. Cybermen in the background of a scene would take it in turns to have the battery packs removed to relieve them of the weight.

On top of the head was a skullcap. Plastic tubing painted silver was mounted on round metal ear pieces and stuck to each side of the head. These 'jug handles', as they have become known, supported a large lamp. Martinus had wanted the lamp actually to work so one of the technicians fitted a halogen bulb – to be operated by a switch on the chest unit. A test shot was set up, the actor flicked the switch and the light bulb exploded, turning the Cyberman's face black. The idea was dropped.

For obvious reasons the headgear was nicknamed the 'hairdryer'. The light was adapted from the headlamp of a large truck and was extremely heavy. There had to be frequent recording breaks while the director, Edwina and Sandra stuck the Cybermen's headgear back on with the ever-useful sellotape:

'We had awful trouble with the head pieces. It's not surprising because I really didn't do a good job on that – it's what I would now call "very Mickey Mouse". There were some very rude comments from people around the Ealing Studios after the Cybermen had been seen in their costumes, taking a coffee break or whatever. I remember somebody coming up to me and saying, "Is it you who's responsible for those strange looking creatures with the piano accordions on their chests?" I took it as a terrible insult!'

In spite of this, the 'jug handles' and the piano

FAR LEFT Sandra and Edwina attending two Cybermen

LEFT Edwina Verner, Derek Martinus and fallen Cybermen

accordions' persisted through many changes of Cybermen design. They have become a kind of Cyber trade mark.

A feature which has changed radically over the years is the Cyberweapon. For this first story it was an extraordinary sight. It looked like a lamp shade fastened over a reflective dish. And that is what it was. In the centre of the dish was a powerful light bulb which could be flashed on and off by flicking a small switch on the side of the gun. Occasionally, these bulbs exploded – particularly when caught in the cold blast of the giant wind machine which was used to create a blizzard of polystyrene snowflakes.

The costumes were constructed in a great hurry after Lloyd's approval of the design. Out of the seven made, three were carefully put together so that they could be in all the major scenes involving Cybermen, while the rest were less well constructed and kept in the background. Sandra Reid had help with the work:

'I think the costumes were made by a lady who lived in Islington. She had miles and miles of this crin tubing. We had some green and some yellow and there might even have been some kind of pinky-magenta colour so that we'd get some variation in tone. Looking at the photographs of them now I would say that was a dismal failure too. But the stuff was the only sort of tubing I could find because we were short on time and pretty low on finance. Not much has changed there, has it?

'There was a lot of mending and running repairs that went on all the time. With the head pieces, we had to keep taking them off in between shots

because the Cybermen got very hot inside and very sweaty. The fabric started to stain and discolour so we had to take them off every few minutes and dry them out before putting them back on again.

'They were absolutely wonderful, these chaps playing the Cybermen – a lot of them were working on Stanley Kubrick's *2001* and we used to hear all sorts of stories of what they were doing at Elstree – but they really were splendid. They never complained and they were thoroughly professional about the whole thing, though I must say they had plenty to complain about if they had really wanted to.'

To achieve the full potential of these new monsters, Innes Lloyd had decided at the beginning of the production that he wanted them to sound very different from other *Doctor Who* monsters. He had been impressed by the Dalek voice work Roy Skelton had done in a Season Three story *The Ark* so he got him to devise a 'robotic yet human' voice for the Cybermen. Roy Skelton came up with a nasal sing-song voice that was continually alternating in pitch. Sitting off-set, watching a monitor relaying pictures from the studio cameras, he dubbed the voices live through a microphone when a Cyberman opened its mouth on a given cue. This created the eerie effect of words coming from the creature's open mouth without any movement of the lips.

For Episode Four, Peter Hawkins joined Roy Skelton as a second Cyber voice for scenes of dialogue between Cybermen. He used a different method: with the assistance of an Electronic Voice

Frequency Modulator he developed a harsh, emotionless, metallic sound; it was to become the Cyber voice of the next three stories.

The BBC's film studios at Ealing were used for the polar surface. Designer Peter Kindred used the available area to great effect. A trap door in the studio floor was incorporated into the set as the hatchway which leads down to the subpolar tracking station – so saving the expense of building a raised stage to achieve the same effect. Time and money was also saved by using the whirling globe which normally introduced every BBC programme. Turned upside down, it provided the 'reverse-image of Earth' which the Tenth Planet, Mondas, was meant to be.

As for the destruction of Mondas, Sandra Reid explains: 'They had to burn up a polystyrene ball. It was meant to be the Tenth Planet frying up in some incredible way. Nowadays, the rules and regulations are so strict about the toxic fumes which come off that stuff, everybody would be out on strike thinking they'd be poisoned by it all. But not then. So there was this great ball of polystyrene being attacked by blow torches and suchlike and it all just went up in flames. Very crude.'

The finished effect was not one of *Doctor Who*'s most successful: pieces of Mondas could clearly be seen dropping off in great melting lumps and falling downwards – an odd phenomenon for a planet which was meant to be disintegrating in the gravity-free conditions of space.

An altogether more successful effect takes place in the final scene in Episode Four – the all-important transformation of the Doctor from old man to young. In fact, Innes Lloyd had a hand in writing this scene as well as directing it. He used a vision mixer to fade gradually from Hartnell's face into Troughton's. The process of rejuvenation seemed to take place as one watched. 'The changeover from Willie to Pat on that first Cyberman story was great fun to do,' says Lloyd. 'Pat was waving to Willie, shouting "hello, Dad" and things like that. And Willie was muttering, "He'll bring more life into the show." Everyone was happy with the way it went.'

On the eighth of October 1966 – at the end of Episode One of *The Tenth Planet* – the Cybermen were seen on television for the first time ever as they strode menacingly out of a polystyrene snow storm. The last shot zoomed in on the Cyberman's human hand, then panned up to its white eyeless face. Soon, children all over the country were lumbering around school playgrounds pretending to be this new monster from *Doctor Who* – while those still loyal to the Daleks skulked off to another corner. Innes Lloyd could count the Cybermen as a success: 'The Cybermen were exactly the kind of villain that *Doctor Who* needed. Instead of just being another pawn in that everlasting battle with

the Doctor, they were more of a King.'

The public wanted to see more of these new mechanical humanoids. It did not have to wait long. Even as *The Tenth Planet* was being filmed, Innes Lloyd was already planning a sequel.

### *The Moonbase*: Metallic Augmentation

Before the last episode of *The Tenth Planet* had been broadcast, Innes Lloyd went to Kit Pedler and told him that he wanted the Cybermen to feature in a second story – even if they failed to catch on with the public in their first story.

But the Cybermen did catch on. Letters were soon flooding into the production office asking when the Cybermen would next appear. 'It's very hard to pin down exactly why the Cybermen were so popular,' admits Lloyd. 'I'd always thought that the Cybermen had some aspect in their appeal that was lacking in the Daleks. By then, the Daleks had definitely had their day in this country and that's why Terry Nation took his creations over to America. The only thing I can think of is that to the adults they were a more plausible creature than the Ice Warriors, for example, and with the kids I think it was because you couldn't escape from them – other monsters you could, but Cybermen just kept going.'

For the next Cyberman story Gerry Davis wanted to have a situation similar to *The Tenth*

ABOVE RIGHT A *Moonbase* Cyberman on the loose in the shopping area of St Pancras

*Planet* – an isolated group of humans menaced by Cybermen and unable to get outside help. "My basic premise for *Doctor Who* stories in that era of miniscule budgets was to limit the usual dozen tatty sets to one major set around which we could concentrate the entire budget. This made a much more exciting and convincing central location for the drama.' So he and Pedler set the story on a weather base situated on the Moon and manned by a handful of scientists.

Despite their close collaboration, Davis was again not credited as a co-writer. 'We had written *The Tenth Planet* together,' explains Davis, 'but because of BBC policy I was unable, as Story Editor, to claim a credit. For *The Moonbase*, Kit was gravely ill in hospital facing extensive surgery and a lot of our collaboration took place over the hospital bed. Again, I was uncredited – although I shared copyright and script fees with Kit. We were both credited on *Tomb of the Cybermen* because by that time I had left the programme!'

Innes Lloyd thought it important to get the look of the Cybermen right: 'Those first ones were very rushed. The costumes were put together in an awful hurry. That's partly why we brought them back so quickly – it gave the costume girls more time to build a better set of costumes for them. I could see the great potential they had as a monster. We brought them back so soon because we felt that there was a lot more that could be done with them. We wanted to change their image, make them more robotic.'

With these thoughts in mind, Lloyd went back to Sandra Reid. She produced three different designs from which he and director Morris Barry chose one. Shortly before filming began, a set of eight of these new-style Cyber suits were taken out on the local village green at Ealing for a photo call. They caused quite a stir. Unfortunately, Sandra was not there to see it. Like Kit Pedler she spent most of the filming time in hospital.

'I think suddenly the Cybermen must have got to me,' she says. 'I was under the surgeon's knife and quite glad to be there! I do think that's a terribly funny photograph – the only one I've got from *The Moonbase* – where there's a Cyberman standing in front of a man who is reeling back in horror. It looks like a deodorant ad. Either that or the Cyberman must have really awful breath!

'Actually, the costumes were pretty high by the time we finished because of the problems of perspiration. I think most of the blokes wore T-shirts underneath – but precious little else – and with rubber boots and all that vinyl and fibreglass and the hot lights, it was jolly uncomfortable. They certainly earned their money.'

The most obvious improvement in the new costume was the body covering: it was now a one-piece jumpsuit made of vinyl. The hands were concealed by three-fingered, claw-like

'Who's invading Ealing?' Cybermen taking a break during the filming of *The Moonbase*, 1967

gloves of the same material.

'I was much happier with the Cybermen Mark II,' says Sandra. 'The people who made them weren't all that happy though. We bought silver vinyl for the costumes and the people who made them up nearly went bananas. They broke machine needles and they – oh, they just went round the bend working on those costumes. Very difficult stuff to sew. It was topstitched and hard to get under the foot of the sewing machines because it would slide. They had to try different tactics to stitch it properly. But the finished articles did look good, I thought.'

Though the suits were going to be dyed a metallic silver, this was found to be too costly and silver car paint was sprayed over them instead. To counter the claustrophobia which had been caused on *The Tenth Planet* by stretching the body stocking over the head, Sandra Reid designed a separate mask which could be removed in a matter of minutes:

'The man who made the headgear was called Jack Lovell, a clever guy who went to endless trouble with the fibreglass and did a jolly good job on it. Looking at it now though, I must say that I could have come up with a much better idea of how the whole thing fitted together. They were constructed in two pieces, the helmet proper and a back panel which was fastened on with little hooks – you can just make them out in some of the photographs. The tubing at either side was made of perspex and we had to put sticky silver stuff round the mouth and eyes to make them more prominent.'

ABOVE Kaftan (Shirley Cooklin) with Cybermat from *Tomb of the Cybermen*

At the mouth was a flap which could be opened and closed by the actor's jaw and so indicate which of the Cybermen was speaking. Because of the previous failure of the effects department to get the head lamp to function, Sandra Reid ensured that, at worst, a small torch could be slotted in as a substitute. Luckily, when they were constructed, the masks had a very powerful light bulb built into it, powered by a battery pack inside the helmet and worked from a switch on the side of the chest units. (This created the eerie glow which emanated from the Cybermen's heads when they were on the lunar surface.) The air supply inside the mask was not so was constricted as before, but the actor still had to put up with seeing and breathing through a layer of black gauze at eyes and mouth.

An attempt was made to suggest exoskeletally-powered limbs – the 'ram-like cylinders acting over the joints' of Pedler's original conception: 'We used bits of the old crin tubing again – but it was black this time – and some sort of practice golfballs for the joints. The large tubing along the limbs came from a manufacturer who normally made them for vacuum cleaners! He was terribly excited about coming to the BBC with his sample of tubing. It was such a big outing for him to be involved with *Doctor Who*.'

The silver wellingtons were replaced by surplus army boots, painted silver. Initially, the trousers were tucked into the boots but because that looked too military, they were left to hang round the ankle.

Most of the long-suffering actors who played Cybermen in *The Tenth Planet* were brought back to play the new-look Cybermen in *The Moonbase*. Peter Hawkins also returned to provide the Cyber voices. Brian Hodgson of BBC's

Radiophonic Workshop devised new voice modulation equipment for him. Though it produced a chillingly cybernetic effect, Hawkins – who had also provided Dalek voices in previous *Doctor Who* stories – had to suffer for his art. 'Given the choice between Dalek voices and Cybermen voices,' he says, 'I'd choose the Daleks. For the Cyber voice I wore a dreadful false palate in my mouth. It was worked by a small buzzer that I worked from a battery pack. The trick was to mouth the words without speaking. The mouth cavity modulated the buzzing into words. It wasn't much fun wandering round with damp lead hanging out of my mouth. I wasn't a pretty sight. Another problem was that the little diaphragm used to get clogged up with spittle – a constant nightmare.' As if that wasn't bad enough, the constant vibration of the palate in his mouth left him with a chronic headache after the recording session was over.

In *The Moonbase* the Cybermen overcame opposition with an energy field which was seen to flow from their fingertips and into their hapless victim. The effect was achieved with the help of a vision mixer. An arc of electricity was created on a spark machine and this image was superimposed on the shot of a Cyberman pointing at its human target. A similar principle was used for the new-look gun (now a short rod with a cylindrical handle.) The image of a candle-flame was turned on its side and superimposed at the end of the gun.

There were two versions of the lunar surface set. One was built full-scale to be used by the actors and one was a much smaller version – built into part of the other – for all the model shots, such as the Cyber spacecraft landing. This was used to great effect for the sequence where the crew of the TARDIS first see the moonbase. Panning from actors to the moonbase model in the smaller set effectively conveyed the impression of the base being several miles away.

Such effects were simple and cheap and, above all, convincing. Just as convincing had to be the sequences on the surface of the moon where the Doctor and his companions take giant leaps in the low-gravity conditions. A system of Kirby wires was used to 'fly' them and the camera was hand-cranked at four times its normal speed to create a graceful, slow-motion effect. In this way too, the Cybermen could be seen to float away from the Moon's surface when the Gravitron neutralises the gravity around them at the end of the fourth episode. According to Victor Pemberton, it was all great fun:

'I played one of the crew on *The Moonbase* and I think I was killed off fairly early on – only to be brought back to life. Black streaking lines were painted onto my face. It took ages. I had to go into Make-up hours before we started filming. There was one scene where I had to go out to the lunar surface with another technician. It involved having to climb a ladder and for some reason we just couldn't get up there without bursting out laughing.'

The viewers certainly enjoyed it. Of all the stories of that season so far, *The Moonbase* was the best received. Innes Lloyd's faith in Pedler and Davis's creations was being repaid. It seemed that the Cybermen might be around for some time.

## *Tomb of the Cybermen*: Sepulchre of Steel

*The Moonbase* was a big hit. The viewing figures were better than Innes LLoyd had ever hoped for and the Cybermen were now a firm favourite with the public. He quickly made plans to conclude the season with a third Cyberman story and asked Kit Pedler and Gerry Davis to make it the best one yet, promising a large budget and plenty of time to write it.

'Innes wanted to move on and offered me the producership,' says Davis. 'But I'd previously stood in for Innes and other producers and preferred to remain on the script side. I recommended Peter Bryant for the job and took up an offer to edit a new Alan Plater series produced by David Rose.' He did, however, continue to work with Pedler on the third Cyberman script.

'When I joined the production team,' recalls Bryant, 'things seemed to move so fast. One moment I was there trailing Gerry who wanted to go onto other things, and practically a week after he'd gone, Innes started to say he was intending to go as well and did I want to take over from him. Of course, I jumped at the chance and he gave me a Cyberman story to do as a kind of test run.'

*Tomb of the Cybermen* was to be broadcast as the first story of Season Five. Innes Lloyd explains, 'I handed over the producer's chair to Peter who was my script editor. We both worked quite heavily on *Tomb* but I left the actual production to Peter.'

Victor Pemberton, actor in *The Moonbase*, was a friend of Bryant's and remembers: 'Peter Bryant got me the job of script editor for that one story he produced while Innes had a short break. We knew each other from our days in radio. After *Tomb*, while Peter was learning the ropes of the job from Innes, I did the next three up until Innes actually left. Peter's wife was in *Tomb*. She played the arch villain called – I think it was – Kaftan.'

Morris Barry was to direct again and had clearly built up a rapport with the Cybermen from directing *The Moonbase*. Victor Pemberton says, 'Morris was a wonderful director. I knew him from the last Cyberman story. He knew Cybermen very well.' And Cyberman Charlie Pemberton (no relation to Victor) adds, 'Morris Barry was a wonderful director. He understood the Cybermen inside out. It was almost as though he had a deep respect for them although he would never speak of it. It was fun to do and I find it incredible that people still remember it after all this time.'

Barry decided to use the Cybermen costumes from *The Moonbase*. Sandra Reid added a few details to make them look slightly different – for example, two thin black pipes were attached at the top of the chest unit and were run over the shoulders – but basically, the design was unaltered. There were eight costumes already made. But to accommodate a new kind of Cyberman, another had to be custom built for the Cybercontroller. Michael Kilgarriff, the actor who played the Cybercontroller, was 6ft 5in tall; he later played the Giant Robot in a future *Doctor Who* adventure. There was no chest unit on his costume and no pipes or tubes. Instead of the normal headgear, the Cybercontroller had an enlarged dome without 'jug handles'. Michael Kilgarriff casts his mind back to the role:

'As regards the Controller, that caused a lot of problems I remember. I had a giant brain which was transparent, with lights inside that pulsated. I had a battery gadget inside the mask which, as with most things, was always going on the blink. You couldn't quite see through it – which made it look like a glowing brain.'

Sandra Reid remembers the lights in the Controller's helmet: 'They were functional. I'm not sure how they turned on and off but I think they were operated by the actor himself. The helmets were pretty uncomfortable to wear. We had to put some foam rubber inside the top so they'd be more comfortable. On the subject of discomfort, if they wanted to go to the loo they had an awful time: they had to get out of the whole jolly thing – helmet, piano accordion and body costume. So before they put their costumes on, it was a case of "have you all been, boys?"'

Actor Hans de Vries still clearly recalls the ordeal: 'Particularly vivid is the sheer discomfort of playing a Cyberman for two weeks. It was all studio work, all inside, and by the end of the day you literally had an inch of sweat in the bottom of your wellies. It was very, very uncomfortable and very claustrophobic.'

Charlie Pemberton has similar recollections. But for him it was all worth it: 'The studio lights made you ever so sweaty – you would quite literally find your wellingtons full of water when you finished in the studio for a day. The pipes on my left arm kept coming away – the poor costume girls kept having to put me back together. But it was a very special thing to do *Doctor Who* – almost a privilege – because it was the ultimate as far as science fiction was concerned in those days. Being a Cyberman was an experience to remember.'

Michael Kilgarriff

RIGHT Special Effects De-signer Michael John Harris (standing) and Designer Martin Johnson working on the set of *Tomb of the Cybermen*

*Tomb of the Cybermen* did not only introduce the character of Cybercontroller. 'Kit Pedler introduced those weird rodents called Cybermats in that story,' points out Victor Pemberton. 'I remember being in the studio and the technicians were chasing them around the place. They couldn't work the radio control system. It was hilarious.'

Though some of them were worked with wires, several were battery controlled. It was up to an off-set technician to point them in the direction of the actors and cross his fingers as the creatures went charging off. Michael Kilgarriff says, 'They were like little mice, always scurrying around your feet. They were always going wrong as well. Direct them one way and they went in the opposite direction.'

Interestingly, Gerry Davis reveals that the inspiration for the Cybermats was not in fact based on a rodent but on 'silverfish, those tiny, ancient-seeming, shy creatures that can be seen scuttling occasionally around the house'. Whatever their origins, the Cybermats certainly impress-ed the viewers. In fact, they to were to reappear in two later Cyberman stories. At the time of *Tomb of the Cybermen*, Pedler and Davis hoped they might interest a toy manufacturer in these endearing creatures but the BBC would not grant the rights. It was not until the mid-eighties that plastic kit and metal cast versions became avail-able – a fact which indicates something of their enduring appeal.

*Tomb of the Cybermen* was the first Cyberman story to afford the luxury of location filming. It was done shortly before the previous *Doctor Who* story had finished production because none of the regular cast was needed for the scene where Professor Parry's expedition first discovers the great doors of the Tomb. Later scenes involving the Doctor, Jamie and Victoria in front of the massive Tomb doors were done in the studio. A transparency of these doors was fitted in front of the camera during location shooting to give the illusion of their being discovered in the distance.

The entrance area of the Tomb allowed desig-ner Martin Johnson to imagine an area intended by the Cybermen to accommodate any humans intelligent enough to have gained access to the Tomb. The table and stools were human-sized and covered with a padded silver material embellished with a darker, smaller version of the Cyber emblem seen on the the doors of the Tomb. The control console which worked on principles of logical progression was also built to human proportions and was a working prop. It was vaguely in the shape of a 1950's radio. Its large, circular, patterned front was transparent and covered in symbols representing the logical language of the Cybermen. These could be illuminated from behind and the level of light varied in intensity as the controls were operated. To each side of the control panel was a huge door – built to Cyber proportions – and set in the floor was a massive hatchway which swung open on a hinge and was meant to lead down to the cryogenic chamber.

To judge by the vivid image of it that remains with those involved almost two decades on, it was the cryogenic chamber which presented the most spectacular sight both in the studio and when the story was actually transmitted. It was a gigantic set of layered catacombs.

Sandra Reid: 'I do remember quite a bit about working on the third story and it was the filming at Ealing I remember most. There was a terrific set, as you'll see from the photographs. It was very clever and it worked extremely well. It was very exciting to see all those Cybermen suddenly start to come to life and burst out of their bee-like hives through all that plastic film. I can remember quite clearly the finished product when it was shown on TV and thinking it looked really good.'

Richard Kerley (a Cyberman): 'The main thing that struck me was just how alien the set looked – a vast honeycombed structure that looked very unearthly. It was a bit cramped inside the little rooms on each level but when we all broke out and started to climb down you could almost sense how good it looked. I saw the finished programme when it was on television and I remember thinking it was all worthwhile.'

Victor Pemberton: 'The tomb itself was incredible. It was vast. Ever so impressive.'

Michael Kilgarriff: 'I was very impressed with the *Tomb* sets. There was this enormous construction almost like a honeycomb with all these Cybermen inside. They weren't all live. There were one or two that just had empty suits inside them which were propped up. They could only be seen faintly. I suppose they hadn't defrosted properly.'

Hans de Vries: 'There was a catacomb of passages. Part of it was a sort of honeycomb with chambers in it that the Cybermen stood in before we were woken up very slowly into life. Bees in the honeycomb slowly being brought to life.' (Here, Hans may be unconsciously recalling Klieg's line from *Tomb*: 'Like a gigantic honeycomb and bees waiting for the signal to arise from their winter sleep.')

The large structure was built up on scaffolding, three storeys high. It rose like a pyramid with each higher level smaller than the one beneath. On each level were the chambers in which Cybermen were stored in what was meant to be frozen suspended animation. Transparent plastic, stencilled with the Cyber emblem, covered the circular entrance of each cell. Sprayed down with paint, it looked as though it was covered in frost. Each of the cubicles had lights inside which could be brought up on cue – giving the actor inside the signal to break through the plastic. Hans de Vries says, 'I was in one of these chambers, as in a womb, and had to burst through some plastic sheeting. No difficulty there: we were all picked for size in those days, all well over six foot tall. I'm 6ft 2in and that was the average size.' As well as this large structure, a smaller version of the set was built to enable Barry to film sequences where the Tombs were being activated and defrosting.

The Controller was housed in a larger chamber at the centre base of the pyramid. When the door opened to reveal the Controller, a powerful light at the back of the cell kept this huge, new-look Cyberman in silhouette until it stepped out fully into the general light of the set. All around the honeycomb structure were set up high walls covered in silver foil to reflect the light and

Director Morris Barry in front of *Tomb* set during filming at Ealing

increase the feeling of being inside a huge cryogenic structure.

Peter Hawkins returned for the third time and on this occasion provided all the Cyber voices. He differentiated the Controller from the other Cyberman voices by adjusting the voice palate. Hans de Vries again: 'I remember Peter Hawkins providing the voices and I think we made some sort of hissing sounds – but you could certainly call mine a non-speaking part!'

Michael Kilgarriff's was technically a non-speaking part too. But, though he did not speak the Controller's lines, he had nevertheless to learn them: 'The Cybermen had movable mouths – like letter-boxes. When you were inside the mask you could open it with your jaw. You learnt the lines and the cues but instead of saying them you opened your mouth, which opened the flap. Peter Hawkins said the line and at the end of it – clunk! – you closed your jaw and shut the flap. It was a very weird and a very alien kind of effect and I think it was a pity it was lost with the newer Cybermen. Also you could tell which one was speaking – with the new ones you keep having to move the shoulders. But when that flap opened and the metallic voice came out, it was really alien.'

Another impressive set was the Cyber Revitalisation Chamber. A giant gun-like device was mounted on a large turret. On it was fixed a giant receiver dish which was balanced by a counterweight system that enabled it to move up and down and from side to side. This was aimed at the

RIGHT *Tomb of the Cybermen* makes front cover of Radio Times

recharging 'form' which looked like a giant coffin set on end with a Cyberman-shaped space inside. The Controller had to be seen breaking out of it at one stage so the cover was made of expanded polystyrene and Michael Kilgarriff was able to smash his fist through the surface. It was an effect which worked convincingly and well.

To suggest the cybernetic surgery Toberman had undergone after being caught by the Cybermen, actor Roy Stewart wore a pair of long silver vinyl gloves. Morris Barry made use of the Kirby wire methods he had learnt in *The Moonbase* to create the effect of Toberman being lifted from the ground by the Controller. This comes at the dramatic conclusion of the story when Toberman and the Controller are engaged in a titanic struggle in which both are electrocuted by the closing Tomb doors. The sequence was shot on film so as to have more control over the final effect. Michael Kilgarriff has reason to remember it:

'I collapsed to the floor – which was not a comfortable thing to do with bits of metal sticking into you at all points of the body. I was lying on the floor and then the effects boys shoved plastic tubes into my costume at various points, through which they pumped smoke – so it looked as though I was burning up. Well, they set all this up and suddenly the lights went up. It was the crew's tea break, which was always on the dot to the very second, no matter what you were doing. Suddenly the place was empty and there I was on the floor, helpless, unable to move an inch. I shouted for help and eventually somebody came to my rescue. Luckily, I didn't miss out on my cup of tea.'

*Tomb of the Cybermen* was transmitted during the September of 1967. The day after the first episode had gone out, Peter Bryant had a phone call which he has never forgotten: 'Sydney Newman rang down to my office and said how great he thought Saturday's episode had been. Coming from the man who created *Doctor Who* that was the ultimate compliment, even more so seeing as it was my first job as producer.'

But from other quarters *Tomb of the Cybermen* came in for strong criticism. On the Tuesday following the last episode, BBCTV broadcast a new programme called *Talkback*, chaired by David Coleman. It was meant to provide a forum for viewers to express their feelings about current television shows. That first programme questioned the morality behind showing such violence on a children's serial. The studio audience, many of them concerned parents, were vociferous in their condemnation. Neither Innes Lloyd nor Gerry Davis could be present and Lloyd felt that Peter Bryant had not been with *Doctor Who* long enough to be able properly to present a case. It was the unenviable task of Kit Pedler alone to defend not only his creation, the Cybermen, but

SEPTEMBER 2–8

**Radio Times**

SIXPENCE          LONDON AND SOUTH-EAST

BBC-1
tv
BBC-2

DR. WHO

and his companions face their old enemies, the Cybermen
SATURDAY BBC-1, see page 3

all the monsters in *Doctor Who*. Before being overwhelmed by angry parents and a less than impartial chairman, he managed to put forward something of his own feelings: 'This is horror, admitted, of a sort. But it is horror perpetrated by unhuman beings. They're not relatable to Dad – at least I hope they're not! – and it's entirely harmless in this context.'

Innes Lloyd feels, 'I should take equal blame with Peter – perhaps even more because I should have known it would have turned out as it did. Peter and I should have taken the blame though. It wasn't Kit's fault.

Peter Bryant, however, did discover an effective way of dealing with the outrage which *Tomb* had generated: 'We had a letter from a distraught mother who was complaining that her little boy had been scared to death by the Cybermen. So when we next did a Cybermen adventure I got her to bring him down to the studio. He came in and saw a Cyberman without its mask on and the problem was over. In fact, he didn't want to leave!'

With the perspective of the years it is evident that *Tomb of the Cybermen* is one of the true classics of *Doctor Who*. Though it no longer exists in the BBC's archives, it is still one of the best remembered of the Patrick Troughton adventures. In many ways it marks the end of an era for the Cybermen. Kit Pedler and Gerry Davis would never again collaborate on a Cyberman story. Neither would Innes Lloyd nor Morris Barry nor Sandra Reid be involved again with Cybermen. At least, that is what Sandra Reid imagined:

'When I came to the end of that last story, I

remember thinking, "That is that. I will never have to have anything to do with the Cybermen ever again." How wrong can you be? It's obvious I'm going to carry the guilt of making those early Cybermen to the grave. I've got a horrible feeling that on my tombstone it will say, "She designed the Cybermen!" I suppose it's very easy to look back and be highly critical. For *Tomb*, as for the two previous stories, it was the same old problem of "we haven't got much money and you've overspent again". One is terribly limited by the amount of money one has to spend. But it's lovely to know that they made enough impact – even as they were – to keep coming back. They look quite spooky, I suppose, don't they?'

## The Men Behind the Cybermen

*Tomb of the Cybermen* marked the end of Gerry Davis and Kit Pedler's contribution to *Doctor Who* as a writing team. However, Pedler was to submit the plotlines for the next two stories; and Davis returned to the Cybermen in 1974 in order to bring them back to the screen after a long absence of their own. Between them, Pedler and Davis established a mythical foundation for the Cybermen, strong enough for other writers to build on and extend. They created the possibility of a never-ending story about the Cyber Race.

In *The Tenth Planet* we learn where the Cybermen come from and why they became cybernetically augmented. Pedler and Davis imagined an almost tragic race of beings desperately seeking, above all else, to survive. In doing so, they had divorced themselves irrevocably from their former humanity. In her designs, Sandra Reid, perhaps unconsciously but very effectively, reflected this tragic quality in the Pierrot-like faces of those first Cybermen.

In *The Moonbase* the Cybermen become more concerned with conquest and destruction. Again, this is reflected in the change to a more robotic, militaristic costume. A human face is no longer suggested under clinging fabric and the human hands have gone.

With *Tomb of the Cybermen* Pedler and Davis showed how insidious a threat the Cybermen were. Five hundred years after they were thought to have died out, they could still be reawakened to threaten humanity once more. In writing it within an established 'Ancient Egyptian horror film' format, they gave the idea an added resonance which was to make it one of the best of the Cyberman

stories and a classic *Doctor Who* adventure.

On their own, they did not produce the same quality of work for *Doctor Who*. Pedler's scientifically-based ideas were good and imaginative: the Cybermen hatched from eggs in *The Wheel In Space* is an example. Davis's feeling for story-telling produces evocative drama: witness witness the 'Marie Celeste' setting of the Nerva Beacon in *Revenge of the Cybermen*. But it is the mix of their separate talents – one for science, one for fiction – which produced the headiest brew: science fiction at its best.

This successful alchemy was not at an end after they finished writing for *Doctor Who*. In the summer of 1969 they brought a new kind of drama to the screen. *Doomwatch* was an SF thriller series with a difference – developing situations out of real environmental crises. Several of the stories, anchored in scientific reality, literally came true in the newspaper headlines even as they were being broadcast.

*Doomwatch* was a smash hit and a second season was commissioned soon after the first was shown. Later, however, both Pedler and Davis left because of irreconcilable differences with the producer, who saw the series more in terms of character clashes than original environmental concepts. Their judgement proved accurate: the second season was nowhere near as good as the first; after a dreary third season, the series was cancelled.

Together, Pedler and Davis produced three novels, published by Souvenir Press, based on the concepts which they had not covered in *Doomwatch*. Then they went their own ways once more. They were destined never again to work together. Kit Pedler died on May 27 1981 at the age of 53.

Gerry Davis now lives in California where he works as a writer with several successful film scripts and many episodes of television series to his name. He returns to England every so often and has novelised several of the *Doctor Who* adventures on which he worked.

Together, Kit Pedler and Gerry Davis created one of the most popular of *Doctor Who's* celebrated cast of monsters. Together, they created the Cybermen.

### *The Wheel In Space*: Round in Circles

Season Five had begun with a Cyberman story so Peter Bryant decided to end it with one. Shortly after the transmission of *Tomb of the Cybermen*, Kit Pedler had submitted a brief storyline called *The Space Wheel*. Bryant hoped to use it when he had fully taken over from Innes Lloyd. It was with *The Web of Fear* that Bryant finally became producer in his own right. Script editing was taken over by Derrick Sherwin.

Because Pedler was not available to work on his plotline, Sherwin contacted *Doctor Who* writer David Whitaker who agreed to work it into a six part serial. Whitaker stuck fairly closely to Pedler's format although he injected several ideas of his own and expanded on some of Pedler's. A case in point was the Cyberplanner: Pedler had wanted one Cyberman who would look totally unlike the others – with a vast domed brain case, supported by a thin weak body; Whitaker envisaged a being similar to the *Dan Dare* Mekon who would float around on a saucer-like chair. In the end, neither idea predominated. Budget restrictions and lack of time led, almost by default, to a structure of wires and metal pipes with an egg-shaped ball at its centre.

Tristan de Vere Cole was hired to direct this fourth Cyberman story which was now to be called *The Wheel In Space*. Relatively new to directing, he had previously worked on *Doctor Who* as production assistant to Rex Tucker on the ill-fated Hartnell story *The Gunfighters*.

The completed script of *The Wheel In Space* arrived ahead of schedule. All was set for production to start. But two days before it was due to go into studio, the scene shifters at the BBC went out on strike. 'This affected us quite seriously,' de Vere Cole recalls. 'One week we would be in one studio and the next we'd been moved not only to a different studio but to a different sound stage, like going to Ealing to Shepperton and back again. I seem to remember it went on throughout that story. Such was the cost of having to move the sets from one place to another, the show went vastly over its tiny budget.'

Another drain on the budget was caused by the refusal of the BBC Special Effects Department to become involved in production. They felt that the complex effects required by the script would leave them no time for their work on other series. Peter Bryant sought out an independent company to undertake the work. He found Bill King and Trading Post. They were expensive but guaranteed to get the job done on time. They were as good as their word and Bryant used them again on the next Cyberman story, *The Invasion*, and in another two *Doctor Who* adventures, *The Krotons* and *The Seeds of Death*.

De Vere Cole was not very satisfied with the look of the Cybermen from *Tomb*. For *Wheel* he

wanted something different: 'A much more complex design – more bits attached to their limbs. I thought they looked a bit dull in the previous story. They looked exactly like men in robot costumes – which is what they were!'

The *Wheel* versions were designed by Martin Baugh. It was his sixth story of the season and he had already designed two of the more notorious of *Doctor Who*'s monsters, the Ice Warriors and the Yeti. 'The designer came up with a kind of framework that went over the main body of the costume,' says de Vere Cole. 'The trouble was that it was so delicate, the joints at the hips and shoulders kept breaking and so the final effect was lost because we couldn't afford to waste time continually fixing them.'

The basic body costume was a version of the 'wetsuit' seen in the last two stories. It was padded to make the limbs seem slightly more weighty and robotic; it also helped to relieve the strain on the costume of the heavier fixtures and fittings.

The chest units were the ones used in *The Moonbase* and *Tomb of the Cybermen*. In order to make them look different they were sprayed with a duller shade of silver paint and fixed on upside down – with straps that were all too apparent in some scenes. The socket for the Cyber-gun which had been added at the bottom of the *Tomb* chest units was cut away and the surface painted over. It was de Vere Cole who wanted the variously coloured light bulbs inside the chest units to indicate when they were in action. Shots had been planned of the Cybermen floating through space with only the lights on their head and chest units at first being visible. Kirby wire and a black 'space' backcloth would again have been used for this effect but the problems caused by the strike meant that this approach had to be dropped.

The delicate framework over the Cybermen costumes was a structure of wire, thin rods and strips of metal so fragile that it often came apart during the filming of a scene. Consequently, the Cybermen are seen to become more immobile as the story progresses – until they are reduced to curt nods with hands by their sides in order not to fall to pieces. Of course, the dressers had with them at all times a roll of sellotape to stick them together again. In fact, the addition of the sellotape was found to be a help – under the bright studio lights it lent the rods a metallic glint!

The three-fingered gloves were augmented by thimble-like metal cups placed over each digit. They looked effective and are caught in all their fascinating detail in a close-up at the beginning of Episode Three when a Cyberman's fist bursts through its 'birth pod'. Inside the costume for this shot, incidentally, was a technician and not an actor.

The silver army boots were back for this story

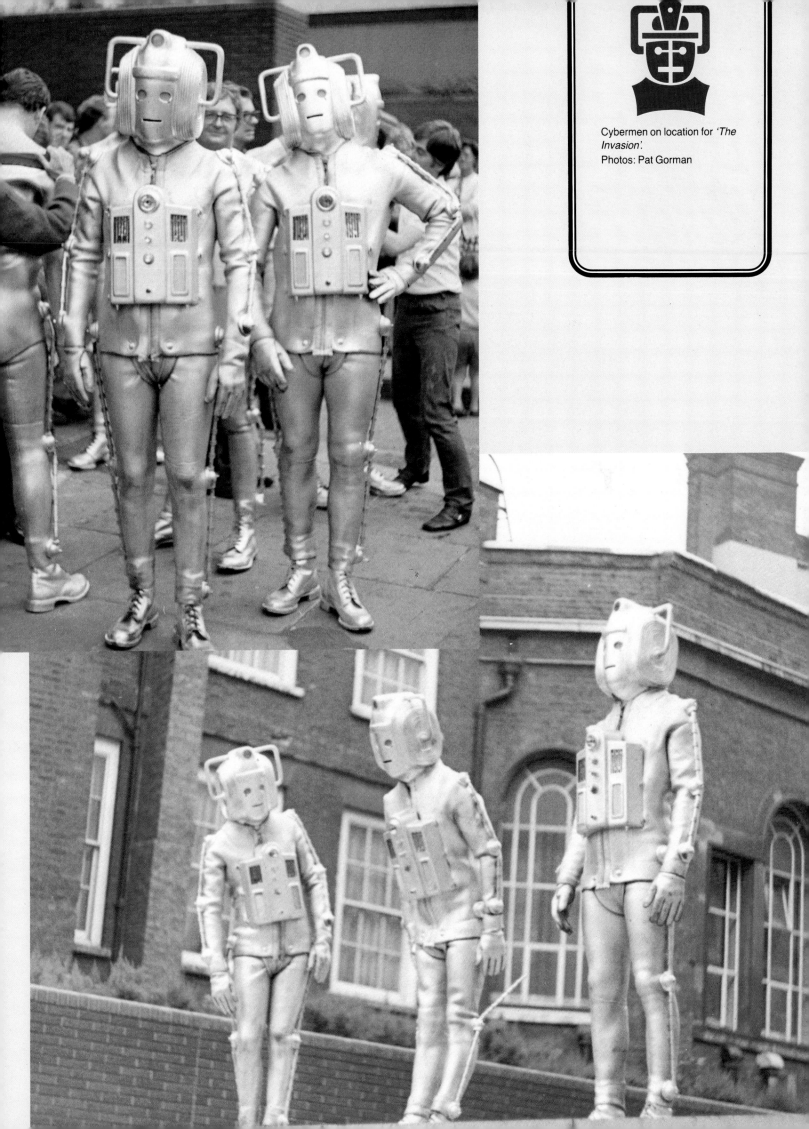

Cybermen on location for *'The Invasion'.*
Photos: Pat Gorman

# FUTUREVIEW
## The Shape of Cybermen
## to come..?

The supreme Cyber Co-ordinator, suspended in the controlled bio-mechanical environment of its impenetrable sanctum deep in space, surveys on a surrounding screen a distant battle front. The Cyberleader – of a deadly new species of Cybermen – communicates progress…

The making of a Cyberleader –
'Silver Nemesis' on location,
London.

Photos: © Patricia Papps

after the silver wellies had appeared in the previous story. As with the boots in *The Moonbase*, the rims had been trimmed down. However, wellies do make an occasional, not to say odd, appearance due perhaps to the confusion of changing recording venues. Added to that, one of the Cybermen recalls that if a scene was to feature only their upper half, they would shoot it without boots to relieve some of the heat.

An interesting detail was added to the Cybermen's helmets which would remain until the big revamp of *Earthshock*. Teardrop holes were drilled at the corner of each eye and at the mouth. Apart from allowing the actor a slightly better air circulation within the mask, it emphasised something of the tragic 'Pierrot' quality suggested in the very first Cybermen. The lights fitted into the dome of the head were seldom used in this story – except for the Cyber hypnosis sequences.

Martin Baugh had originally planned on making a total of seven Cybermen costumes which might then, he hoped, survive to be used for the next Cyberman story. But as it turned out, the budget would only allow two costumes to be put together and, considering the problems that were encountered with them, it was probably just as well they were not used again. One of the Cybermen, however, did return in the next story. De Vere Cole had tracked down the tallest actors he could find to play the two Cybermen in *Wheel* and one of them, Gordon Stothard, went on to appear in *The Invasion*, not as a Cyberman quite, but as a warehouseman whose body had been cybernetically strengthened.

Pedler had originally wanted hundreds of Cybermen to be seen walking through space at the end of the story. In the circumstances only a small group was seen, walking in line, an impression created by overlaying several filmed sequences of the same two Cybermen walking one behind the other.

Roy Skelton returned – after an absence of two stories – to provide one the Cybermen's voices. So, for the fourth and final time, did Peter Hawkins. Skelton used several different kinds of voice modulator to get a rough voice which Brian Hodgson then processed through a prototype sound distortion box recently made for the BBC Radiophonic Workshop. This system broke down while Episode Three was being recorded, so Hodgson had to modulate Skelton's voice through one of the studio boom microphones. Unfortunately, it did not match up with the earlier voice at all well. Hawkins continued to use the palate which had been made for him on *The Moonbase* and provided the voice of the Cyberplanner and the second Cyberman.

*The Wheel In Space* saw the second appearance of the Cybermats. They were an improvement on those in *Tomb of the Cybermen* on two counts. Firstly, they looked better: the spine which ran down their back were now smooth bumps and the fringed skirting was made more flexible; and the black pupils, which formerly gave their eyes a rather endearing quality, were gone. Secondly, they were far easier to control: though they were operated by the same methods – radio control, batteries and 'invisible' wires – the control unit was now vastly improved and all the scenes involving them were shot on film to avoid the difficulties of interference from the television cameras.

A total of four Cybermats were made by Bill King and Trading Post – many fewer than for the previous story. They were also responsible for the sequences depicting the Cybership and the Wheel itself, floating in the blackness of space. Although it was a costly process, the effects were completed in good time, making it easier for de Vere Cole when he came to edit the whole thing together.

Looking back on it all now, Tristan de Vere Cole concludes: 'My main memory of directing *The Wheel In Space* was the atmosphere that was on set. It was so friendly and co-operative. No one caused any fuss. Patrick was super to work with and so was Frazer. Little Wendy was doing it for the first time so she was a bit nervous. It was very relaxed – although it was absolute chaos to do. One week Patrick decided he was off on holiday so a double had to be found fast. I have a feeling it was Chris Jeffries who I knew quite well. But after it was shown I heard from one of my friends working at the BBC that it had done very well in the ratings – highest in the season or something like that. Overall, although there were a lot of problems, it was a very enjoyable story to do.'

### *The Invasion*: Hypnotic Effects

While *The Wheel In Space* was still in production, Peter Bryant requested another Cyberman story from Kit Pedler. What arrived was a short storyline in a six part format called *Return of the Cybermen* in which the Cybermen used a giant computer company to assist them in an invasion of the Earth.

As Bryant prepared Season Six, he knew it would be difficult to better Season Five which had contained so many classic stories. Added to that, he had a restless star: Patrick Troughton was making signs that he wanted to leave *Doctor Who*. Bryant also had to face script complications: the first two stories, *The Dominators* and *The Mind Robber*, were extensively revised at the last minute; then the next story, a four-parter about the invasion of a space station, fell through; finally, a six-part serial by comedy writer Dick Vosburgh was scrapped. Bryant decided that now was the time to use Pedler's storyline.

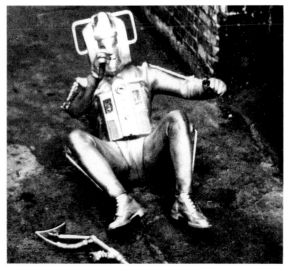

'That first UNIT story,' he recalls, [talking about *The Web of Fear*, though UNIT had not actually been formed then], 'was a big hit, so after a while I thought it would be good if we brought them back. Derrick and I started tossing ideas about on what to give them to fight. We both agreed that the Cybermen were the ideal choice.'

There was a large gap to fill so they decided to expand Pedler's idea to eight episodes. It was decided to bring to the new Cyberman story something of the style of *The Web of Fear*. The director of that story, Douglas Camfield, was brought in to help devise the expanded version of Pedler's storyline. The character of Colonel Lethbridge-Stewart was to be reintroduced – again played by Nicholas Courtney – now promoted to the rank of Brigadier.

Because of the Yeti invasion in *The Web of Fear*, an organisation had been set up to combat any other alien attacks on the Earth. It was named – an idea of Camfield's – UNIT (United Nations Intelligence Taskforce). While Sherwin was combining these ideas with Pedler's and working the mix into eight episodes, Terrance Dicks took over as script editor and Camfield continued to contribute other ideas of his own. The story was now simply to be entitled *The Invasion*, a title which did not give away the identity of the invading monsters.

Another idea of Camfield's was that the characters of Professor Travers and daughter Anne might be reintroduced from *The Web of Fear*. But the actors who had played the parts, Jack Watling and Tina Packer, were unavailable for the filming dates. A speedy rewrite by Sherwin metamorphosed the characters into Professor Watkins and niece Isobel.

The principal villain of the story was retained from Pedler's original format. The name 'Tobias Vaughn' came from a book of Christian names which Pedler had browsed through when trying to find a suitably evil-sounding combination. For the portrayal of such malevolence, Camfield turned to Kevin Stoney. This actor had won the Daily Express award for 'Villain of the Year', playing Mavric Chen in *The Dalek Master Plan* which Camfield had directed.

To achieve a similar quality to *The Web of Fear*, Bryant decided to allow a large section of filming to be done on location. It would be costly but well worth while if the authentic atmosphere of Yeti in Covent Garden could be recreated with Cybermen in and around London generally. As it turned out, the format of *The Web of Fear* and *The Invasion* was to be used throughout Jon Pertwee's Earth-bound time as the Doctor. A total of 21 UNIT stories featured over the next few years, with the Brigadier appearing in 19 of them – each time getting more confused by what he was fighting against!

The Production Assistant on *The Invasion* was Chris D'Oyly John: 'My main task was to choose all the locations that were used – like the steps of St Paul's Cathedral, etc. When it came to Vaughn's offices and the kind of factory he had, I found an old Guinness plant that was partly closed down. So after a bit of negotiation I got the go-ahead to use it. I didn't know at the time what would happen. When we started filming, the owners were so pleased by the publicity it was drawing that every lunchtime they supplied us all with crates of their beer. The afternoon filming took longer than usual because everyone was, shall we say, very happy.'

Actor Peter Halliday, who played Vaughn's sidekick Packer, has similar memories: 'There was a certain well-known beer factory that we filmed at – I think it must have been used by every serial in those days – but while we were there they were very hospitable. Shall we say there was plenty of samples of their product available. Pat, Kevin, Dougie, myself and Chris D'Oyly John used to spend many a happy lunch hour together.'

His view of the character he played is interesting: 'Packer was the ultimate baddie, he was so downright nasty. I think he was the evil that Vaughn couldn't express – that's why Packer respected Vaughn so much.'

How such 'ultimate evil' fared in the studio is described by Pat Gorman: 'I had to go charging into Kevin Stoney's office and kill Peter Halliday. We sent it up terribly in rehearsal – it was getting near the end and it was Peter's chance to have a big death scene. It ended up with us trying to outscream each other. Peter went first, then I got shot, so I went down groaning wildly. Great fun.'

Pat Gorman also enjoyed the location work. 'The Cybermen invading London was great fun to do,' he says. 'There was a great feeling of power when we walked down those steps at St Paul's. It was odd to see the crowds behind the crew looking at you as though the Cybermen were real.'

But Chris D'Oyly John's memory is not so rosy: 'It was a great pity about the crowds. Dougie wanted to go to far more places than we did. It was up to me to keep telling the crowd to stay back and

Kevin Stoney

Nicholas Courtney and Ian Marter

Pat Gorman in one of his
many Who guises!

nine times out of ten they just wouldn't co-operate. It drove Dougie wild. He liked to work at a brisk pace and he hated any delay.'

The idea of filming Cybermen at Tower Bridge and outside the Houses of Parliament, marching across Hyde Park and emerging from underground stations, had to be abandoned. Nevertheless, *The Invasion* was to include more location filming than any previous *Doctor Who* story. Other locations were found away from the public eye and the Guinness factory was discovered to have a lot of useful locations: a railway yard as the packing and transportation area for the 'crated' Cybermen; and various exteriors to represent Vaughn's different premises. Other locations included Ruislip, Blackfriars and – no expense spared – a manhole outside the car park of the Lime Grove Film Studios. All interior sequences were shot at Lime Grove in Studio D.

The location for UNIT's base, first seen at the beginning of Episode Two, was an airfield at RAF Northolt near London. Because the military were being portrayed in a good light in this story, Camfield found the people there very helpful, providing them with a Hercules Bomber that doubled as UNIT's mobile headquarters and also providing a set of jeeps. The sequence where the Doctor and Jamie were first brought onto the plane was filmed on the base airstrip with groundcrew willingly acting as extras, wandering round the background.

Peter Bryant appreciated the way in which Douglas Camfield dealt with the difficult eight part format: 'Dougie was a super director. He knew how to balance suspense and action in exactly the right quantities, never going O-T-T but getting it just right. The Cybermen one gave him the chance to try out things he didn't get time to do with the Yeti story.'

This was the Cybermen's fifth story and for the fourth time they underwent a significant change in appearance. The designer Bobi Bartlett wanted them to look very tough and soldier-like – hence the padded suit and the larger heads. Construction of these new Cybermen was carried out by Bill King and Trading Post who also shot all of the model-effects footage, under Camfield's supervision.

Seven costumes were made. The basic body covering was a very thick two-piece rubber wetsuit, sprayed silver. The boots were all silver-sprayed army lace-ups and the gloves were now ordinary five-finger thick black rubber which had to be continually sprayed silver by the Make-up girls since with any movement the paint cracked. On location, the paint glittered metallically. Unfortunately, this did not show up on film.

New chest units were constructed for this story, mainly because there weren't enough of the old ones left for all the Cybermen who were to appear in *The Invasion*. A lighter, smaller, yet more powerful battery pack meant greater mobility for the actor and greater effectiveness for the sewer scenes when the Cybermen's bright lights emerge from the blackness. Bartlett ensured the chest units were as compact as possible, yet keeping close to the previous look.

Thin hollow metal pipes were used to represent the powered exoskeleton. These were sewn on to the wetsuits and held at the joints by small plastic plugs. This enabled the actor to move his limbs without coming apart – as had been the difficulty with *Wheel* – though close inspection of publicity photographs taken at St Paul's Cathedral shows one of the Cyberman's joints adrift. 'I remember one poor chap got a bit hot under the collar,' says Chris D'Oyly John. 'The sweat inside his suit got so bad that he began to squelch as he walked along. And it was that same poor chap who kept coming apart when they walked down those steps. They had pipes running along their legs and his kept coming away. Bruised another one badly when it hit his leg.'

The Cyber heads were a much better design. They were now made from a light form of fibreglass and were much easier to support on the shoulders. As with the previous versions, the eye-sockets and mouth were covered with a thin layer of black gauze. It was with this version that the 'ear-muffs' made their first appearance. The hole at the dome of the head was left empty, although it had been planned to put in a light for the sewer scenes.

Bill King and Trading Post built eight Cyberguns. On location – it was too dangerous for the confines of a studio – smoke charges were placed inside, activated by a trigger on the base of the gun. The effect of gunfire in the studio was achieved with the aid of an optical printer.

For the few Cyber voices needed for this story, a voice modulator was used not unlike Roy Skelton's in *The Tenth Planet*. As well as playing Packer, Peter Halliday provided these voices, though he was not credited for it. He used the modulator set at high frequency for the Cybermen and at low frequency for the Cyberplanner, which featured more centrally in *The Invasion* than in *The Wheel In Space* – and in a more sophisticated form. It consisted of hundreds of glass and plastic tubes fixed onto a large skeletal structure, fitted with glowing lights. Several of the various parts moved and the finished product looked very effective when viewed in the dark setting behind Vaughn's sliding office wall.

*The Invasion* marked the last time the Cybermen would appear with Patrick Troughton. In fact they were to bow out from *Doctor Who* for almost seven years. But Peter Halliday thinks it was a good story for them to go out on:

'*The Invasion* took a long time to film – round about twelve weeks – far longer than the normal stories. After a while we began to get like a large family. There was a great atmosphere on set. Patrick and Kevin got on so well. They were deadly enemies in the serial but out of the view of the camera they were the best of friends.'

**The Years In Between**

The Cybermen did not appear again in their own story until 1975 when Tom Baker had taken over the role of Doctor from Jon Pertwee. During that time, however, they did crop up in the odd *Doctor Who* adventure to make what might be called 'guest' appearances.

The first of these came in the final Patrick Troughton story –*The War Games* by Terrance Dicks and Malcolm Hulke. In Episode Ten of this epic adventure, the Doctor is put on trial by his own race, the Time Lords. As part of his defence, he has projected onto a large viewing screen images of some of the monsters he has encountered. Among images of a Dalek, a Yeti, an Ice Warrior and a Quark, there also appeared a Cyberman. The costume was from the previous Cyberman story, *The Invasion*. Actor Roy Pearce was called in for the day's filming and joined all his fellow monsters for a publicity photo of the Doctor and his TARDIS surrounded by his worst enemies. Director David Maloney took the opportunity to experiment with this group of famous monsters and had photographs taken with their headgear removed and even with their heads swapped round – the Ice Warrior, for instance, wore the Cyberman's head and vice versa.

The next time a Cyberman was seen on *Doctor Who* was well into the Pertwee era – in *The Mind of Evil* by Don Houghton, directed by Timothy Coombe. At the end of one of the episodes, the Doctor has been strapped to a chair and is being menaced by a series of images of his past foes that the deadly Keller machine is projecting. The images were simply cardboard cutouts of stock photographs of various *Doctor Who* monsters. Along with a Dalek, a Zarbi and a War Machine, was a rather blurred picture of an *Invasion*-type Cyberman.

Almost exactly two years later, in *Carnival of Monsters* by Robert Holmes (director Barry Letts), a Cyberman made another brief appearance. Travelling showman Vorg owns a weird machine called the Mini-scope. Something like a peepshow, it contained a selection of different races from various alien cultures – miniaturised so that many hundreds of them can be accommodated within. As Vorg views his collection, an Ogron from *Day of the Daleks* is seen. So too is an *Invasion* Cyberman standing against a cave surface. Pat Gorman was hired to play the Cyberman in this sequence.

These three appearances filled the seven year gap between *The Invasion* and *Revenge of the Cybermen*. After *Revenge*, a further seven years elapsed during which the Cybermen made only one guest appearances. There was to have been another but the programme was never broadcast.

*Shada* by Douglas Adams (later to be author of *The Hitch-Hikers' Guide to the Galaxy* but at that time script editor on *Doctor Who*) was to feature a 'guest' Cyberman. Due to a BBC strike, filming for this six part story was never completed. The plot concerned the search for the greatest villain in Time Lord mythology, the great Salyavin. In the end the Doctor has to confront the evil scientist who is searching for him on Shada, the Time Lords' prison-planet. Several of the prisoners are set free. Amongst them are a Dalek, a Zygon and a Cyberman. Pat Gorman was again signed up to play the Cyberman but the sequence was never filmed.

*Logopolis* by Christopher H Bidmead faced no such difficulties. It was broadcast in 1981 and in it the fourth doctor was fatally injured. His entire life flashed before his eyes – including a clip from *Revenge of the Cybermen* showing Christopher Robbie as the Cyberleader turning on the Doctor.

With *Earthshock* in 1982 the Cybermen made a dramatic return, and featured in three stories within four years. But even during this period they made a guest appearance in another adventure, *Mawdryn Undead* by Peter Grimwade. One sequence featured the Brigadier (who had also returned after a seven year absence) recalling all his experiences with the Doctor (Peter Davison). This was done in the form of sepia photos taken from the show's past. At one point a Cyberman was seen bursting from a cocoon – a still from the beginning of Episode Five of *The Invasion*.

So the years in between the Cyberman stories were never entirely devoid of Cybermen. The lavish use of clips from previous shows was obviously a good way of tapping the rich *Doctor Who* mythos which had been built up over hundreds of episodes of the programme. This was done to great effect in *Earthshock* itself when clips from previous Cyberman stories were woven together to provide an instant history of the Doctor's involvement with the Cyber race.

But the guest appearances served another, perhaps more telling, function. They reminded the viewing public that the Cybermen were never far away. They could always return – a never-ending threat.

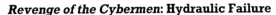

### *Revenge of the Cybermen*: Hydraulic Failure

As the Pertwee era of the series was drawing to a close, producer Barry Letts decided to bring the Cybermen back once more. Hoping to match the popularity the Daleks had newly won after their return in the early 1970's, he contacted Gerry Davis and asked him to write a four part storyline that would reintroduce the Cybermen to the series.

It was at this time that several major changes took place in the show. Jon Pertwee had been the Doctor for four seasons and he decided that his fifth was to be his last. Letts and his script editor Terrance Dicks felt that this was the time for them, too, to leave the show. Tom Baker was chosen to be the fourth Doctor. Pertwee left with *Planet of the Spiders*, while Letts and Dicks stayed on to see the new Doctor through into his first story.

Philip Hinchcliffe replaced Barry Letts as producer. He felt a season of monsters would ensure that the new Doctor was a hit with the viewers. As well as the Cybermen, the Daleks would return once again and Robert Holmes was to bring back his popular Sontarans. Gerry Davis got the go-ahead for his script. The new script editor, Robert Holmes, asked that it feature no more than four Cybermen and that the story be set entirely on a space wheel. Holmes was to link the Cyberman story, *Revenge of the Cybermen*, with a space wheel story, *The Ark In Space*, thus enabling sets to be shared.

Michael E Briant was called in to direct *Revenge of the Cybermen*: 'Whenever I do any filming, I like to go down to wherever the location is and spend several days checking the place out, finding various points where I'll shoot certain scenes, etc. On *Revenge* a sudden budget increase meant we could go on location, so as a setting for the cave system on the planet, Philip decided to splash out on several days' filming in Wookey Hole.'

To accommodate the location scenes, Holmes had quickly rewritten the script – Davis was in America and was unable to do it himself. In fact, Holmes altered a great deal. He introduced the whole of the Voga scenario, changed the characters on the space wheel and added the scenes where the rocket is fired and the beacon nearly crashes into Voga.

'At the time,' says Gerry Davis, 'I wasn't too pleased with the extensive reworking of what was originally a tautly written suspense thriller. But, seeing it now, it seems a fairly creditable effort all round. My original idea was to have the Nerva Beacon doubling as a space gambling casino (later realised in the intergalactic bar sequence in *Star Wars*).'

Briant and Hinchcliffe decided to base the design of the new Cybermen on the *Invasion* versions. Because of the extensive work which was being carried out on the special effects of the other stories of the season, Briant commissioned an independent effects company – the Alistair Bowtell Company – to construct a total of three ordinary Cybermen costumes and one 'Cyberleader' costume. The Cyberleader was a new character which had been central to the storyline since it was commissioned by Barry Letts the previous year. It had always been Kit Pedler's intention to introduce a permanent Leader of the Cybermen and it was with this story that Gerry Davis chose to do it. The character made its mark and has appeared in every Cyberman story since.

The costume was again basically a two-piece wetsuit. This time, however, it incorporated a slight hump between the shoulder blades. The piping which had run along the arms and legs was now made of corrugated rubber tubing and extended from the chest unit to join in the centre of the back at a large metal disc. At knee and elbow was a larger section of tubing to represent 'hydraulic-powered' joints. Large metal epaulettes were stuck on each shoulder to hold the pipes in place. The hands were covered in silver rubber gloves, and on the feet silver wellies made a comeback. *The Invasion* chest units were touched up and used again. But of all the sections of the costume, it was the headpieces which were the most impressive.

The helmet was now bigger than before and it was therefore slightly easier for the actors to breathe. They were constructed in the same basic way but the dome area of the head was different. Instead of a light, there was now what looked like the centre barrel of a four-chamber pistol inserted into the front of the dome. Each of the chambers was filled with powder charges which were worked by a button on the chest unit, linked to the head by wires which ran along the inside of the costume. The result was a series of spectacular flashes which exploded from the head. The chambers had to be reloaded after every shot – a time-consuming task but well worth the patience for it was a good effect, particularly in the battle between Cybermen and Vogans filmed at Wookey Hole. To distinguish the Cyber-leader from the other Cybermen, the 'ear-muffs' of his helmet were painted black.

The costumes were all made in one size and actors were to be hired to fit. As it turned out, one of the actors was slightly shorter than the rest and this can be clearly seen in several scenes where the head wobbles disconcertingly. At one point of the studio recording, one of the Cybermen suddenly began to charge around the set, screaming and clawing at his face. The actor, shut inside his mask, had had a sudden attack of claustrophobia. It took several technicians and a couple of the cast to hold him down and unclamp the headpiece. Another actor was called in to take his place for the day, giving him time to recover and regain his confidence.

Kevin Stoney (Tobias Vaughn in *The Invasion*) returned to play Tyrum, the leader of the Vogans and Christopher Robbie (in his second appear-ance in *Doctor Who* – his first was as Karkas, a comic strip character from the year 2000 AD) had the privilege of creating the role of the Cyber-leader. Unfortunately, this newly-introduced rank of Cyberman came across as rather less than menacing as he strutted around the sets, hands on hips, barking orders at his three melancholy subordinates in a clipped transatlantic accent and making such unlikely declarations as: 'You are about to die in the biggest explosion ever witnessed in this solar system. It will be a magnificent spectacle. Unfortunately, you will be unable to appreciate it.' Robbie turns in what has since been regarded as a very funny perform-ance – though that was not the intention at the time.

*Revenge of the Cybermen* saw the reappear-ance of the Cybermats. It was the third and (to date) last time they featured in a Cyberman story. Perhaps this is because, as Briant admits, they were not so successfully presented as previously: 'The Cybermats didn't work in that story. I tried to do the same effects with them as I had done with the maggots in *The Green Death*. They just didn't look right. We should have stuck to the radio con-trol models instead of hand puppets.'

In *The Green Death* Briant had created very effective sequences showing maggots squirming about on the ground. The maggots were hand-puppets operated from underneath a raised floor. He had plans for Cybermat hand-puppets to crawl over a fallen crewman; acid was to be spilt over them and they would squirm in cybernetic agony. But because the sets were linked with those of *The Ark In Space*, he was unable to incorporate the necessary raised floor. In the end, only one

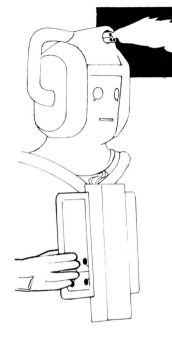

Cybermat was used instead of the planned six – a model which was either pulled along by wire or manipulated by actors.

For the scene where the Doctor's companion Sarah Jane Smith is attacked, actress Elizabeth Sladen had to hold the Cybermat prop and attack herself with it. This sequence took a long time to complete because, understandably, the film crew and actress were unable to keep a straight face. Takes often ended in fits of hysterical giggling.

Another scene difficult to film for the same reason comes near the end of the story where the Doctor and Sarah are about to crash into Voga and have to deliver the line, 'We're heading for the biggest bang in history'.

Despite their long absence, the Cybermen did not fire the public imagination this time round. Perhaps it was the combination of unconvincing Cybermats and strident Cyberleader with his mighty army of three. But interestingly, in 1983, BBC Enterprises decided to release a *Doctor Who* story on video to mark the twentieth year of *Doctor Who*. To find out which adventure the public wanted to see again, questionnaires were sent out. Several thousand were returned. Num-ber one choice was *Revenge of the Cybermen*. It was a surprising result, but it may have reflected the growing popularity of the Cybermen in general at that time. During the previous year, in March 1982, they had suddenly reappeared after another seven year absence. Their return was unexpected, unannounced and undeniably dramatic.

## A Time of Destruction

The BBC has built up a vast stock of film and videotapes of TV programmes which have been broadcast over its 50 year history. Their Film and Videotape Library is the largest of its kind in the world. It contains half a million cans of film and 100,000 spools of videotape. Nevertheless, there are huge gaps. Programmes which were miles-tones in broadcasting history have been lost forever.

Hours of light entertainment – including epi-sodes of *Hancock's Half Hour*, *That Was The Week That Was*, *Steptoe and Son*, and *Till Death Us Do Part* – no longer exist. Little record remains of many important documentaries and current affairs programmes – like *Panorama*, for example – which are now recognised to have been of great historical value. The television dramatists of the 1960's and early seventies (whose reputations are highly esteemed today) were also poorly treated. Plays by Harold Pinter, David Mercer, Alun Owen, Peter Nichols, John Mortimer, David Rud-kin, Dennis Potter, Tom Stoppard, Simon Grey

and Michael Frayn have all been lost to the ether. Included amongst this sorry list are many episodes of *Doctor Who*.

Until the late fifties most television programmes – including drama – went out live. A transmission could be filmed as it went out but the resulting quality was poor and in any case the programmers were more concerned with serving the watching public than worrying about posterity. It is not surprising that little archive material remains from this period. In 1958, however, videotaping of programmes at last became a practical possibility. Theoretically, no programme need now be lost. In practice, the videotape was expensive and since it could be re-used, many recorded programmes were still considered not important enough to keep. They were 'wiped' and the tapes used to record newer programmes.

When colour TV arrived in the early 1970's, archive black-and-white material became even more vulnerable. The majority of the black-and-white serials, it was thought, would seem dull by comparison with programmes in colour. And there was, in any case, the general difficulty of arranging a repeat showing of any material more than two years old. Every artist involved had to be contacted and repeat fees individually agreed. Hence, many black-and-white serials from the fifties and sixties – programmes that are now considered classics of their kind – were wiped. This 'purge' erased more than seventy episodes of the Patrick Troughton era of *Doctor Who*, depleted the William Hartnell stories by almost fifty episodes and even destroyed some of the colour prints of Jon Pertwee as the Doctor.

Early Cyberman stories were affected quite severely. Here, in detail, are the episodes which have been lost:

| | |
|---|---|
| *The Tenth Planet* | Episode 4 |
| *The Moonbase* | Episodes 1 and 3 |
| *Tomb of the Cybermen* | No episodes remain |
| *The Wheel In Space* | Episodes 1, 2, 4 and 5 |
| *The Invasion* | Episodes 1 and 4 |

Episode Four of *The Tenth Planet* was not, in fact, wiped. It 'went missing' in 1973. To mark the tenth anniversary of *Doctor Who*, the children's programme *Blue Peter* showed clips from old adventures including the sequence from this particular episode where the William Hartnell Doctor becomes the Patrick Troughton Doctor. The videotape of the episode disappeared the day it was shown. It is possible that one of the people working on the show might have taken it home with them – in which case it could still turn up again some day.

The episodes from *The Moonbase* and the entire story of *Tomb of the Cybermen* were wiped. *The Wheel In Space*, however, might have

escaped the purge. A couple of years ago, Episode Three was returned in excellent condition and there are continual rumours that other episodes of this story, as well as others, are about turn up. Every so often a previously missing episode of *Doctor Who* does turn up and is returned to the BBC archives.

Fortunately, none of the other Cyberman stories has been affected. *Revenge of the Cybermen*, *Earthshock*, *The Five Doctors* and *Attack of the Cybermen* remain intact and are preserved in the vaults of the BBC awaiting repeat screening (*Earthshock* and *The Five Doctors* were repeated within a year of their first broadcast) or release on video – as *Revenge of the Cybermen* and *The Five Doctors* have been.

Optimistically, Innes Lloyd believes that since nearly all the episodes of *Doctor Who* he produced were exported to other countries, the adventures of the early Cybermen may have been disseminated too widely for the BBC purge to have destroyed all trace. There exists the intriguing possibility that even the Cybermen from the lost tombs of Telos might awake from their long slumber and march onto our television screens to terrify us once again.

### *Earthshock*: Rebirth

In 1980 Graham Williams gave up his job as producer after three years with the programme. He handed over to John Nathan-Turner who had been production unit manager on *Doctor Who* for three years.

John Nathan-Turner (or JNT, as he is widely known) was determined to get *Doctor Who* out of its rut. Viewing figures had been on the downward slide for some time and he decided that the show needed a facelift as it entered the new decade. Early changes under JNT included updated title graphics and theme music, new companions and, most importantly, a new Doctor.

RIGHT JNT on *Silver Nemesis* location

There was also a shifting of the programme from the traditional weekly episode each Saturday to two episodes a week (Tuesdays and Wednesdays).

Tom Baker had been the show's longest serving Doctor. His successor was a younger actor, Peter Davison, well-known at the time for his portrayal of Tristram Farnum in the BBC TV series *All Creatures Great and Small* on which JNT had also worked. Tom Baker had played the role for so long that he was firmly established in the minds of younger viewers as the Doctor. To accustom them to the idea that other actors could portray the Doctor, a series of repeats featuring each of the previous Doctors was screened between Baker's last and Davison's first season, under the umbrella title of *The Five Faces of Doctor Who*.

When Peter Davison had accepted the role, he had asked if it would be possible to bring back the Cybermen since they had not been seen for such a long time. JNT had been thinking along similar lines. 'The Cybermen had always been popular,' he says. 'Historically speaking, the second most popular villains of the piece. I thought it was time to bring them back. We wanted an action adventure. The shape of the script was down to Eric.'

Eric Saward was script editor for the programme. His first *Doctor Who* story, *The Visitation*, was to be screened earlier in the season. He now produced a Cyberman script. JNT was impressed: 'It was a hugely ambitious epic. There were over three hundred scenes. It was the fastest action-packed story the show has ever aimed for – that sheer number of scenes. Changing the camera angle 360 times is an awful lot more time-consuming than the average 60 times. I think, taken from the point of view of action, it was my favourite Cyberman story. I quite like stories that tie in with the show's past. And the whole bit about the dinosaurs appealed to me greatly.'

Eric Saward himself admits to a natural affinity with the Cyberman concept: 'Terrance Dicks once said that I have an obsession with the Cybermen, which is not far from the truth. To me they are much more fascinating than the Daleks and offered a much more plausible, chilling opposition to their enemies.'

To ensure the utmost dramatic impact, it was intended that the title of the story would give no indication that Cybermen were returning. 'It was the first appearance of the Cybermen since *Revenge of the Cybermen* in 1975,' David Banks explains. 'That ended with what seemed to be the last remnants of the Cyber race being blown apart. Fans might have thought that Cybermen would be heard of no more. Pre-show press releases made no mention of their involvement in the story. Perhaps that's why the title was changed from *Sentinel* to *Earthshock*. It was

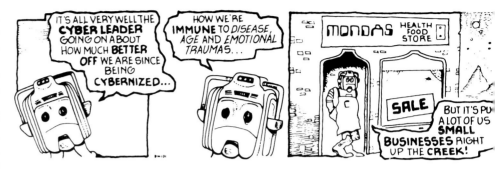

certainly intended to be a shock for the viewers when the Cybermen suddenly appear because up to that point it looks as though it's going to be about dinosaurs!'

Of paramount importance, JNT realised, was to bring the Cybermen up to date: 'I was very keen to retain the essence of what had gone before but to make them look a little more streamlined: I thought that was important dramatically. Some of the early ones looked very clumsy and moved badly – which was fine for that period – but it was something I didn't want to happen with the ones in *Earthshock*. I wanted something with tremendous menace. In some of those early stories they're almost laughable.'

Dinah Collin was the costume designer who was to create a new 'hi-tech' look for the Cybermen. She chose the independent effects company Imagineering to help her. Between them they hoped to capture something of the style of science fiction which had become highly popular with the film *Star Wars*.

'I had a design problem with the head,' she recalls. 'The Cybermen were being resurrected and I wasn't allowed to create a totally new idea of what they looked like. JNT told me to update them but to keep the head as near to the original as possible.

'I saw some photographs from the later stories but that was all. If people had said more about what had gone before, it might have been too confusing – although the actual background to how the Cybermen evolved would have been nice to know, what they can and can't do, what their powers are and so on. I wish I'd seen something of the first Cybermen. From what I've heard of them since, they seem to have been horrifying – and I didn't actually think mine were. However, I do think that as a finished product – the set and the story – *Earthshock* was very good. And of course there was the script to go by which was informative and allowed the imagination to get to work. All of us, designers, actors, directors, really base our work from the script.

'I could understand why John needed to have them recognisable from what had gone before. It would have been quite exciting to have been able to create a new creature with a body inside it but the job I had to do was quite a challenge in itself –

fraught with difficulties because of its attachments to the old.

'One had to find something that technically would work, that people could move in. First and foremost, it is necessary to find out what an actor has got to do in a costume and design round it. That was one of the things that failed to work in the helmets. Because they had to remain more or less the same, I couldn't explore the possibilities of making them more practical to work in for the actor.'

Imagineering is an enterprising group of free-lance visual effects technicians led by Richard Gregory. Their workshop, Unit 22, is in a converted mill at Witney near Oxford. Building Terileptils for *The Visitation* was their first *Doctor Who* assignment. *Earthshock* was their next.

'*Earthshock*,' says Richard Gregory, 'has been our biggest *Doctor Who* to date. For that one we produced nine Cybermen – don't forget the one that got frozen into the wall – fourteen troopers and two silhouettes (the androids), although they were just heads basically. So when you add it all up there were about two dozen costumes for that story, which is rather a lot. When Dinah came to us we were able to offer her a lot advice on the costumes she wanted because we had worked with vacuum formers, fibre glass and latex. She came to us with ideas and together we worked out what could be done. We did a lot of sketches ourselves to show how we thought the Cybermen should look and how they could be made and we were very lucky in that she agreed so many of them.'

Dinah Collin recalls this collaboration with enthusiasm: 'Richard worked very closely with me as we sorted out what changes we could actually make. We had this idea that the body of the actor would become part of the outer skin. Instead of having gloves on the hands, it would have been nice to build them up with make-up. It would have been an extension of this funny suit which had tubes on it already and I thought that if you brought the tubes up over the chin and into the mouth, then the helmet part of it would grow from that. There wouldn't have been any clear division where body ended and helmet began. But I was running out of time because Richard had to cast the helmet and we had to decide whether there was going to be a lower jaw and if we would keep the handles – I didn't like them very much. But JNT was right to keep the links going. Without the handles, the fans probably wouldn't have recognised it as a Cyberman at all.

'On all things technical, Richard was extremely good. I would keep coming to him to say, "If I wanted this, Richard, how could it be done?" For example, he found the G-suit – the lightweight flying suit covered in all those tubes – in an army surplus store in Oxford and he suggested it as a base to work from – so I can't claim any credit for that at all. We put the G-suit onto a cotton boiler suit which had been tailored to the size and shape of the particular actor who was to wear it. I wanted to get away from the previous vinyl suits because it was just a flat surface and anything put on to it doesn't seem to have grown out of it. I talked to Richard originally about having a suit with these tubes built into it – based on an original drawing I did. I didn't keep the drawing, I'm afraid.'

Meanwhile, JNT and his director, Peter Grimwade, were searching for two actors who could play the Cyberleader and his Cyberlieutenant. These two Cybermen were central to Eric Saward's story and had considerably more dialogue than Cybermen in previous stories. But the main consideration was height. Only actors of 6ft 3in and over were seen. David Banks was one of them: 'In the summer of 1981 Peter Grimwade was looking for someone to play the Cyberleader. My agent wasn't sure that I should appear behind a mask and was rather dismissive. However, I thought the part had possibilities and was excited at the prospect of being in *Doctor Who*. I had an idea how the part could be played and when I read at the interview I think Peter agreed. Or perhaps I was just the right height!'

Another was Mark Hardy: 'When I got my first call from the BBC to read for the Cyberlieutenant, I didn't know what they wanted. I went to meet Peter Grimwade. He asked me what height I was. Then he gave me a couple of lines to say and told me to speak them in a kind of monotone voice. I said, "Why the monotone voice?" He said, "Do you know *Doctor Who*?" I said, "Well, yes." He said, "Do you remember the Cybermen?" "Well, I remember the Daleks," I said, trying to be helpful, "but I don't actually remember the Cybermen." He said, "Oh well, never mind. Just try to speak in a deep monotone voice." So I did, and I went away, and then I heard that I'd got the part. I was called in for a costume fitting and suddenly found myself in this silvery, wiry thing covered in pipes and heavens knows what.'

JNT was still keeping a close eye on the development of the new Cyberman costume. 'The glass jaw was totally my idea,' he explains. 'It's the old thing of inanimate objects, a problem we have with any of the monsters – like the Daleks, they are completely expressionless except vocally. We had such a lot of scenes between the Cyberleader and the Cyberlieutenant. I know one has the black pressure cooker handles and the other has the silver ones but you're cutting between two virtually identical objects. We were very well aware that we were going to require the actors to do a lot of nodding work and shoulder movement but I felt that there should be something on the face that moved – activated as they spoke. At the top of their heads was some material that flares and shines in different ways and I thought it would be interesting to get a hint of something underneath. I didn't want to see the jaw or part of the actor's mouth but to see something in there moving that would look cybernetic. The idea was not just to see a chin but a sort of flap, as it were.'

What was also tried out in the pre-production period was a new method of producing the Cyber voice. In *Revenge of the Cybermen* the actors' voices were hardly altered at all to make the exchanges between the Cyberleader and the Doctor more dramatic. For *Earthshock*, JNT wanted to retain the the natural tones of the actor's own voice – but to process it electronically to give it a cybernetic feel. David Banks remembers going up to the studio gallery with Mark Hardy and the sound engineer to see JNT:

'We had a prototype helmet with us, fitted up inside with a radio mike: in the dome at the top was strapped a radio transmitter and next to the transparent jaw was attached a tiny microphone. Mark and I took it in turns to try out different types of voice and levels of pitch. The sound engineer electronically processed the sound, instantaneously lowering and raising the pitch of the voice without slowing it down or speeding it up. After some experiment, the best results seemed to come from keeping the natural voice and combining it with both the lower and higher processed pitches. Even so, there was still an appreciable difference between Mark's voice and mine – and, what was more important with so much dialogue to get across, the natural cadences of the voice were still there.'

For Dinah Collin, there was still much to be done and a deadline to meet: 'We were left with so little time to sort out the front of the helmet that we never got round to sorting the back out. So we ended up using the original head as a base for Richard to cast from, since that was the only way we could get the fourteen – or whatever ghastly number it was – made in time. Those frightful little screws to hold the back panel on was a design fault simply because of lack of time.

'The other thing we'd like to have done was to spray into the bodies. You know how we covered the costume with tubing and mesh and string vests and whatever? Well, I'd like to have gone much further and made it look more like a body with no skin, painting the tubes to make them stand out more, as though we were seeing arteries and capillary veins, even over the boots which had no detail and looked as though they were just stuck on the end of the legs. Again, we ran into this problem of time because, as well as the Cybermen, there were the other actors to costume – including Beryl Reid, who was delightful to work with – and though you might eventually get one Cyberman costume right, all fourteen had

to look the same. In the end we just sprayed them all silver.

'I think my ideas for this open-surgery look really came from a TV programme of the time. It showed a heart replacement operation with clamps and valves and all the veins and arteries exposed. It seemed in line with what the Cybermen were about and was the image I had wanted to carry a lot further with the new Cybermen. But I got bogged down with this head.'

Richard Gregory agrees that the *Earthshock* project was a challenge: 'The Cybermen were a difficult subject because of the way they'd been conceived and the way they'd developed over the years. Nevertheless, whenever somesome saw our version they instantly recognised them, even if only in silhouette – and all because of the jug ears. In all other respects the head is very much different to the originals and the body doesn't resemble the predecessors at all.'

Although he would have liked to distinguish the Cyberleader by extending the idea from *Revenge of the Cybermen* and giving him a totally black helmet with strange runic markings, in the end it was decided to black in only the 'handles'. The gun which had been mounted in the dome of the head for *Revenge of the Cybermen* was replaced by the reflective material mentioned by JNT.

'The helmet was extraordinarily uncomfortable,' recalls Mark Hardy. 'It had to be screwed on. When we had a short break between shots, there wasn't time to have it taken off. It rested on one's neck all the time and it was quite a strain. Looking back at the video, I see I've got a continual stoop: it might be because I've got a continual stoop anyway, but part of it was because the helmet screwed me in at an angle – if you understand me. But when you're in it, you can wiggle your head around inside without moving the helmet and look out in all directions without anybody knowing. In the scenes in Cyber Control, I would look out of my ear if I wanted to check what the Cyberleader was up to.'

David Banks adds: 'The new cybersuits are reasonably light and easy to move about in. But under studio lights they can still become uncomfortably hot to wear. The main problem was that the helmet has a panel on the back which has to be securely screwed in place. Itches cannot be scratched, nor noses blown. It can lead to acute claustrophobia. The sight of a dresser standing by with a screwdriver should help, but somehow doesn't. We lost at least one extra whose nerve failed him as he heard the screws tighten behind him.'

Dinah Collin was well aware of the terrors of donning the Cyber helmet. 'Nobody likes to be screwed into something they can't get out of,' she says. 'One extra – who had been warned he would be wearing something that would enclose

David Banks

Mark Hardy

him completely – actually couldn't take it. He disappeared. The other extras said they were getting itchy noses from the fibreglass helmets – "cybernose". We had to give them nose pads. I do remember talking to Richard about what we could do to solve the difficulty with the screws and Richard saying, "I'll do my best," but at that point we had enough trouble just getting the actual garments out and sprayed, etc.'

Because of the helmet's transparent jaw, the actors had to go through an elaborate and uncomfortable make-up session. The chin and neck were painted silver with crinkled clingfilm glued over this to create the impression of something indefinable – perhaps mechanical, perhaps organic – moving beneath the mask as the Cyberleader or Cyberlieutenant spoke. The lips were painted black and the teeth coated in black enamel, an unpleasant substance which left a nasty taste in the mouth for days afterwards. Mark Hardy:

'It was rather fun going to the BBC canteen. You'd be standing in the queue with silver chins and blacked out teeth and wearing black lipstick – and nobody would take any notice of you – because there was always *Doctor Who* going on, wasn't there, and *Blake's 7* and all that sort of thing. The queue at the BBC canteen is sometimes quite bizarre.'

Martin Bower was responsible for the hi-tech design of the Cyber hardware, of which there was a great deal including the cyberscope, the cyberbomb and models of the freighter (both its gloomy vast interior and the intricately detailed exterior). 'I first got involved with the BBC when I met Special Effects man Ian Scoones at Bray Studios,' says Bower. 'I was working on the film *Medusa Touch* when he turned up to do *Blake's 7*.

'All I was usually given were a few rough drawings, often of the most basic sort, along with a verbal brief from the effects man. Sometimes I did a drawing myself based on this brief before I started work and okayed it with him. But often there wasn't enough time and I would simply go away and make the model. As time went on they used to know the sort of thing I did and trusted me to get on with it.

'I just get an idea in my minds eye. I can visualise what I want pretty quickly. Then I do a few sketches. I did all the Cyberman stuff together. That way you get a uniformity of design. Much of the Cyber hardware was constructed in perspex with aluminium parts added. Also a great many radio spares. I seem to remember I also got through loads of self-tapping screws.'

There was one day of location shooting (at a quarry near Dorking) but it did not involve Cybermen. The first sequence of shots for the Cyberleader and the Cyberlieutenant were all centred around a Cyberscope, an impressive prop built by Martin Bower. Three arms rose out of its console area, which was packed with detailed and realistic-looking instrumentation. From the arms was meant to be projected in 3-D the previous encounters of the Doctor with the Cybermen. Clips of earlier stories – *The Tenth Planet*, *The Wheel In Space* and *Revenge of the Cybermen* – superimposed on the projection area cleverly provided an instant history of the Doctor's meddlesome involvement with the Cyber race.

The sequences where the Cybermen break out of the cargo silos were a deliberate echo of *Tomb of the Cybermen*. The outer shell was made of expanded polystyrene sheeting which was easy for the actors to burst through. The actors were also covered in a thin transparent film to suggest the kind of storage membrane seen in *Tomb*. The sequences showing Cybermen being killed were elaborately set up: the actors were wired up with powder-flash charges.

The first indication in the story that Cybermen are involved comes dramatically in the last few seconds of Episode One. Three Cybermen – including the Leader and Lieutenant – are seen clustered round the Cyberscope. As Mark Hardy has cause to remember, the Cyberlieutenant was not, in fact, present: 'I was meant to be in the last scene of Episode One, in which I didn't actually speak but stood next to the Cyberleader as he said, "Destroy them! Destroy them at once!" To avoid having to pay me an extra episode fee, the dear old BBC kept me out of that scene, though I was in the studio ready to play my other scenes, and put in a stand-in for me. It saved them a teeny-weeny bit of money. But to make up for that – and I think they paid me a little bit extra for it – after being killed off as the Cyberlieutenant, I found myself playing various other Cybermen who had to be bumped off.

'One came through a polystyrene door and was meant to get stuck in it. As two other different Cybermen, I had to do two different death scenes, which both came out very similarly when edited together – and very close to each other. I had to make a terrible noise on an inward breath which was supposed to be a last death throe, but it came out as this kind of hysterical panting as if I found everything hilarious. Anyway, it was a very eccentric sort of death and, because of the tightness of my costume, I couldn't actually fall flat on my face. So I fell to my knees, sounding as if I was suffocating with laughter, and luckily they'd cut before it became too obvious that I was stuck on all fours – showing that I hadn't actually died at all. For the second one, I did an identical death which for some reason they kept in and cut at the identical place. So, in the finished film you get the Cyberleader's death, then me, dying this very strange, identical death, first on the freighter and, a few seconds later, on the TARDIS.'

Peter Grimwade managed to get all the many short scenes shot in the allotted time, though he had to go into overtime on the day the Cyberman extras were hired. To create the illusion of an army, he used a special prismatic lens which trebled the number of marching Cybermen. Because of the tight schedule there was very little time for retakes. 'In one scene,' says David Banks,

At the time it was shown, *Earthshock* caused some surprise among fans because the Cybermen had seemed to have lost something of their emotionlessness, up until that time a fundamental Cyber characteristic. JNT explains how he thought it came about: 'You're caught in a cleft stick, in a way, if you have emotionless creatures – because "emotionless" means they have no expression in their voices whatsoever – which dramatically is just unbearable. An example would be *The Moonbase* Cybermen. I just find them so difficult to swallow. So what we tried to do was to eliminate as many emotional phrases as possible, but to allow the actors to express their emotions both vocally and physically.'

David Banks adds: 'For me the difficulty in representing emotionlessness was an acting problem. I remembered watching the Peter Cushing/Dalek *Doctor Who* film. Whenever the Daleks had more than a few words to say they became boring because of their unvarying tone. I bore this in mind when thinking about the most important aspect of the Cyberleader: his voice. *Earthshock* had many lengthy exchanges between Leader and Doctor, Leader and his men. Emotionless exchange of information can so easily become monotonous.

'Eric Saward's script was exciting and pacy, but it also made clear that the Cyber race found human emotions quaint and illogical. My answer to the problem was this: Cybermen do not have emotions in the full human sense but they have directives and intents; when their intentions are threatened or thwarted they will always react logically but this does not preclude intensity of reaction. It is that intensity which can sometimes be mistaken for emotion – cold anger, perhaps. Their first priority is logical behaviour and what seems like anger may be a logical imperative.'

From the advantage of hindsight we can see more clearly how the move away from total emotionlessness had started much earlier than *Earthshock*, probably as far back as *Tomb of the Cybermen* in the figure of the Cybercontroller, the first real Cyberman to be differentiated from the others – given a personality, in a sense. With *Revenge of the Cybermen*, the Cyberleader was allowed to be even more individualised with Christopher Robbie's idiosyncratic portrayal.

*Earthshock* saw some very fine performances in a story that clearly took a great deal of hard work to make. But the finished product was well worth the toil. '*Earthshock* was a super show to initiate,' says Eric Saward. The story went on to win several awards amongst the *Doctor Who* fan clubs and was also acclaimed by the critics. As with *The Tenth Planet*, the Cybermen had once again helped to inject new life into *Doctor Who* and bring it back to the attention of the public.

*Earthshock* is a example of *Doctor Who* at its very best. The Cybermen had made a spectacular return. The manner of their next appearance was to reflect their new-found popularity.

### The Five Doctors: A Sign of Success

1983 was the twentieth anniversary of *Doctor Who*. To celebrate the series and those who had been connected with it over its two decades, John Nathan-Turner wanted a special adventure which would feature all the Doctors, many of the companions and a selection of the Doctor's most formidable opponents.

It was a tall order to combine all these elements and yet still produce an entertaining and exciting story. When veteran *Doctor Who* writer Robert Holmes found it too daunting, Terrance Dicks was approached. He relished the task of writing for the series again and, working with script editor Eric Saward, he came up with a clever formula – a kind of dungeons and dragons whodunnit – set in the Death Zone of Gallifrey, the Doctor's home planet, into which all five incarnations of the Doctor had been deposited, along with their companions, the Master, a Dalek, a Yeti and three patrols of Cybermen. In a way, the Cybermen were making another 'guest' appearance – *The Five Doctors* was not a Cyberman story as such – but they are the major representatives of the *Doctor Who* monster and play a principal part in the proceedings.

To direct this very special story, JNT chose Peter Moffatt, a freelance director of long experience and highly regarded among his fellow professionals. He was impressed with the script: 'Terrance Dicks did a wonderful job with what

119

was after all a phoney story. All the Doctors have to appear together in one adventure so they are brought to one place and have to surmount many obstacles to reach their goal. But that is the source of all drama, isn't it? – the goal is in sight but you are hindered in getting there. Fairy story time: you've got to go through seven magic gates in order to get there in the end. Perhaps that's what Terrance had in mind.

'The Dark Tower is part of the fairy story and we tried to enhance that feeling with the sounding of the huge alpenhorn every time we see the Tower. It was a real alpenhorn recorded in the Swiss Alps so there was this great echo on it. We got a proper sense of scale there, I think, and I also thought the Tower itself, which was just a model, worked pretty well. It was a big model – about six feet tall – which we filmed in the special effects studio at Ealing.'

Though most of the Cybermen costumes were again constructed from scratch – again by Richard Gregory at his Unit 22 workshop – they were the same in every regard except for one – the boots. 'The wonderful thing about the costume in Earthshock was the boots,' explains Mark Hardy who returned to play the Cyberlieutenant, 'Ski boots sprayed silver. Very comfortable and they looked good. But as we did all our filming in the studio these insulated ski boots got very hot. We looked forward to being able to use them on location next time. Ironically enough, when we went out on location for The Five Doctors – and it was freezing cold on those icy Welsh mountain-sides – the only thing that had changed about the costume were the boots. We had to wear these terrible thin canvas things with laces up the front which let in water – our feet were wrapped in plastic bags to keep them from getting too wet.

'I was the only one to wear exactly the same costume then as I did for Earthshock. It was made fairly tight, which was fine for the studios, but on location there was mountain mist and rain on the hills and in the slate quarries – and freezing temperatures. All the other Cybermen with new, looser costumes could bundle themselves up with thermals and layers of warm clothing underneath, whereas I couldn't wear any clothes – otherwise I would have split the costume. So I merrily froze.'

David Banks had returned as the Cyberleader. He, too, bemoans the loss of good Cyber footwear: 'The snug moonboots we wore in Earthshock were substituted for canvas lace-up overboots for The Five Doctors. Unfortunately, they were too small to go over our own shoes and they let in water. On a freezing February location in a wet Welsh slate quarry, this was not a pleasant experience. If you ever watch The Five Doctors again, some of the menace might evaporate knowing that under the boots the Cybermen were all wearing plastic bags on their feet to keep dry.'

But the work of these two longsuffering actors did not go unappreciated by the production team. 'I thought,' comments Eric Saward, 'that the actors we were lucky in getting to play the Cybermen in Earthshock were so good that they almost demanded to be used again.' And JNT admits: 'We always try and get David Banks and Mark Hardy.'

A new Cyberman type was introduced in The Five Doctors. More compact, presumably for more efficient reconnaissance, the Cyberscout was played by William Kenton. 'I'm 6ft 1in', he says. 'Even so, I was the smallest Cyberman they'd ever had. Of course, there were the six Welsh extras hired to play other Cybermen – they were even smaller than me.' JNT agrees: 'They were all tiny. That's why in so many scenes they stand on the hill in the background, so the main ones don't dwarf them.'

Peter Moffatt sheds some light on the matter: 'Production manager Jeremy Silberston was responsible for hiring the Cybermen extras. They should have been taller but we were filming in Wales and he had to engage Welshmen, who all turned out to be small. The other Cyberman, William Kenton, had a line – "I know where they are" or whatever it was – so we were allowed to engage him in London and take him on location.'

'There's lots of things I remember about that location shooting,' says Kenton. 'Most of them unprintable! One of them was that it was so bloody cold! We had to put BBC plastic bags on under our boots because of all that marshy water.'

Well aware of the discomfort caused by the costumes, Peter Moffatt had the greatest sympathy for the people inside them: 'I remember the costume designer Colin Lavers was down at the bottom of the hill warning "insurrection from the Cybermen", who were freezing. Instead of being in coats of armour they were in nylon or something equally thin and freezing to death. I've just been working again with Colin on 'Eastenders' and he sent me a postcard – a picture of himself alongside a Cyberman – which said: "Even colder than Bridge Street in Eastenders – a reminder of the Cybermen in Wales!"'

William Kenton tells the same story from the Cybermen's point of view: 'Once, I remember, we were all waiting – right out in the wilds in Wales – at the bottom of a cliff. The camera was at the top of the cliff and they wanted us to climb up. It was very, very cold. We were all sitting in the Land Rover, all the Cybermen. We drove up to this spot and they decided up on the cliff that the camera angle wasn't right or something. They said, "No, no, we want you another half mile down the road." We had put on all our helmets and plastic bags and everything and we were fed up and saying, "Cor, bloody hell!" and so on. Colin, the costume chap, was getting really annoyed for us. In the end he really lost his racket and shouted up to them "We've got a Cyber insurrection down here!" on his walkie-talkie.

'You couldn't see down at all when you were wearing the Cyber mask: you could only see straight in front of you. It was very difficult to move about – especially on those steep hills. You had to go over the moves first, before you did the shot, with your head bent right down to try and remember where all the rocks were – and pray to God you got your footing right when the camera started to roll.'

The location shooting was sited at and around Maenturog in North Wales. David Banks: 'It was like a holiday. We had had the luxury of a week of film rehearsal before going on location: usually for films you are lucky to grab a few minutes to rehearse the scene just before you shoot it. The location too was over an unusually long period. We were there for two weeks and there seemed to be a buzz of excitement in everybody. Everyone who was anyone in *Doctor Who* was involved. People who had been in the show years before were meeting old colleagues. Rival Doctors were staying in the same hotel. So were rival monsters and villains. Once in the studio it was the same hot slog of course, though eased by the fact that the director, Peter Moffatt, was a true professional and knew his shooting script inside out.'

*The Five Doctors*, though not his first *Doctor Who* story, was Peter Moffatt's only Cyberman story to date: 'I knew about them and about the divided theories in the history from reading the appropriate section in *The Doctor Who Technical Manual*. Writers have approached them in different ways so there is a divergence of theory about where the Cybermen came from. From a purely technical point of view, I didn't know at the beginning whether the actor spoke the lines at the time of shooting or whether it was dubbed – that sort of thing.

'Monsters in *Doctor Who* are generally at a disadvantage because they don't have a great range of expression, though one monster I directed was very expressive – the Terileptil in *The Visitation* – because various parts of the mask were movable under radio control: the technician operated the controls as the actor was speaking. It was beautifully done. I was worried when we started with the Cybermen because their masks don't register any emotion at all. But I found that David and Mark did so much with their voices that it didn't really matter. Even though their natural voices are distorted by an artificial echo device, the variation they got into their voices still came through quite clearly.

'In fact, I found it astonishing that we didn't use their own voices as they were. When we recorded them on location I thought that they were going to be used in the original form because they sounded fine to me. It turned out that they would have to be dubbed – each of them dubbing their own voice, of course – but I still felt that the original soundtrack was better than the final dub.

'JNT helped out on the direction of shots of the Cybermen exploding and so forth in the "Cyber massacre". I put it all together during editing and thought it turned out rather well considering we shot it on two completely different days – one fine and one rainy.'

'Peter Moffatt wanted an extra day of filming,' recalls JNT. 'I said "no" and he said, 'Okay, can I have a second unit for a day and can you shoot some of the Cyber-death sequence?' I could hardly say no. I did most of the stuff with the Raston Robot doing all the killing, up until the point where he comes down and the row of Cybermen turn round and face him head on. From that bit onwards Peter took over and did the rest – with the exception of a few cutaway shots that I did.

'It was always planned to have the Cybermen in *The Five Doctors*. I seem to remember that the Cyber massacre was in Terrance's first version. We liked it and kept it in. Everything was there with the exception of the Cyberleader being sick – David spitting milk all over the place. I remember him asking – because we had a coffee urn standing by as usual (we'd staged his fall and were ready to go for a take) – "What if I had a mouthful of milk, as if it were the internal fluids of the Cyberleader's body and have them emitting from within?" It was totally his idea.'

Stuart Fell, a stuntman who has appeared in numerous *Doctor Who* stories, played the first Cyberman victim of the Raston Robot attack. The Cyberman is decapitated by a razor-disc. Because Stuart Fell was a good deal shorter than a normal Cyberman, he was able to wear the costume with the helmet balanced on the top of his head. With a disc set into the neck as though it had just struck, an explosive charge inside the neck was detonated and the head blown off. The effect was stunning. But setting up shots like these is not without its dangers, as David Banks explains:

'The special effects team is concerned more than anything else for the safety of the actors, but accidents can happen. Stuart Fell was asphyxiated by smoking green slime daubed on his Cyber helmet. We thought his waving hands and writhing body was a piece of bravura acting but as he explained afterwards (thankfully he lived to tell the tale) he could not get the helmet off – because of the screwed-on panel – and he could not shout for help as he was afraid of gulping in the toxic fumes.'

The rest of the Cyber patrol met with equally spectacular deaths. William Kenton: 'The part I enjoyed most of the whole film. We had explosive charges put onto us and wires running up our

Peter Moffatt

backs. I was surprised how powerful those explosive charges were. They didn't quite knock you off your feet, but rather than wondering, "Has it gone off or not?", you could actually feel it and react to it. And then there were all the paper plates that the people behind the camera threw at us. They were meant to be the deadly accurate discs from the Warrior Robot – but they were flying everywhere. You had to wait till one of them happened to hit us before the explosions were set off. It was great fun.'

During the course of the story, Cyberleader Banks returns from the dead twice. He dies for the second time in the Dark Tower on a giant chess board and then is later seen to be commanding his Lieutenant and the third Cyber patrol which is trying to destroy the TARDIS. This third appearance is speeded up on film to give the impression of their being different Cybermen. But Peter Moffatt came to terms with it in this way: 'I assumed that the Cyberleader must be eternal, that once killed he rose up again like some terrible monster growing up out of its own head. I feel that the Cyberleader is always the Cyberleader, that there will never be another one and that he is always David Banks!

'When we came to the chess board sequence in the studio, it was apparent that a path had not been worked out mathematically according to the Pi sequence. I had to invent a path once we were in the studio but it had nothing to do with what was supposed to be the real mathematical path. It was dramatically very effective if you were seeing it for the first time with the lightning and the Cybermen going up in smoke; but if you stop to think about it, you see that it wasn't quite mathematical!

'We added the green jags of lightning in what they call the "Gallery Only" session. Always on *Doctor Who* there's a time when you're not using the studio, just the gallery – the area above the studio floor where the director normally controls a production and cuts between monitors showing different camera shots. Well, we also use this gallery afterwards to add all the electronic effects – coloured beams, explosions – on Quantel. For lethal rays you run the clip slowly to see what angle is required and plan a path down to the Cyberman you want to zap. Run it again and the beam will strike at the pre-planned position.

'There are various ways of doing the electronic effects: Quantel is the most effective and is often used to squeeze an image and turn it round and so on; there's also a thing called Tipse which freezes the frame and superimposes it on another so that you can make someone disintegrate and disappear. In fact, if there's any particular effect required in *Doctor Who* and the equipment exists to do it, the director has access to it. The BBC offer them to you on *Doctor Who* because the effect is important. Also it's an advertisement for the BBC's own specially developed equipment.

'Not everything can be added on electronically. You sometimes have to have live explosions as when the Cybermen tried to destroy the TARDIS. We cut from one real explosion of flame which engulfed the TARDIS to another which was set off after it had been taken away. The end result looked as though the TARDIS had disappeared as the explosion 'erupted. The actual location explosion was huge but unfortunately it didn't seem as big on the screen, I thought. It's sometimes difficult to convey a true sense of scale on TV.'

The magnitude of that location explosion was such that David Banks thought at first something might have gone wrong: 'It all went as planned – I think – but the intensity of the blast was so great that watching it several hundred yards away, seated inside our location vehicles, we felt its heat through the windows.'

Although *The Five Doctors* was primarily a celebration of the Doctors themselves, it was an accolade of the highest order that the monsters chosen to play such a significant part in this epic adventure should be the Cybermen. Peter Moffatt sums up his feeling about them thus:

'I find the Cybermen more believable than most of the other monsters because they have a closeness to humans. As a director, I sometimes find myself alienated by monsters from outer space, whereas the Cybermen have reactions which are easily understood. I know they are mechanical and electronic but from a director's point of view it's like working with actors who are playing ordinary human beings. Their minds work in a human way, or rather, they understand how a human thinks. They behave like human beings a lot of the time and, unlike other monsters who may look like dragons or whatever, they look something like a human being. For a director, that's half the battle.'

### *Attack of the Cybermen*: The Final Dissolution?

In 1984, after only three seasons, Peter Davison decided to retire from playing the Doctor. JNT cast Colin Baker as the new Doctor. The changeover came in the last story of Season 21. The start of Season 22 was to be the new Doctor's first real adventure and it was a measure of the current popularity of the Cybermen that they were chosen to confront him in this story.

Eric Saward assigned Paula Moore to write a Cyberman story which would contain certain specific elements: the Cybermen were to be seen on their home from home, Telos; the 'tombs' would be revealed as having once been the refrigerated cities of the planet's original inhabitants, the

Cryons, an all-female race of creatures who could only survive at sub-zero temperatures. The return of Halley's comet in 1986 would also feature in the plot, establishing close connections with the very first Cyberman story *The Tenth Planet*.

Director Matthew Robinson was hired after his success with *Resurrection of the Daleks* from the previous season. He had a reputation as an action director and, if anything, that was what was required for this adventure. Two actors from that story appear in *Attack*. The character of Lytton, a mercenary who had worked for the Daleks, was brought into the story and played again by Maurice Colbourne. Terry Molloy had played Davros, creator of the Daleks, in *Resurrection* and Matthew Robinson had next time promised him a part where his own face might be seen. He played Russell, a reluctant villain who was really a policeman.

Nicola Bryant had also taken part in *Resurrection*. She had not long been introduced as Peri, a new companion for the Doctor. This was her first contact with the Cybermen in the 'flesh':

'I'd watched *Doctor Who* from about six years old. My sister hated it and I used to drag her to see it – I couldn't watch it without her because I was secretly petrified too, but I wasn't going to admit it. The Cybermen were one of the things I was petrified of. I used to think that they were hiding in large cupboards in my house because it seemed the kind of logical place that they would be – the airing cupboard or the larder, somewhere like that.

'When I first pick up a script I always ask myself whether I believe the plot I've been written into, the enemies I have to face and how it's resolved. With *Attack of the Cybermen* I felt it was fairly well thought out from my point of view. Of all the monsters I've worked with as Peri, the Cybermen seem to me to be the most difficult to escape from. The Daleks, for example, can't climb stairs. We tried to get around that by making one of them hover but still the overall image of the Dalek is not so terrifying – you think, "Well yes, I could get away from that." But with Cybermen – especially, I remember, when I was in the TARDIS and had to shoot at them and realised the helplessness of having to fire at something like that – they seemed to me one of the strongest enemies that I would possibly have to tackle. With them I felt I stood even less chance than with the Master, say, against whom I could at least use my character's cunning and intelligence. It's like kicking a steel wall.'

Michael Attwell had previously been an Ice Warrior in their debut story seventeen years earlier. He was now cast as one of the two escapees from a working party of 'rejects' – prisoners of the Cybermen on whom the process of Cyber conversion had only partly succeeded.

The Master

This strand in the plot was added at a late stage but JNT was happy with how it turned out. 'Nice performance from Michael Attwell in particular,' he comments. 'The actor who played the other one, Jonathan David, was originally going to play the Cyberlieutenant but the actor who preceded him broke his arm – a guy called Trevor Raymond. We promoted the other guy and brought Brian Orrell in to replace him.' Mark Hardy, Cyberlieutenant in the two previous Cyberman stories, was not able to return to this role because he was working abroad.

Other *Doctor Who* veterans who did return

included Pat Gorman who had played a Cyberman sixteen years earlier in *The Invasion*, and Michael Kilgarriff who had been Cybercontroller in *Tomb of the Cybermen* and now, seventeen years later, recreated his role. He may never have done so, however, if David Banks had not remained loyal to the Cyberleader.

'Matthew was anxious to get the Cybermen right,' David Banks recalls. 'Since I had done the Cyberleader twice before, he would contact me from time to time before rehearsals began to discuss some technical aspect of the Cybermen. At one stage, while the script was still in a very loose draft form, he said that the Cybercontroller was coming back: he was the boss Cyberman – did I want to play him instead of the Cyberleader? It took only a moment's consideration to realise that I couldn't stand by and watch someone else play the Cyberleader. I'd worn the costume so often. I'd got under the Cyberleader's skin, if you like – literally. But it was only then that I realised that, in fact, the Cyberleader had got under mine!'

'Michael Kilgarriff took no persuading to come back to the Cybercontroller,' says JNT. 'I didn't realise he'd put on so much weight. It didn't worry me though, no reason why there shouldn't be a big Cyberman. As he'd been around such a long while he could have had several operations that added more machinery to him.'

The Cybermen costumes were exactly the same in design as for *The Five Doctors*. Several of the masks had to be remoulded and a special suit was constructed for Michael Kilgarriff. Basically, it was a larger version of the normal costume with a specially modified mask to remain in character with the original: no 'jug handles' and an enlarged dome, which no longer contained flickering lights but was just painted silver.

'I was very flattered to be asked to play the Cybercontroller again after so many years,' Michael Kilgarriff admits. 'I had actually been asked back a few years earlier but I wasn't available. The new version of the costume was a lot easier to wear compared to the older one – lighter, much easier to carry, made of a lighter material, not so much metal. When I came back to do *Attack* I thought that the Cybermen had lost all the menace that they used to have, possibly because they had this new design of costume. It

made it rather obvious that there was a body inside, the old costumes were stiff and hard to move in, making them look very robotic.'

Pat Gorman disagrees. 'These new Cybermen were terrific,' he says. 'They were so alien. Being inside that mask was no joke, though. The face plate was right up against your nose. The air was restricted. But the fun thing was you could turn your head around inside the mask. The Cyberman was looking forward but I was looking out of the hole in the ear.'

'I think the idea of these cybernetic creatures is a very interesting one,' says Nicola Bryant, 'and I don't think it was explored fully in *Attack*. The Doctor explained some of their history to me in the story but he never said what they actually were. So from Peri's point of view, they were just enormous heavy-handed robots whose strength was to be treated with respect! But I always met the Cybermen in an enclosed space. Outside, on location, I might have felt differently because I would have had speed on my side. They seem to lumber a bit in the filmed scenes that were supposed to be set on Telos. Their cybernetic sophistication should really make you think of them more as a sort of advanced android than of a clumpy 1960's robot, an awkward heap of metal.'

The location filming took place over several days near Gerrard's Cross on the outskirts of London, with the London scenes being done the following week. In the original script the Cybermen were to wear plastic bubbles over their Cyber helmets. The atmosphere of Telos was meant to be poisonous for them! JNT felt it would have looked 'pretty ludicrous' and it would also have caused severe breathing problems for the actors inside. But the idea was only finally dropped on the morning of the first location shoot.

The quarry was also used to site what appeared to be a full-scale construction – Cyber Control. 'I think it was the same process we used with *Planet of Fire*,' explains JNT. 'It was a model in front of the camera but placed in such a position that it looked further away and blended in with its surroundings. A great deal of time was spent on it. The visual effects boys blended in the sand absolutely brilliantly which is why it was such a success.'

For the worker 'rejects' on the surface of Telos – partly converted humans – basic Cybersuits were worn with black sleeveless jackets worn over the top. For the scene where Bates removes his glove and rolls up his sleeve to reveal a cybernetic arm, a special working forearm was built by Special Effects. Pat Gorman was on location as a Cyberman and also as one of the escapees:

'We all went down to a quarry for a couple of days. I was with two others who had to knock the head off a Cyberman. We charged up to the actor, who was then replaced by a dummy, and Mike knocked his head away. They got away with it but

I was shot. That tends to happen to me.

'When we got into studio I was the "rogue" Cyberman locked in a room who breaks through the door and knocks the head off a Cyberman standing outside. It was carefully planned out but I was a bit worried by the chap outside – he was new to the job and was very nervous. But it worked, thankfully.'

Part of the story was set in the sewers under London, where the Cybermen had massed in *The Invasion*. Down here, a new type of Cyberman was seen, the same in every detail except for colour. They were black. 'They'd painted themselves black to avoid being seen down the sewers,' says JNT. 'Probably painted each other actually.'

Matthew Robinson hoped to create a convincing army of Cybermen by training the new recruits in the reheasal room. 'Normally,' explains Brian Orrell, 'the rehearsal process is the most important part of creating a character. But in the case of Cyberlieutenant you couldn't really begin until you were actually in costume – in the studio – evaporating in the heat. The Cyber costume is all-embalming – it freezes your natural movement and dictates what you can and cannot do. Thus, most of what we did in rehearsal went out of the window. Though I do recall one particularly painful session with the director. He was trying to instil the Cyber-walk into me by making me walk backwards and forwards with a paper bag over my head for nearly an hour! But all to no avail, for without the costume it was an utter waste of time.'

A mysterious change had come about to the jaw of the Cyber helmet. It was no longer transparent as it had been in *Earthshock*. This does not appear to have been a conscious design alteration. Rather, it seems to have happened by default. JNT puts it down to the touching-up job the costumes had to go through for *The Five Doctors*. 'The costumes had been put into our exhibition,' he recalls, 'and as a result they got slightly battered. So most of the paint that was on the jaw – because it wasn't totally transparent, it was sprayed down so you could just get this image of something behind it – most of it had rubbed away. We first discovered this on location so we got Costume and the dressers with their spray cans to respray them. Initially it was a very delicate job. A little more was added and it was less delicate: you could still see the chin underneath – I suspect it was the harsh light of Wales in Winter – and in the end the difference between not seeing anything and seeing something was so remote and the dressers got a little bit over-enthusiastic and in the end the jaws were blocked out.'

But, contrary to what JNT remembers, the jaw was originally entirely transparent, as can quite clearly be seen in some of the *Earthshock*

close-ups. David Banks believes its transparency started to disappear during *Earthshock*. 'Near the end of one gruelling day in studio,' he explains, 'things were getting very hot and wet inside the helmet. We were filming an important sequence of dialogues between the Doctor and the Cyberleader which we had to finish that day. During one take I suddenly realised that the transmitter, usually strapped above my head, had come unstuck in the damp conditions and was slipping down towards my jaw. There was no time to unscrew the helmet and tape it back again, so I had to carry on, regardless of the extremely odd sensation of this heavy object moving against my cheek whenever I spoke. When it became visible at the transparent jaw, Costume had to conceal it somehow, so they sprayed the jaw area with silver paint between takes. Because I was inside at the time it was a rather unpleasant experience. The effect was to make the jaw opaque, and as such it was to appear in *The Five Doctors* and *Attack of the Cybermen*. Unfortunately, because it wasn't an official design decision, the message never got through to Make-up who still insist on applying it even though it's never seen.'

'Sans eyes, sans teeth, sans everything!' cries Brian Orrell at the memory. 'The powers-that-be didn't want any trace of actor to shine through the costume. So we had our eyes and lips blacked out as well as black nail varnish on the teeth. This meant that liquid between takes could only be sipped through a straw. I can still taste the nail varnish remover to this day!' But according to JNT, 'the make-up continues to be applied as a safety, really. I mean it would be awful to have to do a big scene again because teeth could be seen. In *Attack* there are one or two scenes where that happens.'

*Attack of the Cybermen* saw the return of the Doctor to the place he thought he had sealed off for good. But there was no attempt to make the Cyber Tombs look like the original design in *Tomb of the Cybermen*. The new set was basically a corridor system with the cryogenic chambers as rooms off them. Cybermen, wreathed in what looks like cobwebs, are seen to be standing or lying inside. It is in one of these rooms that the Doctor tampers with the mechanism behind a Cyberman's mask and for a moment we get a clear view of a silver protuberance at the jaw area – an intriguing hint of what was vaguely suggested behind the transparent jaw in *Earthshock*.

The fight sequence at the end of the story – a complex chain reaction with the Doctor causing the Cyberleader to shoot his own Lieutenant who in turn shoots his Leader – was so carefully staged that only one take was needed. At the end of the sequence, the Cybercontroller himself is felled and destroyed.

'I was lucky with my death scene,' claims Michael Kilgarriff, 'because when you do fall over in those things you find all sorts of protrusions inside that you never knew existed. I did have a bit of padding in the helmet but of course your head goes clank! I remember when we came to do it I thought, "I've got to go for broke with this, get it right first time." He was going funny anyway – after all, he'd had his tubes cut. So I lurched round the set flailing away, trying not to clout Colin Baker. But then if I didn't get him it would look false. When I was shot I did this great yell and went crashing backwards. Luckily, I got it right on the first take.

'I thought my voice was a bit overdone. You could hardly understand a word I said. I had to watch *Attack* on a very fuzzy portable. That probably made it better than it was! I thought it was a bit nasty when that chap Lytton got his hands crushed – very nasty. And I thought it was odd the way that I kept saying "Excellent" whenever something went terribly wrong. All in all, it's something for the memoirs, I suppose. I was the Cybercontroller.'

For the scene where a Cyberman is killed by a gun fired into its mouth, a special mask was constructed with a section that would come away with the detonation of a powder charge. The resulting effect was quite superb, though the question does arise as to why it is so easy to kill off the Cybermen with bullets that would once have merely been deflected off their resilient surfaces. JNT puts it down to luck:

'I don't think it's stretching the imagination too much to imagine that a lucky shot could finish one off. I mean you do often read dire cases in some of the less reputable magazines of somebody being shot in the wrist and dying from it because it just happened to trigger a nerve or whatever. I think it's reasonable to assume that some of those deaths were executed with a great deal of luck.'

*Attack of the Cybermen* is the last of the Cyberman stories in the *Doctor Who* adventures – so far. It received criticism for being a violent story in a season which, partly because of its violence, led to BBC1 Controller Michael Grade postponing Season 24 of *Doctor Who* for eighteen months. History was repeating itself. The outraged questions about what was suitable for children's viewing, questions which Kit Pedler had to face after the broadcast of *Tomb of the Cybermen*, were surfacing again.

David Banks takes up Kit Pedler's gauntlet and addresses a larger question: 'We need to be alive to the possibility that what we see on television does affect our perceptions and behaviour. But TV is also a mirror. Rather than blotting out a reflection of ourselves which we find unflattering – violence, for instance – perhaps we should ask why we relish seeing our enemies come to a nasty end, or why we are shocked by it, even in the fantasy world of *Doctor Who*.'

## How Will It End?

Over their twenty-one year history, the appearance of Cybermen has changed to reflect whatever technological fashions were current at the time. The behaviour of the Cybermen has changed, too, from totally emotionless robot-like entities whose only concern is to survive, to more individualised creatures with an overweening desire for conquest. What has not changed is Kit Pedler and Gerry Davis's basic premise, a race of human beings altered irrevocably because they replaced bits of themselves with artificial substitutes, because they pursued a desire for mechanical immortality to its ultimate conclusion. And it is in the best of the Cyberman stories – *The Tenth Planet*, *Tomb of the Cybermen* and *Earthshock* – where the premise is explored and its implications demonstrated.

This may partly explain the reason why the Cybermen first caught the public imagination. Kit Pedler and Gerry Davis had given their *Doctor Who* 'monsters' a very believable background. The thought of a society where replacement surgery had taken over everybody's lives unnerved adults because they realised that it was not too far-fetched a picture of the direction our own planet was taking. The Cybermen caught on with children because their appearance was frightening – not quite human but too close for comfort.

The public were intrigued by what they saw in *The Tenth Planet* and wanted more, so Innes Lloyd brought the Cybermen back within a few months, improved – as he saw it – and far more effective. The viewing figures for *Doctor Who* shot up and reviews in the national press praised *The Moonbase* for making the show great once more. The Cybermen had arrived. Within the space of just over two years, they featured in no less than five adventures. Some were good, some not so good – but the Cybermen were always a big audience draw.

Suddenly, they dipped from view. Fourteen years passed with only *Revenge of the Cybermen* and four 'guest' appearances. Then, with *Earthshock*, they came back in a blaze of infamy. It ranked not only with the best of the Cyberman stories but also as a classic *Doctor Who* story in its own right. Such was the effect of their return that it prompted Gavin Millar on BBC2's weekly review programme *Did You See?* to devote part of the show to celebrating past *Doctor Who* monsters and welcoming the return of the Cybermen.

Two more Cyberman stories followed *Earthshock*. The Cybermen have been firmly established once more in the ranks of the most popular monsters on *Doctor Who*. But will they ever march across our screens again to suffer the meddlesome interference of the Doctor, their greatest adversary?

There have been plenty of ideas for stories in which Cybermen feature. Many of them have been considered by *Doctor Who* producers and script writers and have been rejected for one reason or another: *Wargame* featured the Daleks teaming up with the Cybermen; *Hydrogratz* was about the Cybermen's second adopted planet after the destruction of Telos; *Dark Labyrinth* saw the Cybermen return to Ancient Crete – with the help of the Master.

Most probably, none will be seen on TV. But there is one storyline which has been saved from oblivion, *Genesis of the Cybermen* by Gerry Davis, an intriguing speculation about how the Cybermen may have been created. It is published here for the very first time in the fourth and final section of this book – *Datalog*.

Undoubtedly, there is plenty of scope for further adventures. 'I should like a more imaginative use of the Cyber idea,' says David Banks. 'Eric managed it in *Earthshock* – but still created a gripping adventure. The Cybermen have been too much used as "cannon-fodder". But the real excitement and horror of the Cybermen lies deeper – in the entrails of their ideology, if you like – wriggling about in that awful can of cybernetic worms which Kit Pedler opened up over twenty years ago.'

Perhaps the last word should be left to JNT, the producer who has brought three Cybermen stories to our screens. He seems optimistic about the continuance of the Cyber Race. Even the Cybermats might not have gone for good: 'In past stories it's been a matter of money – pounds, shillings and pence. It's yet another effect to add to stories full of effects. But we would certainly consider bringing them back if the right story arrived that featured them in the right way – where they weren't just being used gratuitously.

'As for Cybermen themselves, I think there is always room for development, certainly. I think they are an excellent monster. Excellent!

'EXCELLENT!'

## Silver Nemesis: Hallmark of Excellence

The Cybermen did march across our screens again. Or rather, to be strictly accurate, since this is being written only days before the book goes to press and only days after the filming on this tenth Cyberstory was finished, the Cybermen are scheduled to march across our screens at the end of November 1988.

The story chosen to be the vehicle for their return is, like *The Five Doctors*, an Anniversary Special – this time celebrating twenty-five years of

David Banks as Cyberleader in *Silver Nemesis*

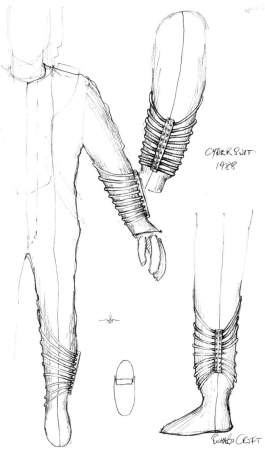

Costume Designer Richard Croft's original drawing for *Silver Nemesis* Cybermen

Location shots from *Silver Nemesis*

RIGHT Sylvester McCoy (the Doctor) disguised as Cyberleader with Sophie Aldred as a perplexed Ace

FAR RIGHT David Banks and Mark Hardy – Cyber double act

Cyberleader unmasked

Doctor Who. It was thought, naturally enough, that the Cybermen would make it an appropriately Silver Anniversary for the Doctor.

It's a three-part adventure called *Silver Nemesis*, the first episode being screened as close as scheduling will allow to 23 November 1988. That is twenty-five years to the day after the first ever *Doctor Who* episode, *An Unearthly Child*, was broadcast to an unsuspecting public.

None of *Silver Nemesis* was recorded in studio. As well as being a hallmark of its prestige, this was also fortuitous. All the main BBC TV studios were out of commission around this time. Crumbling white asbestos had been discovered lining the air conditioning ducts!

Almost a hundred people were involved over a period of three weeks on location at Arundel Castle and Greenwich Gasworks. This was the largest cast and crew since *The Invasion*, as a glance over the credits clearly demonstrates (see *Datalog*). The cast list for *Silver Nemesis* also reveals a subtle tribute the the programme's history. Disguised as 'tourists', a number of well-known names connected with *Doctor Who* actually appear, Hitchcockwise, in the story – including Peter Moffatt, director of the 20th Anniversary Special *The Five Doctors*.

But what about the Cybermen? How had they changed and why? Who was responsible and how did they go about it? So much to tell and so little time or space to do it in. The full story must wait till it can be properly told by the people who actually made the programme. But there is room for one final point.

*Silver Nemesis* is the last of four stories in the 25th Season. It is also the last to be produced by John Nathan-Turner after almost a decade with *Doctor Who*. It is a decade which has seen the re-establishment of the Cybermen, in no less than four separate adventures, to the position they held in the late sixties – most popular of *Doctor Who* monsters. Doubtless, this is due in no small part to the vision and dedication of JNT: a producer, it might be said, of excellence.

# DATALOG

FILE I: LEGEND

Genesis of the Cybermen
by Gerry Davis

FILE II: SPIN-OFFS

1. The Novelisations
2. The Merchandise
3. The Comic Strips

FILE III: PROGRAMMES

1. The Transmission Dates
2. The Programme Credits

'I need more data...'

Tobias Vaughn – THE INVASION

# FILE I : LEGEND

## Genesis of the Cybermen by Gerry Davis

Back in the twilight days of prehistory, the Earth had a twin planet called *Mondas*. Orbiting further away from the sun than Earth, Mondas lacked many of its rich minerals and resources. Consequently, early astronomers considered Mondas to be a barren planet, like Mars – until the Doctor happened to make one of his habitual miscalculations and landed there.

To their surprise, the Doctor and his young companion – pretty, blond *Felicity* – found an advanced civilisation ruled by an old and wise monarch, *King Paulus*. He had two sons: *Prince Dega*, a dark, saturnine and serious man of twenty-five and, younger by three years, his handsome and carefree brother, *Prince Sylvan*. The two youths were being raised to take care over the kingdom as joint rulers. Dega, a scientist and technician, was given responsibility for Mondan science, technology and medicine: Sylvan, the more imaginative one, had custody of the arts, crafts and the agriculture of the planet.

The Doctor and Felicity were favourably impressed with everything (especially, in Felicity's case, by the handsome Sylvan) although the Doctor felt a twinge of apprehension – where had he heard the name 'Mondas' before? Shaking off his qualms, the Doctor turned back to his work and took his faulty Zero Regulator, the vital rejuvenator that kept him alive throughout his numerous transformations, into one of King Paulus's workshops. The different gravitational pull on Mondas provided the Doctor with a rare opportunity to repair the machine.

In the Doctor's absence Felicity, charmed by Sylvan into disobeying the Doctor's orders, brought the young Prince aboard the TARDIS. When the Doctor returned for a replacement part for the Regulator, Sylvan, showing off to Felicity, mistakenly activated the take-off mechanism. The TARDIS dematerialised!

Luckily, the Doctor, for once showing his complete mastery of his craft, took control and landed back on Mondas in exactly the same place – close to the Royal Palace. Only when the time travellers emerged did they find out that the five minute trip in their time had translated to fifty years Mondan time. The Doctor, Felicity and Sylvan stepped out to a greatly changed planet. Heavily armed guards immediately surrounded them and led them before the new king – Dega.

Now fifty years older, Dega finally recognised his brother and the others. He had taken over as absolute ruler of Mondas since their father's death. Lacking the skills of artistry and the emotion of a poet, Dega had transformed the country into a soulless, authoritarian state with technological advances the only officially permitted goal.

The civilisation's most spectacular achieve-ments had been in cybernetics. Dega proudly showed off his massive plastic and metal bionic arms and legs and his colossal strength – not bad for a man of seventy-five! Thanks to the Doctor's Zero Regulator, Dega was now ready for the ultimate transformation – the replacement of his head and trunk by a helmet, computer and chest unit.

With horror, the Doctor recognised what the transformation was leading to. His memory clearing, he begged Dega not to surrender his humanity and turn himself into the prototype of one of the worst scourges the world would ever face – the unfeeling, terrible Cybermen!

Dega, not used to being contradicted, was furious and ordered the Doctor to be taken away by the guards. In the confusion, Felicity managed to slip out of the Palace into the surrounding forest while Sylvan, torn between new friends and the elder brother he always looked up to, stood irresolute.

Dega explained to Sylvan how the complete transformation into Cybermen would give him immortality. When any part of his body wore out, he could be given an indestructible replacement. He would soon have superhuman strength, greatly increased brain function and be impervious to cold, heat or the vacuum of space. A race of such beings could conquer the Universe – starting with their sister planet the Earth!

When Sylvan queried what the people's reaction had been to this, Dega reassured him that they were all behind him. The Mondans were in need of Earth's superior resources in order to survive. A fleet of space rockets were assembled near the Palace to undertake to conquest as soon as a sufficient Cyberman army was ready. Dega offered his brother the joint rulership of the planet with the stipulation that he become a Cyberman as well. He explained to Sylvan how different his friend the Doctor would feel, once he too had become a Cyberman: the Doctor's immense knowledge would be of great value to them.

Meanwhile, lost in the forest, Felicity was captured by a group called the Sylvans. They were the descendants of the artists and artisans who had worked under Prince Sylvan fifty years before. Since Sylvan's mysterious departure, they had become enslaved by Dega's technocrats and forced to give up their artistic pursuits. Now, their sole remaining function was to supply food to the Palace. They were also herded up and treated little better than cattle by their rulers.

Sympathising with their plight, Felicity let them know Prince Sylvan had returned and was being kept in the Palace – a virtual prisoner. The Sylvans led Felicity to a well-hidden cave to meet the leaders of the Sylvan resistance: *Rolf*, aged thirty-five, and *Erde*, thirty.

They told Felicity that they were aware of

KEITH WATSON

Dega's plan to turn his followers into Cybermen. Many of the Sylvan group members were women who preferred to live out their lives naturally rather than achieve a cold immortality as sexless, unloved and unloving robots. Only one Mondan woman had accepted cybernetics -- Dega's wife, *Queen Meta*. A tall, blond, Nordic woman of forty, she now possessed the same bionic arms and legs as her husband.

Felicity suggested that they first rescue the Doctor and Sylvan. They had to act fast because once Dega and his followers were converted into Cybermen, they would be virtually invincible!

Back in the Palace, the Doctor, Sylvan and Queen Meta were escorted to the recharging room to witness Dega's transformation into a Cyberman. The Transformer opened and with horror the Doctor saw the creation of the world's first Cyberman! Dega, now a Cyberman, rose up and was congratulated by his men – the experiment was a success: now the Doctor would become the second Cyberman.

Refusing to comply, the Doctor struggled to get free but was felled by a spark from Dega's metal gauntlet and placed inside the coffin-like Transformer. The switch was pulled and the lid started to close down upon him.

Meanwhile, the Sylvans and Felicity infiltrated the Palace – breaking in and overpowering Dega's men. Released in the nick of time, the Doctor persuaded Sylvan that Dega did not represent the will of the majority of the people of Mondas. The joyful Sylvans acclaimed their long-lost Prince. But their triumph was short lived. Queen Meta, leading the guards in a counter attack, drove the Sylvan rebels from the Palace and captured Felicity and Sylvan. The Doctor disappeared in the mêlée.

Dega, restored to power, issued two directives: to start mass producing the Cybermen army, and to ready the spaceship for launching. Before their departure, Dega planned to release a deadly gas that would wipe out the remaining Mondan people. The Earth was to become the Cyberman base for further conquests.

Led by *Krail*, Dega's chief of staff, Dega's followers began to file into the Transformation Rooms. Only Meta stood aside, deeply troubled, while Felicity and Sylvan were dragged off to prison to await their turn in the Transformation Room.

Meanwhile, the Doctor had contacted the Sylvans. Rolf's plan was to head for the mountains and hide out until the Cybermen had left on the spaceships. The Doctor disagreed – Dega, leave behind a hostile population that could build further spaceships and follow him to Earth? Never! Dega was now a Cyberman, a creature without a shred of compassion: he was probably planning some reprisal to annihilate the people of Mondas

after his departure. The best plan was to return to the Palace and find out – and save Prince Sylvan and Felicity.

Felicity, next in line to be converted, desperately appealed to Meta. The Queen was still a woman with a woman's capacity for love, nurturing and compassion. As she stood irresolute, Krail, now a Cyberman, entered and promised Sylvan he would spare the girl if the Prince disclosed the location of the TARDIS. Sylvan told him, despite Felicity's appeals, but Krail still refused to let Felicity go. Instead, he lifted the girl, placed her in the Transformer and clamped down the lid. Then he told Sylvan it was not logical that he keep his word – he, Krail, had nothing to gain from it – therefore his promise was worthless.

Krail raised his hand to the switch, but Queen Meta stopped him, angered by his duplicity. As the Queen, she order Krail to release Felicity and get out. After a moment's hesitation, Krail obeyed but told her he would have to report to Dega for further orders. As soon as the Cyberman had gone, Meta showed Felicity and Sylvan a secret passage through the Palace – used by Dega to get to the launch site.

The Cyberman army emerged from the Transformation Rooms in a steady stream and were lining up before Dega. Krail entered and informed Dega of what had taken place. Meanwhile, the Doctor and his party were entering the Palace by a hidden door known to Rolf. They reached an underground laboratory filled with black canisters – cyanide gas! There was only one thing for it now, the Doctor told them: they had to get to the spaceships before the Cybermen and force the commanders to start the countdown to launch.

Back in the Transformation Room, Dega arrived to confront Meta and find out where Sylvan and Felicity had gone. Furious, she refused to answer but she was unable to keep the information from him: he read her mind. He raced to the passage, followed by Krail, Meta and a line of Cybermen.

At the other entrance to the passage, Sylvan and Felicity had just emerged. Someone was waiting for them. A Cyberman? No, it was the Doctor! As they hurried off to the spacecraft, the steady tramp of Cybermen was heard coming down the passage after them. At the launch site, the Sylvans had already taken over the spaceships. The long countdown to launch began.

As the last Sylvans entered the leading spacecraft, Sylvan turned to the Doctor and Felicity and urged them aboard. The Doctor shook his head. They had to find their way back to the TARDIS. There was a sad moment of farewell between Sylvan and Felicity, broken by a warning cry from the Doctor – the spaceship was surrounded by Cybermen!

Suddenly, Dega appeared, cutting off Sylvan's way to the entry hatch. The Doctor intervened but the Cyberman sent him spinning with a slight flick of his metal hand. Dega turned and accused his brother of being a traitor. He raised his hand to give Sylvan the lethal Cyberman chop with his massive arm.

With the flash and rattle of a cyberweapon, Queen Meta shot the Cyberman King. Smoke reeking from his metal shoulder joints, Dega crashed down – dead.

Meta shouted to Sylvan to escape. The Prince begged her to come with them. She refused. As the Doctor began to come to, Sylvan ran to help him to his feet. The Doctor brushed off the offer of help and told Sylvan to go while he could. Sylvan ran off and reached the entry hatch just in time to slam it shut as Krail arrived and examined his dead King. There was a moment's confrontation between Meta and Krail. Then the Cyberman raised his weapon and cut her down.

The rocket motors of the spacecraft ignited with a thunderous roar, throwing up clouds of dust. One by one the spacecraft were launched.

When the dust began to settle, the Cybermen discovered that the Doctor and Felicity had disappeared.

Approaching the TARDIS, the Doctor and Felicity found it surrounded by Cybermen sent to guard it. At that moment there was a sound like thunder and the planet began shaking as if in the grip of an earthquake. The explosion-like tremor threw the heavy Cybermen off balance. The lighter and more agile Doctor and Felicity darted between the stricken giants and got safely into the TARDIS.

As the Doctor feverishly worked the controls, he yelled to Felicity that the massive impact of the six giant rocketships must have thrust Mondas out of its orbit in the solar system. Outside, the Cybermen were recovering. They levelled their weapons at the TARDIS, then stood back in confusion as it dematerialised.

The Doctor and Felicity anxiously watched the scanner showing six rocketships moving towards the blue-white globe of Earth. The Doctor then turned the scanner back towards the planet they had just left. Mondas was slowly spinning away out of the Solar System and into deep space.

Felicity turned to the Doctor and asked if Mondas would ever return. The Doctor nodded. 'Yes, some day. I wish I could remember what happened – I must look up my diary!'

'And the Sylvans? Won't they have a great effect on the Earth?' asked Felicity anxiously. 'Won't they change Earth history?'

The Doctor thought, then shook his head. 'The Sylvans will have an immediate effect upon the people they meet and probably leave a few artifacts around for future archeologists to puzzle over – then they will be absorbed into the prevailing culture and forgotten. But they will have made their contribution, never fear. The Earth people will derive a great deal from them. Sylvan and his people are part of your heritage!'

Venice, California
January 1986

# FILE II: SPIN-OFFS

## 1. The Novelisations

The *Doctor Who* television series has generated a library of books, each an adaptation of one complete adventure. They have been published by Target Books – a division of W H Allen – and the selection of titles now numbers more than a hundred. They have come to be known as the 'novelisations'.

All the Cyberman stories have been, or are in the process of being, novelised. They are listed in the order in which they were first published:

*Doctor Who and the Cybermen*
by Gerry Davis
Based on *The Moonbase*
by Gerry Davis and Kit Pedler
Cover by Chris Achilleos
Illustrations by Alan Willow
Published February 1975
No. 14 in the *Doctor Who* library

*Doctor Who and the Tenth Planet*
by Gerry Davis
Based on *The Tenth Planet*
by Gerry Davis and Kit Pedler
Cover artwork by Chris Achilleos
Published March 1976
No. 62 in the *Doctor Who* library

*Doctor Who and the Revenge of the Cybermen*
by Terrance Dicks
Based on *Revenge of the Cybermen*
by Gerry Davis with Robert Holmes
Cover artwork by Chris Achilleos
Published May 1976
No. 51 in the *Doctor Who* library

*Doctor Who and the Tomb of the Cybermen*
by Gerry Davis
Based on *Tomb of the Cybermen*
by Gerry Davis and Kit Pedler
Cover artwork by Jeff Cummins
Published May 1978
No. 66 in the *Doctor Who* library

*Doctor Who – Earthshock*
by Ian Marter
Based on *Earthshock*
by Eric Saward
Cover: photo-montage
Published August 1983
No. 78 in the *Doctor Who* library

*Doctor Who – The Five Doctors*
by Terrance Dicks
Based on *The Five Doctors*
by Terrance Dicks
Cover artwork by Andrew Skilleter
Published November 1983
No. 81 in the *Doctor Who* library

*Doctor Who – The Invasion*
by Ian Marter
Based on *The Invasion*
by Derrick Sherwin
Cover artwork by Andrew Skilleter
Published October 1985
No. 98 in the *Doctor Who* library

*Doctor Who – The Wheel In Space*
by Terrance Dicks
Based on *The Wheel In Space*
by David Whitaker
Cover artwork by Ian Burgess
Published August 1988
No. 130 in the *Doctor Who* library

*Doctor Who – Attack of the Cybermen*
by Eric Saward
Based on *Attack of the Cybermen*
by Paula Moore
To be published Summer 1989

*Doctor Who – Silver Nemesis*
by Kevin Clarke
Based on *Silver Nemesis*
by Kevin Clarke
To be published 1990/91

## 2. The Merchandise

In 1967 the Cybermen began to feature in the merchandise associated with *Doctor Who*. There is no doubt that their profile would have been much higher had it not been for the BBC's refusal to allow Kit Pedler and Gerry Davis to fully exploit the idea of Cybermen commercially – as Terry Nation was able to do with the Daleks. Nevertheless, their popularity has always been celebrated by a wide variety of merchandise.

Top of the league must be the Cyberman doll, distributed by Palitoy in 1975. It was one of a collection which included Tom Baker as the Doctor. Around ten inches high, it had sophisticated joint movements, a nylon silver suit and grey plastic fittings. The design, however, left something to be desired: it was a hybrid of several Cyber types and, most unfortunate of all, the face sported what was undeniably a nose! These were the days when merchandising was relatively unsupervised. One could not imagine the design passing through the *Doctor Who* Office today.

In the sixties and seventies, *Doctor Who* merchandise was often associated with product promotion. The Daleks dominated but Cybermen were not left out in the cold. Games, chocolate figures, even chewy bars, have all depicted the Cybermen in some form. Typhoo tea offered a wallchart and cards which featured Cybermen; and in 1975, Weetabix gave away a series of cards featuring

DOCTOR WHO MARVEL ADVENTURE COMIC
PLUS! The Doctor's Data Base
from Golden Wonder
No. 1. 'REVELATION'

*Invasion*-type Cybermen as part of an 'Action Zone' board game which described the Dalek's rivals as:

> Power-hungry silver giants from planet Telos. Strong and highly intelligent robot-like creatures with no human feelings. Fought the Doctor in many different times and places.

Much of the Cyber merchandise appeared post-*Earthshock* (1982) following the renewed interest in the Cybermen. There have been badges, prismatic stick-ons, T-shirts, a jigsaw and even a credit card bearing the *Ghostbusters*-inspired emblem of a cartoon Cybermen climbing through a crossed-out red circle. And at a recent *Doctor Who* convention, a badge (not originally designed as Cyber merchandise) was given to the Cyberleader by an astute fan. It read:

> I am not a trained killer.
> I *lead* trained killers.

Items which are currently available include a posterprint, bookmarks, artcards and a plastic Cybermat kit. There is a wide range of metal and plastic models of various Cyber types (including one diminutive figure of the dying Cyberleader from *The Five Doctors* in the act of disgorging internal fluid!). And in 1986 the American comany Fasa produced a Cyberman version of a role-playing board game complete with a short, somewhat fanciful, history of the Cyber Race.

Most recently, at time of going to press, there have become available plastic model kits of various Doctor Who 'personae', among which are free-standing Cybermen and the head of the Cyberleader. Even more spectacular, perhaps, is the new set of Doctor Who holograms. You can now hang on your living room wall a chillingly lifelike picture of a Cyberman - in glorious 3D!

The *Doctor Who* Calendar has been published annually since 1985 by Who Dares and has always featured the Cybermen. In 1986/7 the Calendar and the Cybermen appeared as part of a *Doctor Who* Golden Wonder crisp promotion costing more than £200,000. The number of crisp packets involved was 108 million! Perhaps, at last, the Cybermen have achieved their aim of invading every home in the nation.

### 3. The Comic Strips

Also featured in the Golden Wonder crisp promotion were six different *Doctor Who/Marvel* mini-comics. One of them featured the Cybermen in *Revelation!*, a story adapted from an adventure recently published in *Doctor Who Monthly* – the latest of a long line of Cyberman stories told in comic strip form.

On November 14th, 1964 – less than a year after the Doctor was first seen on TV – his picture strip adventures began to appear in *TV Comic*; and when the Cybermen made their popular debut, *TV Comic* was quick to include them in the strip. The Cybermen fought their old enemy the Doctor in no fewer than five different stories – though they remained in their *Tenth Planet* guise throughout. The publishers had sent artist John Canning a batch of *The Tenth Planet* production stills and asked him to use them as reference for a series of Cyberman stories, even though the TV

A complete Cyberman comic strip from TV Comic Annual, 1970

Cybermen had already evolved into their more metallic post-*Moonbase* versions.

Such indifference to detail is not surprising: cult interest in the programme was in its infancy; the comic strip adventures were targeted at children. When the series came to an end it was to be nearly ten years before the Cybermen appeared in a comic strip again. But this time the impetus came from the fans who had grown up with *Doctor Who* and their contribution was to be much more interesting.

In the meantime the same publishing group launched (in 1975) a glossy new TV based comic called *Countdown* which featured Jon Pertwee as the Doctor. This title was not to last long, however, and merged into *TV Action* where the Doctor was promoted to front page status. *TV Action* was then taken over by *TV Comic* again. In 1979 under Polystyle Publications and featuring Tom Baker as the Doctor, the strip came to an end.

But the fans need not have feared that they would never see the good Doctor 'framed' again. In October of the same year *Doctor Who Weekly* (DWW) hit the newsagents, published by Marvel Comics. After Issue 43 it became a monthly publication (DWM) and is still flourishing. Adventures inspired by the *Doctor Who* television series have been depicted in picture strip form in every issue and the Cybermen have featured strongly. In fact, the Cybermen adventures did not at first involve the Doctor at all: interest in the Cybermen as an alien race sustained three 'solo' adventures before they were again to meet up with the Doctor.

And, of course, apart from the official *Doctor Who* publications, there are dozens of 'fanzines' published each year. Many of them have incorporated strips of their own. The Cybermen are often included in these diverse adventures. Due to these 'maverick' adventures, as well as the 'official' ones, the continued existence of the Cybermen, with or without the Doctor to confront, is probably more assured in comic strip form than anywhere else.

Here, then, we present an account of the 'official' comic strips – what might be termed the Further Adventures of the Cybermen:

*The Return of the Cybermen*
(*TV Comic* 824-827 – art/story John Canning)

The TARDIS becomes trapped on board a Space Carrier. The Doctor discovers that the Cybermen are about to launch a cybermissile at Earth. They are intent on colonising the planet and turning surviving humans into Cybermen. It is up to the Doctor and his two young companions John and Gillian to stop the Cybermen before it is too late. They succeed but put their own lives at great risk in the process.

*Flower Power*
(*TV Comic* 832-836 – art/story John Canning)

The Doctor and his two companions land on a planet that appears almost too peaceful to be true. Lush flowers and trees stretch for as far as the eye can see but there seems to be no wildlife. The Doctor discovers a de-activated Cybermat. They decide to find out what is going on and meet a rather eccentric character called Professor Gant who agrees to help them in their quest. Together, they soon locate a city of Cybermen and through their combined knowledge are able to rid the planet of the metallic menace.

*Cyber-Mole*
(*TV Comic* 842-845 – art/story John Canning)

The Cybermen have landed a fleet of their ships on Earth. Using their latest technology, a tunnelling machine called the Cyber-mole, they steal a gigantic bomb known as the Doomsday Device. They plant it at the centre of the Earth and threaten to explode it unless the humans give up their planet to them. The Doctor once more brings his wits to bear and saves the day.

*Empire of the Cybermen*
(*TV Comic* 850-853 – art/story John Canning)

The Doctor accidently lands the TARDIS in the principal city of the Cybermen's home planet. He is brought before the Cybercontroller. He agrees to fight for his life on the condition that if the Cybercontroller loses, he must free the thousands of human beings held captive on the planet. The Doctor manages to win through and the humans escape with him from the deadly city of the Cybermen.

*Conflict on Ice*
(*TV Comic* 903-906 – art/story John Canning)

The Cybermen invade a planet whose sole

inhabitants are a race of beings similar to the Eskimos of Earth. The Cybermen kill some of the natives and capture others. Fortunately for the planet, the Doctor, with the assistance of an inventor called Joe, is able to defeat the threat of the Cybermen and set free the captives.

*Throwback – the Soul of a Cyberman*
(DWW 5-7 – no art or story credits)

Part 1: The setting is Modaran, a planet recently taken over by the Cybermen. The cities are in ruins. Cybermen patrol the area continually to wipe out all resistance. A group of rebel guerrillas led by the man Pendar and the woman Marilka attack a lone Cyberman and destroy him. To avoid suspicion they break up and plan to meet in three days time. At Cyber Headquarters Command Cyberleader Tork notes that twenty-three of his troops have now been destroyed by the guerrillas. He informs fellow Leaders that he has requested reinforcements from Telos to 'solve the problem' of human resistance.

On Telos, Cyberleader Kroton is to lead the reinforcements. His junior officer, Liron, suspects his Leader may be malfunctioning when he finds Kroton gazing skywards for no explicable reason. Arriving on Modaran, Kroton intervenes when he finds a Cyberman beating a girl. Her father, Willoway, has been taken away to be questioned for suspected resistance activities. To her surprise the girl is released by Kroton.

Pendar meets with the other members of the rebel force at the agreed time. He discovers that Willoway has died under questioning by the Command Cyberleader. They decide to disperse but find their exit blocked by a Cyberman.

Part 2: It is Kroton. He has come to make peace and help the guerrillas. Terrified, they attack him and escape but are soon apprehended by two patrolling Cybermen. Kroton appears and calls them off. Pendar begins to wonder whether this Cyberleader could really be on their side. Back at Cyberbase, Kroton is informed by the Command Cyberleader that a human informer has brought interesting news.

Pendar has been caught again by a Cyberpatrol and this time placed in a cell at Cyberbase. Late at night, Kroton frees him and takes him to the safety of the wastelands beyond the Modaran city. There he explains that the Cybermen know of the planned uprising. He tells Pendar to halt the rebellion and save the lives of his friends. Pendar thinks it is a trick and prepares to smash Kroton's head with a rock.

Part 3: But Pendar realises that if he destroys Kroton it would make him no better than the Cybermen he was fighting. He takes his leave of Kroton who is puzzling over why he should be experiencing these strange feelings – emotions. Pendar takes Mirilka to see Kroton but they encounter a Cyberpatrol sent by the Command Cyberleader to find Kroton. When Kroton destroys the patrol to save the humans, Pendar concludes that this Cyberleader is really human inside his metal body.

Marilka wishes they had a pilot amongst the rebel force: they could steal a battle cruiser and leave the city far behind. Kroton offers to pilot the ship – his place is with Cybermen no longer. The guerrillas gather together and Kroton leads a successful attack on the Cyber space-port. He takes the humans to the Forest of Lorn on the far side of the planet but knowing his power will soon run out, he goes on alone into deep space. There, his batteries fade and his motionless body is left to drift endlessly through space in a pilotless space ship.

*Deathworld*
(DWW 15-16 – story Steve Moore – art David Lloyd)

Part 1: The Ice Warriors are on a routine patrol of space. Heading towards planet Yama 10, their instruments indicate traces of trisilicate on the planet's surface – a valuable power source. They land and set up a base. During reconnaissance one of the Ice Warriors is killed by a wild animal with poisonous fangs. The leader orders the forest to be burnt down.

That night a bright light crosses the skyline. Commander Yinak thinks it must be a meteorite. But at dawn the ground is found to be infested with Cybermats. They are an unknown menace to the Ice Warriors and several of them die before they realise how lethal they can be.

The Ice Warriors, led by Yinak, begin to mine for trisilicate. Their efforts are interrupted by a group of Cybermen who proclaim they have taken over the planet.

Part 2: Yinak's party manages to escape and get back to base. Within an hour everything has been packed away and their ship has been made ready for battle. As a group of forty Cybermen is seen approaching, Yinak decides to face them on the polar region of the planet so that the Ice Warriors will not suffer heat exhaustion.

They set a careful trap in the form of a pit in which the battle takes place. When the Cybermen attack, their weapons melt large volumes of ice bringing watery destruction on themselves. But the plan backfires when the Ice Warriors become trapped in an avalanche. All is not lost, however. They are well suited to surviving the coldest conditions. Come the Spring thaw, they will be free.

*The Ship of Fools*
(DWW 23-24 – story Steve Moore – art Dillon)

Part 1: Cyberleader Kroton's cruiser is drifting through space. The ship enters a miasmic cloud and is picked up by a gigantic spaceliner. The crew recharge Kroton's body and he comes back to life. He is shown round the liner which, he is told, is on a pleasure cruise. Strangely, all clocks are stuck at 7.17. Then he comes across a writer who has produced reams of paper with nothing but 'boredom' written on them. Kroton's guide, a blind artist called Leonart, explains that time stands still on this ship. Its name is Flying Dutchman II.

Part 2: Kroton learns that on Earth the name means a ship of the damned. Kroton determines to break the ship free from its time trap. Breaking into the control cabin with the help of a cybergun from his own ship, he discovers that the pilot is a robot. Kroton figures out how to free the ship from its time warp and as it begins to emerge into real-time, the instruments tell him it has been trapped for 628 years. All around him the bodies of the passengers, ageing rapidly, are disintegrating. For them the voyage is over. Kroton is alone once more.

*Black Legacy*
(DWW 35-38 story Steve Moore art David Lloyd)

Part 1: The Planet of Goth was once ruled by the Deathsmiths of Goth, a race who were skilled in developing the deadliest weapons imaginable. Their entire race vanished mysteriously overnight. Their world is now a dead planet. It holds many secrets that would be desirable to other war-mongering races such as the Cybermen.

An expedition from Telos lands on Goth, lead by Cyberleader Maxel and his second in command, Loktar. They have come to discover the secrets of the Deathsmiths to aid them in their conquest of the galaxy. As Maxel contemplates the vast array of deadly devices, he is watched by something in the nearby undergrowth.

During the night, Loktar has a vision of some

foul creature chasing him. Maxel, who thinks his subordinate is malfunctioning, orders Loktar to stay behind and preserve his power while the rest of the Cybermen go and explore the city of the Deathsmiths. All they find of the Deathsmiths themselves are piles of ash and a few bones. But their war museum is intact and full of every weapon the men of Goth ever created.

Back at their base, Loktar hears something which he knows cannot be a fellow Cyberman. Suddenly the creature from the undergrowth attacks him.

Part 2: Exploring the war museum, Maxel comes across an empty chamber. A sign on the open door indicates that it once contained an ultimate weapon, the Apocalypse Device. All the hundreds of ships in the city's spaceport have been destroyed. Maxel reasons that through such destruction the Deathsmiths must have desperately wanted to stop something from ever escaping the planet.

Maxel and his Cybermen return to base with many of the museum's weapons and devices. They discover Loktar, his metal case rotting away as they watch. A Cybertechnician examines him and concludes he will cease to exist within the hour. The technician advises Maxel to abandon the planet. Maxel refuses to do so until he has found the missing Apocalypse Device.

Part 3: One Cybermen after another succumb to the strange rusting symptoms which destroyed Loktar. Some have nightmares, some go 'rogue' and start to kill other Cybermen. Soon only Maxel remains. Reasoning that whatever destroyed his men must have the form of a living being, he decides to confront it. Carrying as many weapons as he can manage, he strides out into open ground

and challenges whatever it is that has killed his men to reveal itself and fight. A rotting humanoid figure emerges – a Grim Reaper – and announces itself as the Apocalypse Device.

Part 4: Maxel uses every weapon at his disposal against the creature – to no avail. He now realises what destroyed the Deathsmiths but also why they destroyed all their spaceships and why the Apocalypse Device allowed Maxel to survive. Maxel's cybership would provide the creature with a means of reaching other planets. To ensure that it could never escape to bring annihilation to the rest of the galaxy, Maxel destroys his own ship and himself with it.

Years later, a Sontaran battle cruiser lands on the planet of Goth. The creature looks on from the undergrowth in delight. Another means of escape has arrived.

*Junkyard Demon*
(DWM 58-59 – editor Alan McKenzie – story Steve Parkhouse – art Mike McMahon/Adolfo Buylla)

Part 1: The TARDIS is picked up by a wandering space salvage craft whose two crewmen, Flotsam and Jets, mistake the Doctor's mode of transport for a piece of junk. As the craft's robot, Dutch, attempts without success to gain access to the TARDIS, the Doctor emerges. The crew apologise and ask if he is in need of any spares. As it happens he wants a Variable Oscillator for his vending machine. As they search through piles of junk he uncovers a *Tenth Planet* type of Cyberman. The Doctor, panicking, throws a spanner at the Cyberman's head before he realises that it is inactive. But as Flotsam, Jets and the Doctor go into the TARDIS the Cybermen comes to life and follows them, proclaiming, 'Resistance is useless'.

Part 2: Dutch comes behind the Cyberman and shoots. The Cyberman retaliates and Dutch is badly damaged. As he Doctor and Flotsam run to help Dutch, the Cyberman takes control of the TARDIS. It disappears with Jets still on board.

They land on a planet where a Cybernaut (sic), the great Zogron, is lying seriously damaged. The Cyberman commands Jets to repair him. Jets succeeds in re-activating Zogron but his programming is faulty and he talks nonsense. Jets is trying to avoid the Cyberman's retribution when the Doctor and Flotsam arrive in the salvage craft. Dutch, now repaired, de-activates the Cyberman with spray paint. The Doctor takes his leave, observing that it was lucky they hadn't found any Daleks.

*Exodus!*
The people of the planet Sylvaniar are fighting for survival. The poorer part of the planet has suffered nothing but famine and drought. Peasants gather together what few belongings they have and try to get away in ramshackle space ships to some other planet where they will be able to lead more fruitful lives.

The Doctor is trying to repair some damaged circuits on board the TARDIS with the assistance of his companion Frobisher, a Shape-shifter stuck in the guise of a penguin. In one of the rooms in the TARDIS Frobisher comes across Peri who is rummaging through a hamper of clothes. They hear a strange scratching coming from an empty room down the corridor and investigate. Within is a family of Sylvaniar farmers and their old space car.

When the Doctor is told, he guesses that the Sylvaniars must have passed through the TARDIS time stream as they travelled in space. The family explain about conditions on Syvaniar. People in the mysterious 'Castle' were always better off than any of the land workers. Also members of their community would simply vanish in the middle of the night. The Doctor stocks the family up with food and clothing and sends them on their way. He then sets a course for Sylvaniar determined to find out why their farmers vanish and who the people in the Castle are.

*Revelation!*
Professor Verdeghast is working in his rooms in the Castle when a strange figure creeps up behind him and breaks his neck. It takes the book that the Professor was working on. Minutes later the TARDIS appears in the same room. The Doctor, Peri and Frobisher discover the Professor's dead body. Suddenly Captain Krogh and two guards burst in. He accuses them of murder and has them locked away. After questioning the Captain agrees to let them go if the Doctor helps to find the murderer. Peri and Frobisher remain locked up.

As the Doctor and Krogh search for clues they bump into the sinister figure of Dr Kravaal. As they leave him, a Dr Sovak staggers into their path. He has been attacked in a similar way to Verdeghast. The Doctor and Krogh go immediately to report the attacks to the Director, Professor Rukh. As they enter they find him being strangled by a Cyberman with a human arm and leg.

*Genesis!*
The Cyberman escapes through a secret passageway. They follow. To their surprise they find it is Dr Sovak who is changing humans into Cybermen. He explains how the farmers found a wrecked cybership and how he rebuilt their army using farmers' bodies. Sovak tries prematurely to activate the Cyber army. They explode and he is killed in the process. Fire courses through the Castle. Saving his companions from the flames, the Doctor, Krogh and the other survivors make for the safety of a hill from where they watch as the Castle is razed to the ground.

# FILE III : PROGRAMMES

## 1. THE TRANSMISSION DATES

### A NOTE ON SERIAL CODES

Because *Doctor Who* has been such a long running series (now well into its third decade), the form of code used to distinguish each separate serial has undergone considerable change. It has expanded from a simple single-letter identification to a more complex arrangement of letter and figures.

William Hartnell's Doctor lasted for 29 stories. The first 25 are catalogued A – Z (in this system the letters I and/or O are sometimes skipped over to avoid confusion with the numbers 1 and 0), so *The Daleks* is coded B because it was the second one to be broadcast. *The Gunfighters* is Z because it was the twenty-fifth.

The twenty-sixth story therefore began a run of double-letter codes. The story was called *The Savages* and coded AA. *The War Games*, Patrick Troughton's final story as the Doctor, happened to coincide with the end of the double-letter run. As the fiftieth adventure of the series it was coded ZZ.

Thus, Jon Pertwee's era ushered in the use of three letters. His first story was *Spearhead From Space* (code AAA) and his last, again coinciding with the end of a sequence, was *Planet of the Spiders* (code ZZZ). Tom Baker's first story marked the beginning of the four letter sequence. For ease of use it was written not as AAAA but as 4A. At the beginning of each subsequent cycle of stories the number was increased by one, leading to codes such as 5X, 6T, 7B and so on.

Here is a summary of the codes used for each era of the seven Doctors so far:

| First Doctor (William Hartnell) | A – DD |
| Second Doctor (Patrick Troughton) | EE – ZZ |
| Third Doctor (Jon Pertwee) | AAA – ZZZ |
| Fourth Doctor (Tom Baker) | 4A – 5V |
| Fifth Doctor (Peter Davison) | 5Z – 6R |
| Sixth Doctor (Colin Baker) | 6S – 7C |
| Seventh Doctor (Sylvester McCoy) | 7D – ? |

### CYBERSTORY TRANSMISSION DATES
A catalogue of the nine Cyberman stories shown on BBCTV to date in order of their appearance:

**The Tenth Planet (Serial DD)**
by Kit Pedler and Gerry Davis

| Episode 1 | 8 October 1966 |
| Episode 2 | 15 October 1966 |
| Episode 3 | 22 October 1966 |
| Episode 4 | 29 October 1966 |

**The Moonbase (Serial HH)**
by Kit Pedler and Gerry Davis

| Episode 1 | 11 February 1967 |
| Episode 2 | 18 February 1967 |
| Episode 3 | 25 February 1967 |
| Episode 4 | 4 March 1967 |

**Tomb of the Cybermen (Serial MM)**
by Kit Pedler and Gerry Davis

| Episode 1 | 2 September 1967 |
| Episode 2 | 9 September 1967 |
| Episode 3 | 16 September 1967 |
| Episode 4 | 23 September 1967 |

**The Wheel In Space (Serial SS)**
by David Whitaker (story Kit Pedler)

| Episode 1 | 27 April 1968 |
| Episode 2 | 4 May 1968 |
| Episode 3 | 11 May 1968 |
| Episode 4 | 18 May 1968 |
| Episode 5 | 25 May 1968 |
| Episode 6 | 1 June 1968 |

**The Invasion (Serial VV)**
by Derrick Sherwin (story Kit Pedler)

| Episode 1 | 2 November 1968 |
| Episode 2 | 9 November 1968 |
| Episode 3 | 16 November 1968 |
| Episode 4 | 23 November 1968 |
| Episode 5 | 30 November 1968 |
| Episode 6 | 7 December 1968 |
| Episode 7 | 14 December 1968 |
| Episode 8 | 21 December 1968 |

**Revenge of the Cybermen (Serial 4D)**
by Gerry Davis with Robert Holmes

| Episode 1 | 19 April 1975 |
| Episode 2 | 26 April 1975 |
| Episode 3 | 3 May 1975 |
| Episode 4 | 10 May 1975 |

**Earthshock (Serial 6B)**
by Eric Saward

| Episode 1 | 8 March 1982 |
| Episode 2 | 9 March 1982 |
| Episode 3 | 15 March 1982 |
| Episode 4 | 16 March 1982 |

**The Five Doctors (Serial 6K)**
by Terrance Dicks

| 90-minute feature | 25 November 1983 |

**Attack of the Cybermen (Serial 6T)**
by Paula Moore with Eric Saward

| Episode 1 | 5 January 1985 |
| Episode 2 | 13 January 1985 |

**Silver Nemesis (Serial 7K)**
by Kevin Clarke

| Episode 1 | Still to be announced |
| Episode 2 | at time of |
| Episode 3 | going to press |

### GUEST APPEARANCES
Episodes of other *Doctor Who* adventures in which the Cybermen figure briefly (as discussed in Section III – 'The Years In Between'):

**The War Games (Serial ZZZ)**
by Malcolm Hulke and Terrance Dicks

| Episode 10 | 21 June 1969 |

**The Mind of Evil (Serial FFF)**
by Don Houghton

| Episode 3 | 13 February 1971 |

**Carnival of Monsters (Serial PPP)**
by Robert Holmes

| Episode 1 | 27 January 1973 |

**Logopolis (Serial 5V)**
by Christopher H Bidmead

| Episode 4 | 20 March 1981 |

**Mawdryn Undead (Serial 6F)**
by Peter Grimwade

| Episode 2 | 2 February 1983 |

## 2. THE PROGRAMME CREDITS

*THE TENTH PLANET*

**regulars:**
| William Hartnell | The Doctor |
| Michael Craze | Ben Jackson |
| Anneke Wills | Polly |

**Cybermen:**
| Gregg Palmer | Shav and Gern |
| Reg Whitehead | Krail and Jarl |
| Harry Brooks | Talon and Krang |

**Cyber extras:**
| John Haines | Bruce Wells |
| | John Knott |

**voices:**
| | Roy Skelton |
| | Peter Hawkins |

**additional:**
| Robert Beatty | General Cutler |
| Dudley Jones | Dr John Dyson |
| David Dodimead | Dr Tom Barclay |
| Alan White | Astronaut Dan Schultz |
| Earl Cameron | Astronaut Glyn Williams |
| Shane Shelton | Tito |
| John Brandon | American Sergeant |
| Steve Plytas | Wigner |
| Christopher Matthews | Radar Technician |
| Ellen Cullen | Technician at Geneva |
| Glenn Beck | TV Announcer |
| Christopher Dunham | R/T Technician |
| Callen Angelo | Terry Cutler |
| Peter Pocock | Soldier |
| Nicholas Edwards | 2nd R/T Technician |
| Sheila Edwards | Secretary |
| Alec Coleman | Corporal |
| Patrick Troughton | Rejuvenated Doctor |

**soldiers:**
| | Ken McGarvie |
| Terence Jones | Freddie Eldrett |
| Nick Hilton | Roy Pierce |

| officers: | Richard Lawrence |
| --- | --- |
| Morris Quick | Gordon Lang |
| Bill Gosling | |

| engineers: | Roy Pierce |
| --- | --- |
| | Freddie Eldrett |

doubles:
Gordon Graig for William Hartnell
Peter Pocock for Michael Craze

| technical: | |
| --- | --- |
| Peter Kindred | Designer |
| Gerry Davis | Story Editor |
| Gillian James | Make-up Designer |
| Sandra Reid | Costume Supervisor |
| Adrian Bishop-Laggett | Sound |
| Howard King | Lighting |
| Jenny McCarther | Assistant Floor Manager |
| Edwina Verner | Production Assistant |
| Derek Martinus | Director |
| Innes Lloyd | Producer |

*THE MOONBASE*

| regulars: | |
| --- | --- |
| Patrick Troughton | The Doctor |
| Michael Craze | Ben Jackson |
| Anneke Wills | Polly |
| Frazer Hines | Jamie McCrimmon |

| Cybermen: | Reg Whitehead |
| --- | --- |
| Keith Goodman | John Clifford |
| Barry Noble | Sonnie Willis |
| Ronald Lee | John Wills |
| Peter Greene | |

| voices: | Peter Hawkins |
| --- | --- |

| additional: | |
| --- | --- |
| Patrick Barr | Hobson |
| Andre Maranne | Benoit |
| Michael Wolf | Nils |
| John Rolfe | Sam |
| Mark Heath | Ralph |
| Alan Rowe | Dr Evans |
| Ron Pinell | Jim (no. 5) |
| Edward Phillips | Bob (no. 7) |
| Robin Scott | Charlie (no. 8) |
| Alan Wells | Joe (no. 9) |
| Victor Pemberton | Jules (no. 10) |
| Derek Calder | Peter (no. 11) |
| Leon Maybank | Ted (no. 12) |
| Barry Ashton | Franz (no. 13) |
| Arnold Chazen | John (no. 15) |

| voices: | |
| --- | --- |
| Alan Rowe | Space Control |
| Denis McCarthy | Controller Rinberg |

| extras: | Sonnie Willis |
| --- | --- |
| Derek Shafer | Declan Cuffe |
| Bernard Reid | Mike Britain |
| Terry Wallis | Paul Harrington |
| John Levine | |

| technical: | |
| --- | --- |
| Colin Shaw | Designer |
| Gerry Davis | Story Editor |
| Peter Hamilton | Film Cameraman |
| Ted Walter | Film Editor |
| Gillian James/Jeanne Richmond | Make-up |
| Sandra Reid/Daphne Dare/Mary Woods | Costume |
| Gordon Mackie | Sound |
| Dave Sydenham/Brian Clement | Lighting |
| Peter Cambell/Mike Healy | Floor Assistants |
| Ian Easterbrook | Vision Mixer |
| Alan Boyd/Dave Baumber | Grams Operators |
| Glenys Williams | Assistant |
| Lovett Bickford | Assistant Floor Manager |
| Desmond McCarthy | Production Manager |
| Innes Lloyd | Producer |
| Morris Barry | Director |

*TOMB OF THE CYBERMEN*

| regulars: | |
| --- | --- |
| Patrick Troughton | The Doctor |
| Frazer Hines | Jamie McCrimmon |
| Deborah Watling | Victoria |

Cybermen:
Michael Kilgarriff (Cybercontroller)

| Tony Harwood | John Hogan |
| --- | --- |
| Reg Whitehead | Ronald Lee |
| Charlie Pemberton | Hans de Vries |
| Richard Kerley | Kenneth Seeger |

| voices: | Peter Hawkins |
| --- | --- |

| additional: | |
| --- | --- |
| Roy Stewart | Toberman |
| Aubrey Richards | Professor Parry |
| Cyril Shaps | John Viner |
| Clive Merrison | Jim Callum |
| Shirley Cooklin | Kaftan |
| George Roubicek | Captain Hopper |
| George Pastell | Eric Klieg |
| Alan Johns | Ted Rogers |
| Bernard Holley | Peter Haydon |
| Ray Grover | Crewman |

| extra: | Frankie Dunn |
| --- | --- |

| technical: | |
| --- | --- |
| Martin Johnson | Designer |
| Victor Pemberton | Story Editor |
| Gillian James | Make-up Supervisor |
| Sandra Reid/Dorothea Wallace | Costume Supervisors |
| Michael John-Harris/Peter Day | Visual Effects |
| Alan Martin | Film Editor |
| Peter Hamilton | Film Cameraman |
| Ray Hider | Technical Manager |
| Brian Hiles | Sound |
| Graham Southcott | Lighting |
| Bob Haines | Floor Assistant |
| Ian Easterbrook | Vision Mixer |
| Laurie Taylor | Grams Operator |
| Pat Harrington | Assistant |
| Sue Willis/Catherine Sykes | Assistant Floor Managers |
| Snowy Lydiard-White | Production Assistant |
| Peter Bryant | Producer |
| Morris Barry | Director |

*THE WHEEL IN SPACE*

| regulars: | |
| --- | --- |
| Patrick Troughton | The Doctor |
| Frazer Hines | Jamie McCrimmon |
| Wendy Padbury | Zoe Herriot |

| Cybermen: | Jerry Holmes |
| --- | --- |
| | Gordon Stothard |

| voices: | Peter Hawkins |
| --- | --- |
| | Roy Skelton |

| additional: | |
| --- | --- |
| Freddie Foote | Servo Robot |
| Eric Flynn | Leo Ryan |
| Anne Ridler | Dr Gemma Corwyn |
| Clare Jenkins | Tanya Lernov |
| Michael Turner | Jarvis Bennett |
| Donald Sumpter | Enrico Casali |
| Kenneth Watson | Bill Duggan |
| Michael Goldie | Elton Laleham |
| Derrick Gilbert | Armand Vallance |
| Kevork Malikyan | Kemel Rudkin |
| Peter Laird | Chang |
| James Mellor | Sean Flannigan |

| extras: | Gordon Pitt |
| --- | --- |
| Tony Harwood | Ken Gibson |
| Dorothy Su | John Taylor |
| Yinka Adebeyi | Kenn Senton |
| Angela March | Harry Fielder |
| Chris Konylis | |

doubles:
Chris Jeffries for Patrick Troughton
Dorothy Ford for Anne Ridler

| technical: | |
| --- | --- |
| Derek Dodd | Designer |
| Derrick Sherwin | Story Editor |
| Radiophonic Workshop | Incidental Music |
| Gillian James | Make-up Supervisor |
| Martin Baugh | Costume Supervisor |
| Brian Hodgson/Radiophonic Workshop | Special Sound |
| Bill King & Trading Post | Visual Effects |
| Ron Fry | Film Editor |
| Jimmy Court | Film Cameraman |
| Peter Valentine | Technical Manager |
| John Holmes | Sound |
| Michael Jeffries | Lighting |
| Tony Hare | Floor Assistant |
| Clive Doig/Shirley Coward | Vision Mixers |
| Laurie Taylor/Dave Thompson | Grams Operators |
| Rita Dunn | Assistant |
| Marcia Wheeler | Assistant Floor Manager |
| Ian Strachan | Production Assistant |
| Peter Bryant | Producer |
| Tristan de Vere Cole | Director |

*THE INVASION*

| regulars: | |
| --- | --- |
| Patrick Troughton | The Doctor |
| Frazer Hines | Jamie McCrimmon |
| Wendy Padbury | Zoe Herriot |

| Cybermen: | Pat Gorman |
| --- | --- |
| Ralph Carrigan | Charles Finch |
| John Spradbury | Peter Thornton |
| Richard King | |

| voices: | Peter Halliday |
| --- | --- |

| additional: | |
| --- | --- |
| Murray Evans | Lorry Driver |
| Walter Randall | Patrolman |
| Sally Faulkner | Isobel |
| John Levene | Benton |
| Geoffrey Cheshire | Tracy |

| | |
|---|---|
| Kevin Stoney | Tobias Vaughn |
| Peter Halliday | Packer |
| Ian Fairbairn | Gregory |
| Nicholas Courtney | Brigadier Lethbridge-Stewart |
| James Thornhill | Sergeant Walters |
| Robert Sidaway | Captain Turner |
| Edward Burnham | Professor Watkins |
| Edward Dentith | Major-General Rutledge |
| Peter Thompson | Workman |
| Dominic Allen | Policeman |
| Stacy Davies | Private Perkins |
| Clifford Earl | Major Branwell |
| Norman Hartley | Sergeant Peters |

**voices:**

| | |
|---|---|
| Sheila Dunn | phone operator/computer |

**UNIT/bunker men:**

| | |
|---|---|
| Ross Huntley | Roy Pearce |
| Leslie Conrad | Steve Kelly |
| Richard Kitteridge | James Holbrook |
| Barry Dupres | Gary Dean |
| Clark Reed | Charles Finch |
| Crawford Lyle | Victor Munt |
| John Kirtly | Peter Roy |
| Mike Lee | Tony Manning |
| Derek Slater | David Pelton |

**IE guards:**

| | |
|---|---|
| Brian Nolan | Leslie Bates |
| Maurice Brooks | Kenneth Hale |
| Ron Conrad | Alistair McFarlane |
| Dave Carter | Derek Slater |
| | Terry Duggan |

**warehousemen:**

| | |
|---|---|
| Miles Northover | Gordon Stothard |
| | John Lord |

**patrolmen:**

| | |
|---|---|
| | Peter Pocock |
| | Roy Ford |

**stuntmen:**

| | |
|---|---|
| Terry Walsh | Billy Horrigan |
| | Alan Chuntz |

**extras:**

| | |
|---|---|
| Bobby Beaumont | Robert Pearce |
| Derek Chafer | Reg Cranfield |
| Trevor Shewring | Terence Denville |
| Roy Denton | Simon Stapely |
| | Lyn Denton |
| The Coldstream Guards (2nd Battalion) | |

**technical:**

| | |
|---|---|
| Richard Hunt | Designer |
| Terrance Dicks | Script Editor |
| Don Harper | Incidental Music |
| Sylvia James | Make-up |
| Bobi Bartlett | Costumes |
| Brian Hodgson | Special Sound |
| Bill King & Trading Post | Visual Effects |
| Bill Chesnau | Film Sound Recordist |
| Martyn Day | Film Editor |
| Alan Jonas | Film Cameraman |
| Don Babbage/Peter Valentine | Technical Managers |
| Alan Edmonds/Bryan Forgham | Sound Technicians |
| Robbie Robinson | Lighting |
| Michael Ward | Floor Assistant |
| David Langford/John Barclay | Vision Mixers |
| Ron Arnett/Dave Silk | Grams Operators |
| Sue Sly | Assistant |
| Sue Willis | Assistant Floor Manager |
| Chris D'Oyly John | Production Assistant |
| Douglas Camfield | Director |
| Peter Bryant | Producer |

## REVENGE OF THE CYBERMEN

**regulars:**

| | |
|---|---|
| Tom Baker | The Doctor |
| Elizabeth Sladen | Sarah Jane Smith |
| Ian Marter | Harry Sullivan |

**Cybermen:**

| | |
|---|---|
| Christopher Robbie | Cyberleader |
| Melville Jones | First Cyberman |

**additional:**

| | |
|---|---|
| Alex Wallis | Warner |
| William Marlowe | Lester |
| Ronald Leigh-Hunt | Commander Stevenson |
| Jeremy Wilkin | Kellman |
| David Collings | Vorus |
| Michael Wisher | Magrik |
| Kevin Stoney | Tyrum |
| Brian Grellis | Sheprah |

**extras (inc Cyber extras):**

| | |
|---|---|
| Tony Lord | Pat Gorman |
| Lesley Weekes | Cy Town |
| Harry Fielder | David Billa |
| Roy Caesar | Barry Summerford |
| | David Sulkin |

**stuntmen:**

| | |
|---|---|
| | Terry Walsh |
| | Alan Chuntz |

**technical:**

| | |
|---|---|
| George Gallaccio | Production Unit Manager |
| John Bradburn | Production Assistant |
| Carey Blyton | Incidental Music |
| Dick Mills | Special Sound |
| James Ward | Visual Effects Designer |
| Prue Handley | Costume Designer |
| Cecile Hay-Arthur | Make-up |
| Derek Slee | Studio Lighting |
| Norman Bennett | Studio Sound |
| Elmer Cossey | Film Cameraman |
| John Gatland | Film Sound |
| Sheila S Tomlinson | Film Editor |
| Robert Holmes | Script Editor |
| Roger Murray-Leach | Designer |
| Philip Hinchcliffe | Producer |
| Michael E Briant | Director |

## EARTHSHOCK

**regulars:**

| | |
|---|---|
| Peter Davison | The Doctor |
| Janet Fielding | Tegan |
| Matthew Waterhouse | Adric |
| Sarah Sutton | Nyssa |

**Cybermen:**

| | |
|---|---|
| David Banks | Cyberleader |
| Mark Hardy | Cyberlieutenant |

**Cyber extras:**

| | |
|---|---|
| Graham Cole | Jeff Wayne |
| Steve Ismay | Peter Gates Fleming |
| Norman Bradley | David Bache |

**additional:**

| | |
|---|---|
| James Warwick | Scott |
| Clare Clifford | Clare Clifford |
| Steve Moreley | Walters |
| Snyder | Suzi Arden |
| Ann Holloway | Mitchell |
| Anne Clements | First Trooper |
| Mark Straker | Second Trooper |

| | |
|---|---|
| Beryl Reid | Briggs |
| June Bland | Berger |
| Alec Sabin | Ringway |
| Mark Fletcher | First Crew Member |
| Christopher Whittingham | Second Crew Member |

**troopers:**

| | |
|---|---|
| Stephen Whyment | Jonathan Evans |
| Ian Ellis | Nikki Dunsford |
| Miles Ross | Kevin O'Brien |
| Lynne Brotchie | Lisa Clifton |

**androids:**

| | |
|---|---|
| | Carolyn Mary Simmonds |
| | Barney Lawrence |

**crew members:**

| | |
|---|---|
| John Towns | David Melbourne |
| Val McCrimmon | Tim Goodings |

**technical:**

| | |
|---|---|
| Malcolm Clarke | Incidental Music |
| Dick Mills | Special Sound |
| Geoffrey Manton | Production Manager |
| Angela Smith | Production Associate |
| Jane Ashford | Production Assistant |
| Nicholas Laughland | Assistant Floor Manager |
| Keith Hopper | Film Cameraman |
| John Gatland | Film Sound |
| Mike Houghton | Film Editor |
| Steve Bowman | Visual Effects Designer |
| Dave Chapman | Video Effects |
| Alan Jeffery | Technical Manager |
| Alec Wheal | Senior Cameraman |
| James Gould | Vision Mixer |
| Rod Waldron | Videotape Editor |
| Fred Wright | Lighting |
| Alan Machin | Sound |
| Dinah Collin | Costume Designer |
| Joan Stribling | Make-up Artist |
| Antony Root | Script Editor |
| Bernard Lloyd-Jones | Designer |
| John Nathan-Turner | Producer |
| Peter Grimwade | Director |

## THE FIVE DOCTORS

**regulars:**

| | |
|---|---|
| Peter Davison | The Doctor |
| Janet Fielding | Tegan |
| Mark Strickson | Turlough |

**Cybermen:**

| | |
|---|---|
| David Banks | Cyberleader |
| Mark Hardy | Lieutenant |
| William Kenton | Cyberscout |

**Cyber extras:**

| | |
|---|---|
| | Lee Woods |
| Richard Naylor | Mark Whincup |
| Gilbert Gillian | Emyr Morris Jones |
| Myrddin Jones | |

**additional:**

| | |
|---|---|
| Jon Pertwee | Third Doctor |
| Patrick Troughton | Second Doctor |
| Richard Hurndall | First Doctor |
| Tom Baker | Fourth Doctor (archive) |
| William Hartnell | First Doctor (archive) |
| Elisabeth Sladen | Sarah Jane Smith |
| Carole Ann Ford | Susan |
| Nicholas Courtney | The Brigadier |
| Lalla Ward | Romana (archive) |
| Anthony Ainley | The Master |

| | |
|---|---|
| Philip Latham | Lord President Borusa |
| Dinah Sheridan | Chancellor Flavia |
| Paul Jerricho | The Castellan |
| Richard Mathews | Rassilon |
| Frazer Hines | Jamie |
| Wendy Padbury | Zoe |
| Caroline John | Liz Shaw |
| Richard Franklin | Captain Yates |
| David Savile | Crichton |
| Stuart Blake | Commander |
| Stephen Meredith | Technician |
| Ray Float | Sergeant |
| John Tallents | Guard |
| Keith Hodiak | Raston Robot |
| Lee Woods | Yeti |

voices:
| | |
|---|---|
| John Leeson | K9 |
| Roy Skelton | Dalek |

extras: — Norman Bradley
| | |
|---|---|
| Lloyd Williams | Johnnie Mack |
| Frederick Wolfe | Charles Milward |
| Graham Cole | Alan Riches |
| Ian Marshall-Fisher | Mark Bassinger |

stuntman: — Stuart Fell

technical:
| | |
|---|---|
| John Scott Martin | Dalek Operator |
| Peter Howell | Incidental Music |
| Dick Mills/Radiophonic Workshop | Special Sound |
| Jeremy Silberston | Production Manager |
| June Collins | Production Associate |
| Jean Davis | Production Assistant |
| Pauline Seager | Assistant Floor Manager |
| John Baker | Film Cameraman |
| John Gatland | Film Sound |
| M A C Adams | Film Editor |
| Shirley Coward | Vision Mixer |
| John Brace/Mike Kelt | Visual Effects Designers |
| Dave Chapman | Video Effects |
| Alec Wheal | Camera Supervisor |
| Derek Thompson | Technical Manager |
| Jean Peyre | Design Effects |
| Ian Hewett | Graphic Designer |
| Hugh Parson | Videotape Editor |
| Robert Fleming | Properties Buyer |
| Don Babbage | Studio Lighting |
| Martin Ridout | Studio Sound |
| Colin Lavers | Costume Designer |
| Jill Hagger | Make-up Artist |
| Eric Saward | Script Editor |
| Malcolm Thornton | Designer |
| John Nathan-Turner | Producer |
| Peter Moffatt | Director |

## ATTACK OF THE CYBERMEN

regulars:
| | |
|---|---|
| Colin Baker | The Doctor |
| Nicola Bryant | Peri Brown |

Cybermen:
| | |
|---|---|
| David Banks | Cyberleader |
| Michael Kilgarriff | Cybercontroller |
| Brian Orrell | Cyberlieutenant |
| John Ainley | Cyberman |

Cyber extras: — Pat Gorman, Thomas Lucy

additional:
| | |
|---|---|
| Maurice Colbourne | Lytton |
| Brian Glover | Griffiths |
| Terry Molloy | Russell |
| James Beckett | Payne |
| Michael Atwell | Bates |
| Jonathan David | Stratton |
| Stephen Churchett | Bill |
| Stephen Wale | David |
| Sarah Berger | Rost |
| Esther Freud | Threst |
| Faith Brown | Flast |
| Sarah Greene | Varne |

Policemen: — Michael Braban, Michael Jeffries

Cryon extras: — Trisha Clark
| | |
|---|---|
| Irela Williams | Maggie Lynton |

technical:
| | |
|---|---|
| Malcolm Clarke | Incdental Music |
| Dick Mills/Radiophonic Workshop | Special Sound |
| Andrew Buchanan | Production Manager |
| June Collins/Sue Anstruther | Production Associates |
| Llinos Wyn Jones | Production Assistant |
| Pennie Bloomfield | Assistant Floor Manager |
| Godfrey Johnson | Film Cameraman |
| Barrie Tharby | Film Sound |
| M A C Adams | Film Editor |
| Chris Lawson | Visual Effects Designer |
| Dave Chapman | Video Effects |
| Nigel Finnis/Dinah Long | Vision Mixer |
| Alan Arbuthnot | Technical Co-ordinator |
| Alec Wheal | Camera Supervisor |
| Hugh Parson | Videotape Editor |
| Henry Barber | Lighting Director |
| Andrew Stacey | Studio Sound |
| Anushia Nieradzik | Costume Designer |
| Linda McInnes | Make-up Designer |
| Eric Saward | Script Editor |
| Marjorie Pratt | Designer |
| John Nathan-Turner | Producer |
| Matthew Robinson | Director |

## SILVER NEMESIS

regulars:
| | |
|---|---|
| Silvester McCoy | The Doctor |
| Sophie Aldred | Ace |

Cybermen:
| | |
|---|---|
| David Banks | Cyberleader |
| Mark Hardy | Cyberlieutenant |
| Brian Orrell | Cyberman |

Cyber extras: — Danny Boyd
| | |
|---|---|
| Paul Barrass | Scott Mitchell |
| Tony Carlton | Bill Malin |

additional:
| | |
|---|---|
| Gerard Murphy | Richard |
| Fiona Walker | Lady Peinforte |
| Leslie French | Mathematician |
| Anton Diffring | De Flores |
| Metin Yenal | Karl |
| Martyn Read | Security Man |
| Christopher Chering | First Skinhead |
| Symond Lawes | Second Skinhead |
| Delores Gray | Mrs Remington |

non-speaking parts:
| | |
|---|---|
| Security Man | Derek Van Weenan |

| | |
|---|---|
| Hitchhiker | Ricardo Mulhall |
| Gardener | Terry Duran |
| Maid | Jacquella Tew |
| Jazz Quartet | Courtney Pine's |
| Her Majesty the Queen | Mary Reynolds |

paramilitaries — Jon Baker
| | |
|---|---|
| Steve Ausden | Sean Barry-Weske |
| Andrew Searle | David Howarth |
| Julian Redmond | Keith Harvie |
| Jamie Durdy | Sean McCrory |
| Jack Talbot | |

walkmen — Dave Ould, John Ould

policemen — Christian Fletcher
| | |
|---|---|
| Daryl Brook | Anthony Gilding |

tourists — Andrew Morgan
| | |
|---|---|
| Peter Moffatt | Ian Fraser |
| Fiona Cumming | Jane Busby |
| Katy Jarrett | Sharon Granville |
| Sandra Granville | Audrey Joyce |
| Pat Worth | Gary Webb |
| John Lewery | Tony Stewart |

stuntmen — Nick Gillard
| | |
|---|---|
| Double for Sylvester McCoy | Paul Heasman |

technical:
| | |
|---|---|
| Keff McCulloch | Incidental Music |
| Dick Mills | Special Sound |
| Les Runham | Production Operator Supervisor |
| Derek Waite/Ken Robins/Mickey Cox | Prod Operatives |
| Richard Croft | Costume Designer |
| Leah Archer | Costume Assistant |
| Riley Clark | Senior Dresser |
| Michael Johnson/Debbie Roberts | Dressers |
| Dorka Nieradzik | Make-up Designer |
| Jayne Buxton/Sara Ellis | Make-up Assistants |
| Perry Brahan | Visual FX Designer |
| Paul McGuiness/Mike Tucker/Russell Pritchard | Visual FX Assistants |
| Doug Needham | Armourer |
| John Asbridge | Designer |
| Philip Harvey | Design Assistant |
| John Charles | Properties Buyer |
| Barry Chaston | Camera Supervisor |
| Alan Jessop | Cameraman |
| Roger Neal | Sound Engineer |
| Dave Thwaites/Mark Robinson | Vision Engineers |
| John Nottage | Sound Supervisor |
| Pete Hales | Deputy Sound Supervisor |
| Ken Osbourn | Sound Operative |
| Brian Jones | Planning E M |
| Ian Dow | Lighting E M |
| Lorraine Godding | Producer's Secretary |
| Hilary Barratt | Finance Assistant |
| June Collins | Production Associate |
| Andrew Cartmel | Script Editor |
| Jeremy Fry | Trainee/Runner |
| Lynne Grant | Assistant Floor Manager |
| Jane Wellesley | Production Assistant |
| Gary Downie | Production Manager |
| Chris Clough | Director |
| John Nathan-Turner | Producer |